Meaningful Arrangement

Functional Linguistics

Series Editor: Robin Fawcett, Cardiff University

This series publishes monographs that seek to understand the nature of language by exploring one or other of various cognitive models or in terms of the communicative use of language. It concentrates on studies that are in, or on the borders of, various functional theories of language.

Published:

Functional Dimensions of Ape-Human Discourse
Edited by James D. Benson and William S. Greaves

System and Corpus: Exploring Connections
Edited by Geoff Thompson and Susan Hunston

Forthcoming:

Text Type and Texture
Edited by Geoff Thompson and Gail Forey

Systemic Functional Perspectives of Japanese:
Descriptions and Applications
Edited by Elizabeth Thomson and William Armour

The Texture of Casual Conversation: A Multidimensional Interpretation
Diana Slade

A Multimodal Approach to Classroom Discourse
Kay O'Halloran

Reading Visual Narratives: Inter-image Analysis of Children's Picture Books
Clare Painter

Meaningful Arrangement
Exploring the Syntactic Description of Texts

Edward McDonald

Published by

UK: Equinox Publishing Ltd., Unit 6, The Village, 101 Amies St.,
London SW11 2JW
USA: DBBC, 28 Main Street, Oakville, CT 06779
www.equinoxpub.com

First published 2008
Reprinted 2009, 2010

British Library Cataloguing-in-Publication Data
A catalogue record for this book is available from the British Library.

ISBN   9781845531478   (hardback)
           9781845531485   (paperback)

Library of Congress Cataloging-in-Publication Data

McDonald, Edward, 1963-
  Meaningful arrangement : exploring the syntactic description of texts
/ Edward McDonald.
      p. cm. -- (Functional linguistics)
  Includes bibliographical references and index.
  ISBN 1-84553-147-7 (hb) -- ISBN 1-84553-148-5 (pb) 1. Grammar,
Comparative and general--Syntax. 2. Discourse analysis. I. Title. II.
Series.
  P295.M33 2006
  415--dc22
                                    2006010175

Typeset by Catchline, Milton Keynes (www.catchline.com)
Printed and bound in Great Britain and the USA

Contents

Acknowledgements

Any book like this is merely the tip of a large iceberg of previous reading, research and teaching; and no less significantly, discussions with and feedback from students and colleagues. Earlier versions of the material contained in the book were used for courses in Comparative Syntax at Peking University in 1992–93; Comparative Language Studies (Chinese and English) at the University of New South Wales in 1995–1997; English Grammar and Meaning at the National University of Singapore in 1999–2000; and Syntax at Tsinghua University in 2002–03: and I would like to thank the students from all of those classes for the stimulation and challenge they provided. My own thinking on syntactic questions has been greatly influenced by discussions over more than two decades with Michael Halliday, Jim Martin, Michael Walsh, Jane Simpson, Licheng Zeng, Arlene Harvey, Chris Clèirigh and the late Dr Raymond Hsu at Sydney University; with Lance Eccles, Ruqaiya Hasan, Christian Matthiessen, Rhondda Fahey, Danny Kane and David Butt at Macquarie University; with the late Prof. Ye Feisheng, the late Prof. Xu Tongqiang, and Hu Zhuanglin, Jiang Wangqi, Guo Rui, Gao Yihong, Qian Jun and the Linguistics Circle at Peking University; with Graham Lock at the City University of Hong Kong; with Lionel Wee, Ni Yibin, Kay O'Halloran, and Desmond Allison at the National University of Singapore; and with Fang Yan and He Honghua at Tsinghua University.

Emily Purser reintroduced me to Old English and provided the two examples used here; Katie Graham introduced me to Scottish Gaelic, and generously helped me translate the Chinese text into Gaelic in Chapter 8, as well as checking all the Gaelic examples throughout. I am also grateful to Rhondda Fahey from Macquarie University, David Cram from the University of Oxford, and Nick Riemer from the University of Sydney who read this book in draft and were both appreciative and encouraging. I would particularly like to thank Anne McCabe, from St Louis University, Madrid, who carefully read her way through the whole book from the point of view of the 'naive reader', and helped me to make sure my message was getting across clearly and consistently. These teachers and colleagues might not recognise their own ideas in the following chapters, but their contribution has nonetheless been crucial for the approach put forward here, which of course inevitably reflects my own particular concerns and limitations.

Grateful acknowledgement is made to the following sources for material used in this book:

p.13, Opening the Cage: 14 Variations on 14 Words, by Edwin Morgan, reproduced by permission of Carcanet Press Ltd

p.75 Hornpipe, by Edith Sitwell, reproduced by permission of David Higham Associates

p.136, Cù Dubh Mhic-A-Phì, narrated by Alastair MacDonald, transcribed by William Lamb, reproduced by permission of William Lamb.

p.90 ff. Dreams, from *Poisonous Weeds: A People's Reader* (unpublished), by Yang Lian and Liu Youhong, reproduced by permission of the authors.

Briefing

The subtitle of this book promises an 'exploration' that brings together two concepts – syntax and text – normally treated separately, and shows how they can best be understood in relation to each other. It offers an intellectual journey to take apart and problematise the whole process of understanding the patterns formed by words with other words in connected discourse. As such, it covers a rather different range of questions, and deals with them in different ways, from most books which explain how to 'do syntax'. So before we set out exploring, it would be useful to examine how 'syntax' is usually defined and how it tends to be 'done'.

If we take a number of introductions to the study of syntax published recently, they tend to cover a fairly consistent range of concerns. Radford's *Syntax: A Minimalist Introduction* (1997) gives a widely accepted definition of the scope of the subject with its stress on distinguishing grammatical from ungrammatical sentences, in other words, what can be said and what can't (Radford 1997: 1):

> Syntax is concerned with the ways in which words can be combined
> together to form phrases and sentences, and so addresses questions like
> 'Why is it OK in English to say *Who did you see Mary with?*, but not
> OK to say **Who did you see Mary and?*'... 'What kinds of principles
> determine the ways in which we can and cannot combine words together
> to form phrases and sentences?'

Sag and Wasow's *Syntactic Theory: A Formal Introduction* (1999) adds a familiar note when it distinguishes between the traditional 'prescriptive grammar' that is (or used to be) taught in schools and the 'grammar' (in this sense subsuming syntax) that they are concerned with (Sag & Wasow 1999: 1):

> As modern linguists we think that prescriptive grammar is for the most
> part a pointless activity. We view human language as a phenomenon
> amenable to scientific investigation, rather than something to be regulated
> by the decrees of authorities.

Sag and Wasow then go on to specify the 'authority' to which they will be appealing in sorting out the 'grammatical' (also known as 'well-formed') from the 'ungrammatical' (Sag & Wasow 1999: 3):

> Every normal speaker of any natural language has acquired an immensely rich and systematic body of unconscious knowledge, which can be investigated by consulting speakers' intuitive judgments.

This then allows them to define what sort of 'science' it is they are doing (Sag & Wasow 1999: 3):

> Languages are phenomena of considerable complexity, which can be studied scientifically. That is, we can formulate general hypotheses about linguistic structure and test them against the facts of particular languages. The study of grammar on this conception is a field in which hypothesis-testing is particularly easy: the linguist can simply ask native speakers whether the predictions regarding well-formedness of crucial sentences are correct.

So the study of syntax is concerned with 'hypotheses' as to what is 'well-formed' or not, and these 'facts' are to be determined by consulting 'normal speakers'? Put this way, the so-called 'scientific investigation' of language begins to look not so different from the laying down of rules practised by traditional grammarians. Where do these 'facts' come from? Who counts as a 'normal speaker'. Who or what decides whether something is 'well-formed' or not? Is the process of forming and testing hypotheses like that practised in the physical sciences, as the use of those terms would suggest, or is it of a different nature? Why the focus on 'linguistic structure' rather than, say, 'linguistic meaning'? And what are the understandings of language and language use that lie behind the way these questions are framed and answered?

I believe that the way such questions are answered in many current treatments of syntax simplifies the genuine complexity involved here, and that we have in fact been rather premature in claiming a 'scientific' status for this branch of study. There are three main reasons why I would argue that the study of syntax needs to be broadened beyond its currently accepted boundaries. These reasons relate to the three pillars of scientific method – data, description, and theory – and are dealt with respectively in the three parts of this book under the headings of processing the text, analysing the clause, and theorising syntax.

Firstly: **data – processing the text**. Most accounts of syntax start off by assuming a division between syntax (how words are combined) and morphology (the forms words take). Not only does such a division have clear roots in one particular linguistic tradition – that of Graeco-Roman antiquity – which will not necessarily be relevant for the particular language or languages we are dealing with, it also begs a whole range of questions. It depends on getting the data in such a form that we can define what a 'word' is (see Chapter 4 for an example of the complexity of this in one language, Mandarin Chinese), and tends to utilise a particular 'bricks-and-mortar' model of language that is not at all the 'common-sense' it is normally taken to be (see Chapter 5). But more than that, it also requires a whole lot of prior 'cleaning up' of the data which in itself embodies – and normally disguises – a whole lot of theoretical and descriptive assumptions (see Chapter 2). So Part 1 of this book focuses on the process of getting texts ready for syntactic analysis, and making explicit the choices that have to be made in doing so. The point is not that we can somehow access the 'real data' directly – we can't. The data needs to be mediated through our processing of the text, so we have to be aware of the nature of that processing and its effects on our subsequent analysis.

Secondly: **description – analysing the clause**. This part deals with what would normally be expected to be included in any syntactic description. It attempts to give an idea of the relevant phenomena that need to be explained and the sorts of concepts used to explain them. As the main focus of 'syntax proper', this is an area where concepts and frameworks proliferate to a confusing degree. The strategy adopted here to open a path through the tangled forest of syntactic theories has been to rely on two main guides: Lucien Tesnière and P.H. Matthews.

Tesnière is someone whose work is not as well-known in English-language scholarship as it deserves to be, and the fact that he died before the publication of his main work, *Éléments de syntaxe structurale* (1959), as well the overlap of its appearance with that of Chomsky's highly influential *Syntactic Structures* (1957) perhaps explains his relative neglect. But Tesnière's work is a wide-ranging and original re-evaluation of the nature and goals of syntactic analysis which provides a bridge between traditional ideas about grammar in the Western tradition and the more systematic focus of modern linguistics. His basic metaphor of the clause as a little 'drama' involving 'actors' and 'setting' (Tesnière 1959: 102) has proven to be a highly influential – if often unacknowledged – model, and provides a very insightful way of linking syntactic structures to their meanings. P.H. Matthews in effect takes up where Tesnière left off. As one of the most perceptive observers and critics of the 'explosion' in syntactic theorising in the second half of the twentieth century, and in particular the most famous 'brand' of syntax, transformational-generative grammar, as it developed through the 1960s and 1970s, his textbook *Syntax* (1981) both sums up the achievements and limitations of that tradition and provides a still unsurpassed general account of what he calls 'the nature of syntactic relations and the fundamental types of construction' (Matthews 1981: xvii).

But syntactic analysis is not just about theories, it is about languages. One of the unfortunate side-effects of the move away from 'description' to 'explanation' in much syntactic work since the 1960s, with the concomitant focus on so-called 'universal' features of language, has been a comparative neglect of the ways in which languages differ. In its extreme form, this has led to the notion that syntax can somehow be 'carried out' on just one language, as Radford explains in justifying the restriction of his data to English examples: 'many students on syntax courses are primarily interested in English, and may have a relatively limited knowledge of (or interest in) the syntax of other languages' (Radford 1997: i). As I noted above, and explain in more detail in Chapter 1, many of the assumptions of syntax in the Western tradition derive from the specific form of the Latin and Greek languages, and it would be naive to suppose that the 'language under description' does not have an effect on the 'language of description' (see Chapter 2) and the theories that are written in it.

Van Valin's *An Introduction to Syntax* (2001) provides a salutary contrast to this descriptive monolingualism, billing itself as 'first and foremost an exploration of the variety of human languages, with examples drawn from every part of the globe'; and Lockwood's *Syntactic Analysis and Description* (2002) takes a similar approach. The current book's focus on texts as data doesn't allow it to be quite so wide-ranging. It therefore confines itself to (a) analysing texts in two languages I am reasonably familiar with, and which coincidentally happen to derive from the two opposite ends of Eurasia – Scottish Gaelic and Mandarin Chinese; (b) using the language of description – English – as the language under description, with the occasional excursion into Old English; and (c) making regular reference to Latin, as one of the key influences in the development of syntactic theories in the Western tradition.

Thirdly: **theorising syntax**. The experienced reader may have already noted a more 'ideological' tone to the current book than is customary. This is not, I believe, because it *is* more ideologically slanted than most such books, only that it is more upfront about the stance it takes. Just as the nature of the processing of the text reveals – or conceals – particular notions about language, so the analysis of the clause depends inescapably on a certain conceptualisation of syntactic categories and relations. While introductions to syntax tend to be more explicit about the assumptions of their analysis than they are about their processing, they are still faced with the problem of the 'tangled forest' of syntactic theories referred to above.

Given this situation, most such books adopt one of a number of strategies. They concentrate on one particular theory and deal with others only in passing if at all: for example, Radford 1997 and Sag and Wasow 1999 each cover different brands of generative grammar; Halliday 1985 / 1994 and Fawcett 2000 different brands of systemic functional grammar. Alternatively they treat a number of theories, in most cases, ones that are theoretically fairly inter-consistent: for example, Van Valin 2001 provides an introduction to basic syntactic concepts shared by theories deriving from the generative tradition, and finishes up with brief accounts of how four particular theories differ at a more specific level. Very occasionally they attempt a synthesis of different theories: for example Lockwood 2002 draws on stratificational grammar, tagmemics, and systemic functional linguistics to provide an account 'centered around the notion of the syntactic construction' (Lockwood 2002: ix).

This book takes a different approach by focusing not so much on constructing a theory as on identifying the range of phenomena any theory has to deal with. However, this does not mean it is 'pre-theoretical' or 'non-theoretical': such terms are basically nonsensical. Even the most avowedly descriptively-oriented account takes a theoretical stance – however implicitly – in its aims and techniques. The approach taken here can be summed up in the title of a 1966 article by Halliday 'Syntax and the Consumer'; or more gnomically 'syntax is as syntax does'. The form taken by any theory of syntax reflects the purposes for which syntactic analysis is envisaged, and the wider concerns to which it relates. So Part 3 tries to give a sketch – and it can only be a sketch – of the range of approaches available for the 'consumer', some of the themes that have emerged in syntactic studies over the last half-century, and what different theories set out to do. In the study of syntax, as in any area, a historical perspective is a valuable corrective to theoretical blinkeredness: I would even go so far as to say that is an essential element of the genuine understanding of any one single theory. As the historian of science Thomas Kuhn (Kuhn 1962 / 1970: 10 22) has described in relation to the physical sciences, the messiness of historical developments in a discipline is often hidden from the student in the way introductions to the 'state of the art' are written, with all predecessors seen as leading inexorably up to whatever framework is being put forward as the 'right' one.

The present book tries to find a way of giving a sense of developments in the field not by dealing with the usual 'schools' of formalism versus functionalism, but by showing how some traditional morphological concepts have been reinterpreted for syntactic analysis (Chapters 14–15), and by picking up on concepts already introduced in earlier parts – such as the key complementarity between syntagmatic and paradigmatic (Chapters 16–17) – to characterise the emphases and biases of different theories. To bring things back to earth, this account of different theories finishes up with a case study of one particular theory being applied to a particular descriptive challenge – developing a functional account of the verb in Chinese (Chapter 18).

The overall approach taken in this book – what it sets out to provide that most such studies don't – can be summed up by unpicking the key words in the title.

The first key word is **arrangement**. This is a fairly close translation of the Greek *syntaxis* from which the term 'syntax' derives, applied originally to soldiers lined up for battle, and then subsequently to words lined up in order. As a semiotic system linking sound and meaning, language exhibits patterning on many levels. The type of arrangement dealt with in this book is that where sound and meaning come together into meaningful 'chunks' that vary and interact in meaningful ways. Such a formulation suggests that the second key word must be **meaningful**. The general approach adopted here is that of J.R. Firth, who saw meaning as involved in all levels of language, not just to be hived off in a separate box called 'semantics'. So for Firth there was phonetic meaning and phonological meaning – how we interpret and distinguish sounds; lexical and grammatical meaning – how we interpret different patterns of wording; and contextual meaning – how we make sense of wordings in their contexts of use.

Firth's approach to analysing lexical and grammatical meaning was what he referred to as 'the word process in the sentence' (Firth 1957 / 1968: 175), and this provides a pretty good definition of the third key word **syntactic**. If we look at the sentence – or more technically what will here be called the clause – as meaningful, what sorts of patterns do we see? Firth pointed out that these patterns are of two kinds: lexical relations between words – what he referred to as 'collocation'; and grammatical relations between categories – 'colligation' (Chapter 3). If we take two words like 'say poetry' (see Chapter 1) they relate lexically in a way we could paraphrase as 'uttering words'; as well as grammatically in terms of functions we can call 'predicator' and 'complement' (see Chapters 7 & 8). The notion of 'syntactic' is most commonly taken to cover only the second type of relation, but both types have separate and equal contributions to make to the meaningful patterning of sentences.

And so to the fourth key word: **texts**. In contrast to perhaps the majority of approaches to syntax, this book sees syntactic organisation as one of the levels of organisation of texts, that is, of coherent pieces of discourse functioning in context. Isolated sentences taken out of context may be adequate for explaining certain features of syntactic patterning, but accounts based on such examples tend to fall down when it comes to explaining *why* a particular syntactic pattern is chosen instead of another. Traditional descriptive accounts of syntax have always used texts as sources of examples, but the move to self-proclaimed 'explanatory' models of syntax in the last half century for some reason seems to have seen texts regarded as a distraction rather than the basic data which need to be accounted for.

Which brings us to the fifth key word: **description**. Why should we be interested in understanding syntactic patterning? Again, there are as many answers to this question as there are definitions of 'syntax', but the starting point for this book is a desire to describe both the forms syntactic patterning takes and how they are used. This approach assumes that we are interested first of all in making sense of the meaningful patterning of texts, in ways that can be related to their material expression in sound or visual symbols, on the one hand, and their contexts of use, whether social or cognitive, on the other.

The final key word is an unusual one as such book titles go: **exploring**. It's unusual for a couple of reasons. It suggests a rather *tentative* approach, as though we're setting out on a journey without being exactly sure what will turn up. It also suggests a *process* of finding out, rather than a delimiting of what is already known. It is written in the spirit of Hockett's (1987) reflective reconsidering of the American linguistic tradition subtitled *Elementary linguistics from an advanced point of view*: to borrow the description by Yuen Ren Chao of his *Grammar of Spoken Chinese* (1968: viii), this is 'a discussion book and not an instruction book to learn [syntax] from'. As I noted above, I believe that we have been somewhat hasty and over-confident in claiming a scientific status for this subject, and that some of what Hockett recommended as *Refurbishing our Foundations* (1987) is urgently necessary here. So this book can perhaps be seen as a 'prelude' rather than an 'introduction' to the study of syntax: it does not provide a ready-made framework that can be immediately taken away and applied to the data, rather it explores the main 'themes' that are developed more technically in other syntax textbooks, such as the ones already mentioned above.

The approach taken here also departs from tradition in that it deliberately does *not* employ the favored scientific mode of explanation in the West since the 17th century, the reductive method, which works by breaking down large structures into their component bits. In practice, this tends to mean 'building up' from small pieces into large structures; in linguistics, the reductive approach has been taken to its logical extreme in Zellig Harris's *Methods in Structural Linguistics* (Harris 1951). Instead it takes the opposite mode of starting off with the broad brush general picture and then gradually 'focusing in'. For example, rather than starting with words and 'building them up' into phrases and clauses, it works the other way: starting by analysing whole clauses, and only discussing the structure of words and phrases after the structure of the clause has already been sketched in. This method of explanation goes along with, and is in many ways required by the emphasis on using as data whole texts, rather than single sentences. An explanation of a text, a piece of discourse, needs to be itself discursive, to be 'worked through' rather than 'taken in' at a glance. The use of texts also highlights the complexity of the whole process of dealing with language syntactically, and the contingent nature of making descriptive decisions, of weighing up different tendencies in the data against each other.

The general approach taken in Parts 1 and 2 could thus be characterised as 'processual' rather than 'declarative': in other words, the discussion attempts to lead the reader through the process of establishing syntactic categories and developing syntactic descriptions, rather than simply putting them forward as givens. Such an approach is not uncommon in syntax textbooks, where the focus tends to be on argumentation as much as – or sometimes more than – description; but this book does not first establish the relevant categories and then proceed to employ them, it instead attempts to derive categories in the course of the discussion. This may occasionally cause the reader some headaches, but hopefully the pay-off will be a better understanding of the genuine complexity of the process of coming up with a description of any language.

Part 3 takes a more reflective approach in exploring the implications of Firth's notion of linguistics, and therefore of syntax as one part of linguistics, being 'language turned back on itself' (Firth 1950 / 1957: 181). Having already gone through a process of necessary linguistic navel-gazing to develop a **metalanguage** for this purpose in Parts 1 and 2 – that is, a language to talk about language, a theory of language – Part 3 attempts to develop what we might call a 'meta-metalanguage': in other words, a language to talk about theories of language. For this purpose, it is important to understand the **historical context** of the development of ideas about 'doing syntax', to get an idea of the previous and concurrent work different scholars have drawn on in devising their own theories of syntax, and to be aware of the sorts of rhetorical strategies theoreticians use to promote their own ideas and (just as importantly) downgrade those of their opponents. It is also crucial to understand the **context of application** for syntactic theories: that is, the purposes for which theorists have seen their theories being useful, in line with Halliday's notion of a theory as a 'means of action', a way of carrying out particular work. An essential element of 'doing syntax', in my view, is developing a cross-theoretical awareness: to understand that not only are some of the *answers* different – something already widely acknowledged – but that often the *questions* are different as well.

In the last fifty years, the term 'syntax' has become inextricably associated with the name of Noam Chomsky. It may therefore strike many readers as strange that no mention of Chomsky's work is made until we reach Part 3. There are a number of reasons for this apparent omission. Firstly, Chomsky has tended to set himself against the idea that there might be different questions, as well as different answers, in doing syntax, characteristically dismissing other accounts of syntax, even those developed by scholars working within his own general framework, as being of little or no significance. So Chomsky does not have much useful contribution to make to an account of syntactic study that seeks to go across different theories, particularly those stemming from traditions different to his own. Secondly, from the very beginning of his work on syntax, Chomsky took over the categories of traditional (Latin) grammar without justification, and saw his task as formalising the insights contained in that framework, which he explicitly cast as universal. He therefore has little to say on the question of problematising those categories, or whether the description of different languages may in fact call for different categories. Thirdly, in a book like this that seeks to reevaluate current wisdom in the field of syntactic studies and to call for rethinking on some key points, I wanted to show that there *are* actually viable syntactic frameworks outside the Chomskyan tradition. Once we reach Part 3, Chomsky must of course make an appearance; not, however, in the role of revolutionary in which he is usually cast, but as a development of a particular theoretical tradition within linguistics, a tradition which must be taken seriously, but not regarded as the be-all and end-all of syntax. To rephrase Saussure's dictum on linguistics and linguists, 'syntax is too important to be left to the (usual) syntacticians'.

All in all, this is a book for raising questions, not providing answers; for suggesting different possible alternatives, not defending one entrenched position; for problematising rather than assuming. I hope that it may contribute to broadening the debate on the nature and uses of syntactic study, and suggest some ways out for a discipline that seems to have driven itself into a corner.

Part 1

Data – processing the text

To start our exploration of the syntactic description of texts, we first need to take a close look at our data – **texts**, in the broad sense of coherent pieces of discourse, spoken or written, which function in a context – and see what needs to be done to them before they can undergo syntactic analysis. As in any area of study, the data comes to us as part of what the philosopher William James referred to as the 'bloomin', buzzin' confusion' of experience (James 1890 / 1950: 456) – or in Firth's terms the 'mush of general goings-on' (Firth 1957 / 1968: 199) – and we need to select and edit that experience in order to focus in on the particular aspects of it that are at issue. In Part 1 of this book, we start off in Chapter 1 with a brief look at what is understood by 'syntax' in the Western tradition, and see how that depends on a particular understanding of texts, and of language in general. Chapter 2 takes a close look at the challenges of 'glossing' a text – that is, presenting it for interpretation, normally only necessary when the language being analysed is different from the one in which the analysis is being done, but in fact an essential part of any syntactic description – and see how the choices made there can affect any further descriptive claims made for the text. In Chapter 3, we examine how language conceals a layered complexity beneath its ostensible 'one word after another' form, and what sorts of concepts are needed to reveal that complexity. Then in Chapters 4 and 5, we focus on the challenges of identifying syntactic units – at the very least, words and clauses – and see how this again often unexamined step has huge implications for description.

1   Meaning and structure

What do we mean when we talk about *meaningful arrangement* in language, i.e. that sort of organisation for which the technical term is **syntax**? Some preliminary answers to this question can be gained from examining a poem by the Scottish poet Edwin Morgan given below:

Opening the Cage: 14 variations on 14 words

I have nothing to say and I am saying it and that is poetry.

John Cage

I have to say poetry and is that nothing and am I saying it
I am and I have poetry to say and is that nothing saying it
I am nothing and I have poetry to say and that is saying it
I that am saying poetry have nothing and it is I and to say
And I say that I am to have poetry and saying it is nothing
I am poetry and nothing and saying it is to say that I have
To have nothing is poetry and I am saying that and I say it
Poetry is saying I have nothing and I am to say that and it
Saying nothing I am poetry and I have to say that and it is
It is and I am and I have poetry saying say that to nothing
It is saying poetry to nothing and I say I have and am that
Poetry is saying I have it and I am nothing and to say that
And that nothing is poetry I am saying and I have to say it
Saying poetry is nothing and to that I say I am and have it

Edwin Morgan (1968) *The Second Life*
Edinburgh University Press

What exactly is Morgan doing here? Well, he takes as his starting point a statement by the composer John Cage which contains exactly fourteen words, and then he simply rearranges those fourteen words in different orders. But is that 'rearrangement' as 'simple' as it seems? Let's try paraphrasing the original statement, and the first five lines of the poem, and seeing how they differ (the paraphrases are not intended to be definitive in any way, just a way of saying the same thing in different words):

I have nothing to say and I am saying it and that is poetry
There is nothing I can say, and I am still saying it, and in doing so I am writing poetry

I have to say poetry and is that nothing and am I saying it
I am obliged to say poetry, and (I ask) is that nothing? and (I ask) am I saying it?

I am and I have poetry to say and is that nothing saying it
I exist, and I possess poetry which I can say and (I ask) does saying it amount to nothing?

I that am saying poetry have nothing and it is I and to say
I, the person saying poetry, possess nothing, and [that nothing] is me and [it] is saying [poetry]

And I say that I am to have poetry and saying it is nothing
And I say that I will possess poetry and that saying poetry amounts to nothing

Now some of these lines seem to make more or less sense, or are more or less easy to interpret, but I don't think we could deny that they could all 'be said' – whether or not we would want to call them 'poetry'! What the poet is doing here is playing with the syntactic potential of English: that is, the different ways words can be ordered in relation to each other, and the different meanings these orders express. (We will see later that this 'reordering' is really a type of 'restructuring' which involves changing not just the order but the syntactic relations between the words.) This is not the only type of organisation present here: there is also an organisation of sounds, represented here by the combinations of written letters and the gaps between them; there is also in a less determinate sense an organisation of meanings, the conventions by which we interpret this sort of word play as having some sort of function. So in order to focus on exactly what *syntactic* organisation is, we need to think about how we would define language as a whole.

One way of looking at this would be to say that language is a type of meaningful behaviour. In the most basic terms, it consists of a stream of sound which we produce in response to particular situations and which we interpret according to certain conventions. More technically, it is a semiotic mediation between two features of our living context: the material context of the human body which is capable of expressing itself through sound and / or gesture; and the social context of a range of meaningful behaviour, including besides both spoken and signed language, 'body language', facial expression, movement, spatial relations between speakers, and so on.

We experience language as a meaningful whole, as a complex but coherent package of sound / gesture and meaning. However, in order to understand it, we need to break it down, as the linguist J.R. Firth suggested, by a 'dispersion into modes, rather like the dispersion of light of mixed wave lengths through a spectrum'. Firth suggested the following 'modes' as necessary (1951 / 1957: 174–175):

> First there is the verbal process in the context of situation… The
> technique of syntax is concerned with the word process in the sentence.
> Phonology states the phonetic and prosodic processes within the word and
> the sentence, regarding them as a mode of meaning. The phonetician links
> all this with the processes and features of the utterance.

Firth here identifies at least four levels on which language can be analysed, regarding all of them as meaningful, but in different ways. These levels were summed up by one of his students, M. A. K. Halliday, as follows (1961: 243):

contextual
syntactic
phonological
phonetic

The level we will be looking at in this book is the syntactic one. This can be seen as a sort of 'internal' level of language, that comes 'in between' the context in which language is used and the sounds of which each utterance is made up. Since this is often taken as a study in its own right, and regarded by some linguists as having no essential connection to any of the other levels, it is worthwhile first taking some time to explore the particular features of this level, and how it differs from the others.

We can start by tracing the derivation of the term *syntax* and some related terms. In the European tradition, dating back to the linguistic enquiry of the Ancient Greeks, what Firth characterised as 'the word process in the sentence' was dealt with under two separate headings:

1. **Morphology**: literally the study of word 'shape' (Greek *morphē*). In early Greek grammars this was known as *ptōsis* 'falling', from which was derived the Latin *casus*, 'case' (from the verb *cadere* 'to fall'), this eventually becoming specialised for referrring to the inflection of nouns. From this same metaphor of 'falling' was derived the general term in Latin grammars *accidentia*, 'accidence', i.e., the forms words 'fell into' (*accidere*). The term *morphology* itself, a 19th century coining, was taken over from biology, where it is still used to describe the physical structure of entities, at a time when linguistics was very influenced by biological models.

2. **Syntax**: literally the 'arrangement' (Greek *syntaxis*) of words into larger units such as phrases and sentences. This of course begs the question of how all these units – words, phrases, sentence – are to be defined, and what sort of 'arrangement' we are talking about here, issues that we will come to in later chapters.

This twofold model needs to be understood in terms both of the nature of the Ancient Greek and Latin languages, and of the linguistic tradition which was derived from them. Greek and Latin, like many other members of the Indo-European family of languages to which they belong, were highly inflected languages: that is, they made great use of changes in word endings, as well as associated changes in the basic form or stem of a word, to indicate its function in connected discourse. The first task for a linguist describing one of these languages, therefore, was to deal with the shape of words, which were set out for pedagogical purposes in what were called in Greek *kanones*, or 'patterns' (Robins 1993: 111), such as the following one for the Latin noun *carō* 'meat, flesh':

> carō
> carnem
> carnis
> carni
> carne

According to the particular role the noun *carō* was playing in a larger unit, it would take on one of these five forms. For historical reasons, inflection in these languages, particularly for nouns and verbs, were enormously complex, with nouns in Latin falling into at least five subtypes or 'declensions', and verbs into four 'conjugations', with a lot of exceptions left over. This meant that for these languages a lot of the descriptive work had to go into covering what we now call the morphological shape of words, before you could move on to describing how they were put together in syntactic patterns.

As a sideline of this morphological complexity, however, the syntax of these languages was relatively flexible. It was not, as has been erroneously claimed, a case of 'free word order': Latin and Greek, like the ancestral Proto-Indo-European from which they were descended, seem to have had what is called a basic SOV, or Subject-Object-Verb, order. In other words, unless there were good reasons otherwise, a situation would be presented linguistically in the order Actor-Acted-upon-Action (in contrast to the SVO – Actor-Action-Acted-upon – order of its descendants like Italian). However, for reasons of emphasis, this order could be varied, because the endings of the individual words showed the syntactic relationships between them. For example, a sentence like *carnem linque in culinā*, literally 'meat leave in kitchen', i.e. 'Leave the meat in the kitchen' could be equally well expressed as *linque carnem in culinā* or *in culinā carnem linque*, because the shape *carnem* showed that the meat was being left, not doing the leaving, in which case it would have taken the form *carō*. For such languages, then, a two-way division into morphology and syntax works very well. It does not work so well for Modern English, where word shape is much less complex and word order much more constrained; and it works even less well for a language like Chinese, where word shape in almost invariable.

Such a model, however, also needs to be understood in terms of the basic Graeco-Roman theory of language as *vox articulāta* or 'articulated sound'. This model was in effect a theorisation of the alphabetic writing system, which the Greeks were the first to invent and which was then taken over by the Romans. In the form this took in the writing of the Latin grammarians, language could be *articulated* or broken down into a number of units of differing sizes, these units forming an unbroken succession from the smallest, the written letter which represented the spoken sound, up to the largest, the complete utterance or sentence:

litera	*syllaba*	*dictiō*	*oratiō*
'letter / sound'	'syllable'	'word'	'utterance / sentence'

As summed up by the famous grammarian of the 5th century, Priscian, 'just as letters combining appropriately form syllables, and syllables words, so too do words form a sentence' (quoted in Matthews 2001: 82).

In fact, modern linguistics has shown this to be an oversimplified picture. There are actually two different kinds of articulation involved, which the French linguist Andre Martinet dubbed the 'first' and 'second' articulation respectively.

Martinet defines the first articulation as that of experience into meaningful form (1960: 22):

> The first articulation of language is that whereby every fact of experience
> to be communicated…is analysed into a succession of units each of which
> is endowed with a vocal form and a meaning.

Martinet uses the French example *j'ai mal à la tête*, literally 'I have pain at the head', in other words, 'I have a headache'. Here we have six units – *j(e)*, *ai*, *mal*, *à*, *la*, *tête* – which in combination are the way the language represents the experience of a pain in that area (in this situation, English makes do with only four, or perhaps five if you count *headache* as two).

As Martinet goes on to explain (1960: 24, phonemic transcription added):

> Each of these units of the first articulation presents…a meaning and a
> vocal…form. It cannot be analysed into smaller successive units endowed
> with meaning. The totality *tête* /tɛt/ means 'head' and we cannot attribute
> to *tê* and to *te* a different meaning, the sum of which would be 'head'.
> But the vocal form itself is analysable into a series of units each of which
> makes its contribution to distinguishing *tête* /tɛt/ from other units such
> as *bête* /bɛt/, *tante* /tãt/, or *terre* /tɛr/. This is what we propose to call the
> second articulation of language.

Thus we have the basic perceptible phenomenon of a stream of sound, which is articulated first into what Martinet referred to as **significant** units, each of which has a sound and a meaning. These significant units are themselves articulated into what Martinet called **distinctive** units, i.e. sounds with no meaning in themselves, but with the capacity to distinguish particular significant units from each other, as in the examples above of /tɛt/, vs /bɛt/, /tãt/, and /tɛr/.

Looking at the problem from the opposite point of view, an American linguist of an earlier generation, Leonard Bloomfield, made a similar division of the units of language into the 'distinctive' (sounds) and the 'semantic' (the meaning-carrying words and their shapes and combinations) (Bloomfield 1914, quoted in Hockett 1968: 19):

> The first task of the linguistic investigator is the analysis of a language
> into distinctive sounds, their variations, and the like. When he has
> completed this, he turns to the analysis of the semantic structure – to
> what we call the morphology and syntax of the language, its grammatical
> structure.

Syntax, including morphology, can thus be taken as the study of the first articulation of language, of the patterning of the significant units of language. As I explained above, from a cross-linguistic point of view there is no need to separate the study of the form words take from how they combine into larger structures, and we will thus deal with both in this book under the general heading of syntax. Furthermore, in line with both Martinet's and Bloomfield's definition, as well as the general approach recommended by Firth above, we will not be separating the study of the structures into which these units enter from the meanings that they have: structure and meaning are in fact two sides of the same coin.

For one final perspective on this question, we can refer to the work of the American linguist Charles Hockett, who put as one of the basic issues of linguistic research the following question (1987: 15):

> What is the nature of the collusion between the structure of utterances
> and the strategy of listeners by virtue of which correct interpretation and
> understanding are possible?

From this point of view, that of the listener's perception of language, Hockett identified two stages in the processing of an incoming utterance (1987: 96):

1. parsing: identifying words and distinguishing them from other words

2. construing: understanding how those words fit together

Traditionally, only the second would count as a strictly syntactic study, since in written texts – the object of traditional analysis and pedagogy – the first task is already performed by the writing system, or by reference to the dictionary. However, the first is also crucial to our understanding of the patterning of significant units, as we will see in the following chapter.

2   Processing the text

Language data does not lay itself out for our inspection and analysis: it needs to be processed. The starting point for this is usually a representation of a text in written form, with the stream of sound 'captured' by symbols such as the letters of the alphabet used for English, or the International Phonetic Alphabet (IPA). Certain of these symbols are then grouped together, by the use of blank spaces, into larger units such as words, and the words are further grouped, using extra symbols such as punctuation, into phrases and sentences.

The linguist A.L. Becker, in a very thoughtful essay on the analysis of Burmese, points out that this processing is in no way theoretically or descriptively 'neutral'. In fact, by the time a linguist publicly presents a description of a language, much of the initial theorising has already been done and hidden away. Firstly, the transcription, i.e. the rendering of a text into graphs (letters and punctuation) and larger units (words, phrases and sentences), makes a whole lot of assumptions about how the language works. As Becker points out for Burmese (1993: 64):

> A Burmese typewriter does not automatically move along to the next space when a letter is struck. It sits still. One strikes a central symbol, the syllable 'initial' consonant in most cases, and then one may modify it by adding marks above, below, behind and in front of it…The central cultural metaphor, the figure of Burmese writing itself, is much more one of center and periphery than linear sequence…The point here is that putting Burmese words into linear, phonemic writing (romanizing it) obliterates a very deep metaphor (center and periphery) which resonates widely in Burmese culture. Much traditional phonology and modern linguistics depends on this romanization as a first step…in analysis. The illusion is that nothing important is lost.

The sorts of issues involved here will be touched on in Chapter 4, when we look at a Chinese text, and see how transcribing the text into a romanised form, i.e. using the Roman alphabet, in fact changes the whole reading strategy by which we interpret it.

Secondly, if the language *of* description (the language in which the description is being written) is different from the language *under* description (the language which is being described), then the original text needs to be 'glossed': that is, each significant unit of the original must be given a (rough) equivalent in the language of description. As Becker again points out (1993: 62):

> …glossing, a kind of 'literal', word by word, morpheme by morpheme translation…though it might be done with care, almost never is. Most of the analysis is done in the glossing, for the reader's understanding and hence, the analyst's argument depend on the familiarity of those glosses.

Thus, here again, distortion is involved. By the very nature of language, it is in principle impossible to find exact equivalents in the language of description for the morphemes and words of the language under description.

The best way to explore the issues involved here is to break this process into stages. The following text extract from a textbook of Scottish Gaelic (Boyd & Robertson 1993: 189) has been scripted to represent a spoken conversation. I present it first below in an unglossed form, which we can call 'Version A':

Version A

(1)R   De nì sinn a-nochd ma tha?

(2)D   Nach teid sinn gu disco neo gu dannsa?

(3)M   Cha teid mise co-dhiù. Tha mi ro sgìth. Bha mi air mo chasan fad an latha. B'fheàrr leam fuireach a-staigh a-nochd.

(4)S   Nach fhuirich sinn a-staigh 's nach coimhead sinn air film air bhidio?

In this first version of the text, there are several things we can tell from the transcription even without understanding the language. Listening to the spoken version, the first division that suggests itself is one into each speaker's turns or **moves**. Using a common convention in transcribing conversational texts, one borrowed from play scripts, we start each new move on a separate line. In this case, I have also identified the speaker by initial (*R*aibeart, *D*ughall, *M*agaidh, and *S*ara), and numbered the moves for easy reference. Since Gaelic uses an alphabetic orthography, the conventions for indicating words, phrases etc. are very similar to English, though as we will see the notion of 'word' is in fact a little different.

The next version starts the glossing process, though in order to dissect this process a little more, what I have provided below are not **glosses**, as normally understood, i.e. word for word equivalents, but rather a **translation**, i.e. a contextually appropriate English equivalent of each move:

Version B

(1)**R** De nì sinn a-nochd ma tha?
What'll we do tonight then?

(2)**D** Nach teid sinn gu disco neo gu dannsa?
Why don't we go to a disco or to a dance?

(3)**M** Cha teid mise co-dhiù.
I'm not going anyway.

Tha mi ro sgìth.
I'm too tired.

Bha mi air mo chasan   fad an latha.
I was on my feet all day.

B'fheàrr leam   fuireach a-staigh a-nochd.
I'd rather stay home tonight.

(4)**S** Nach fhuirich sinn   a-staigh
Why don't we stay at home

's   nach coimhead   sinn air film   air bhidio?
and watch a film or a video?

This version introduces a number of further conventions, intended to make the text more appropriate for syntactic analysis. Firstly, I have broken each move into **clauses**, again a standard convention, and put each one on a separate line. I won't go into the basis on which I've made the breaks here – again a theoretically highly significant one – but we'll have a look at the arguments for doing this in another language, Mandarin Chinese, in Chapter 4. Secondly, I've grouped the words into **phrases** or **groups** (again I won't argue for these groupings for the moment – see Chapter 9 for further discussion) since it is strictly speaking these units, not words, that are directly relevant for syntactic analysis. The use of a smaller font for the English is partly for ease of distinguishing it from the Gaelic, but it may also suggest that it is the Gaelic that is the main centre of attention – an implication that is perhaps deceptive, if we accept Becker's argument about glossing quoted above.

With a translation, we can start making educated guesses, at least, as to the meaning of each group. We can note, for example, the repetition of *sinn* in 1. and 2., and 4., and that of (*nach*) *teid* and (*cha*) *teid* in 2. and 3. We can also, particularly for a language like Gaelic that has close cultural links with English, note what look like borrowings in *disco* and *dannsa* in 2., as well as *film* and *bhidio* in 4. We can note partial similarity between *mise* and *mi*, *mi* in 3., and between *fuireach* and (*nach*) *fhuirich* in 3. and 4. Finally we can note what seem to be regular patterns of co-occurrence, such as that of *nach* with *teid* in 2., and with *fhuirich* and *coimhead* in 4.; or of variation, as between *nach* (*teid*) and *cha* (*teid*) in 2. and 3., and perhaps even between *tha* and *bha* in 3.

Such an exercise can only take us so far, of course, but it is useful in highlighting the sorts of evidence on which we can begin to base glosses. The next version of the text is a glossed one, with English equivalents set out directly underneath each unit of the original:

Version C

(1)R De   nì   sinn   a-nochd   ma tha?
     what   will-do   we   tonight   then

(2)D Nach teid   sinn   gu disco   neo   gu dannsa?
     not-Q will-go   we   to disco   or   to dance

(3)M Cha teid   mise   co-dhiù.
     not-S will-go   I-EMPH   anyway

     Tha   mi   ro sgìth.
     be   I   too tired

     Bha   mi   air mo chasan   fad an latha.
     was   I   on my feet   long the day

     B(u)' fheàrr   leam   fuireach   a-staigh   a-nochd.
     were better   with-me   staying   at-home   tonight.

(4)S Nach fhuirich   sinn   a-staigh
     not-Q will-stay   we   at-home

     's   nach coimhead   sinn   air film   air bhidio?
     and   not-Q will-watch   we   on film   on video?

In this version, I have introduced several more conventions. Unless otherwise indicated, one orthographic unit ('word') on the line above is equivalent to one on the line below: if the English takes more than one word for a word of Gaelic, then the words are joined by hyphens, as in 'with-me' for *leam*. (The hyphen in Gaelic orthography is normally used to mark word stress, indicating that the stress is not on the first syllable, as is normal in Gaelic, but on the second, i.e. following the hyphen: e.g. *a*-STAIGH as opposed to FUIR*each*.) In some cases, however, there is a bit of fudging involved, because of there being no clear English equivalent for a Gaelic word. Take for example the gloss 'I-EMPH' for *mise*. If we refer back to the translation in Version B, we can see that this word is rendered as *I*, i.e. in italics, a standard English convention for indicating emphasis. This gives us the clue as to what EMPH stands for: it glosses the 'emphatic particle' (for want of a better term) -*se* or -*sa* that can be attached to pronouns, as here, nouns, or even verbs; its English equivalent is usually a marked intonation pattern, which is what the use of italics is intended to convey.

A more complex example is in the rendering of *nach* and *cha* as 'not-Q' and 'not-S' respectively. It is probably obvious from the context that Q here stands for 'question' and S for 'statement': in other words, that Gaelic has a different word for 'not' depending on whether it appears in a question or a statement. That this is in fact only a half-truth can be seen by examining the immediately following segment of the text:

(5)R   Am bu toil   leibh   idir   a dhol   a-mach
         Q-were pleasure   with-yous   at-all   to-go   out

         a dh' àite   air choireigin?
         to place   of some-kind
         'Wouldn't you like to go out somewhere or other?'

(6)D   Bu toil   leamsa   sin   co-dhiù.
         were pleasure   with-me-EMPH   that   anyway
         '*I'd* like that anyway.'

Now according to the gloss, the *bu* in 6. simply means 'were', with *am* added in 5. to turn it into a question: this is what the glossing seems to be telling us here. However, if we try to systematise the contrasts that are being expressed by these different forms into what would conventionally be called a grammatical system of **mood** in Gaelic, we can see that the pattern is for there to be a clearly indicated distinction between polarity (positive and negative) in both declarative mood (i.e. expressing statements) and interrogative mood (expressing questions). This pattern can be tabulated as follows into a type of paradigm, in other words, a systematic table of contrasting alternatives, where the amended glosses show the parallelism in the Gaelic:

polarity	mood	
	Declarative	**Interrogative**
positive	*bu* s-were	*am bu* Q-were
negative	*cha bu* not-s-were	*nach bu* not-Q-were

Furthermore, when we look at similar patterning in other parts of the text, we can see the contrast even more clearly, for example with the forms of the verb 'go', where the positive declarative form of the verb, *theid*, is different from the form of the verb in the three other mood types, *teid*:

polarity	mood	
	Declarative	**Interrogative**
positive	*theid* s-will-go	*an teid* Q-will-go
negative	*cha teid* s-not-will-go	*nach teid* Q-not-will-go

Becker comments on this kind of process (1993: 62):

> The second step in analysis [after glossing]…is abstraction…[1] – putting the glossed language into a grammatical framework, the terms of which are terms in the language of the glossing. This language about language or metalanguage is…rarely if ever seen as equal in power in the two languages, and so there is an interesting politics here…which is only beginning to be unfolded: the politics of claiming universal explanations from within a particular language.

The whole question of the 'power relations' between the language of description and the language under description relates, as Becker points out, to the question of 'universal' features of languages. This comes up particularly when we are looking at grammatical categories: what Firth referred to as colligational relations between words (see discussion in next chapter). In other words, what features do (all) languages share, and how similar does a category like 'noun' or 'subject' need to be in two or more languages for us to give it the same name? This is something that is very much a live issue in linguistics generally, but for the time being, I will adopt the careful but practical position recommended by Halliday (1993: 5):

> Since we know that all human languages have much in common, we naturally use the descriptive categories of one language as a guide when working on another. But if a descriptive category named 'clause' or 'passive' or 'Theme' is used in describing, say, both English and Chinese, it is redefined in the case of each language.

This further extract, 5–6, given above, also raises a further issue. What, for example, do we make of glosses like:

(5) Am bu toil   leibh
     Q-were pleasure   with-yous

or indeed of

(3) B(u)' fheàrr   leam   fuireach
     were better   with-me   staying

If we refer back to the translations in version B., we see that these are translated as 'would(n't) you like' and 'I'd rather' respectively. Such idioms are what Becker calls the 'root metaphors' of a language, and these pose yet another challenge for glossing (1993: 62):

> Glossing is clearly a political process. How often do two languages meet as equals, with equal and reciprocal authority? How often, for instance, are the root metaphors of the 'exotic' language considered equal in analytic power to those of the language of analysis? Many find the deepest metaphors of another language poetic and defamiliarising, but few find them to be as useful in analysis as one's own, i.e. as pictures of the world 'as it is'. It takes considerable effort even to see one's own root metaphors as metaphors.

For example, clause 3 in Gaelic clearly involves a comparative construction, 'it would be better with me', which is obscured for us in the English gloss by the fact that *rather*, although in shape like a comparative, is probably no longer understood as one; while the most common alternative (*I'd*) *prefer* is a metaphor borrowed from a different language (Latin *prāeferre* 'to bring before') and thus for most English speakers not considered as one. Gaelic contains a whole set of such 'metaphors' for referring to personal inclination and capacity: as well as *is toil leam* 'is pleasure with me – I like to', it also has *is urrainn dhomh* 'is capability to me – I can', *is còir dhomh* 'is decorum to me – I should', and so on. The question, then, for the analyst is how far does one go 'unpacking' the metaphors, i.e. representing them in terms of their components in the original language, which in the case of the Gaelic examples just discussed seem to be highly systematic.

In fact, the stage of 'unpacking' represented by version C is by no means complete. Gaelic contains a whole lot of other systematic features that were not seen as germane to the analysis of this text (the glossing here was originally designed for looking at mood distinctions). Below I give an example of the opening of another Gaelic text (Ò Maolalaigh & MacAonghuis 1996: 200) where the glossing is far more detailed, and of what seems like a fearsome level of technicality (the numbering here is by clauses; a key to the abbreviations of grammatical terms is given following the text).

(1) uair   dha   robh   an saoghal
     time   to-it be+PAST+DEP   the+MASC world
     'Once upon a time'

(2) bha   iolaire   anns na beanntan
     be+PAST+IND   eagle   in the+PLUR mountain+PLUR
     'there was an eagle in the mountains'

     a-muigh   taobh   Loch Trèig
     away   side   Loch Treig
     'away beside Loch Treig'.

(3) bha   i   a' fuireach ann an coire   an-sin
     be+PAST+IND   she at live+NOM   in   corry   there
     'She was living in a corry [depression in the side of a mountain] there'

(4) ris   an can   iad   An Coire Meadhain.
     to-it REL say+FUT+DEP   they the corry middle+GEN
     'which they call the Middle Corry.'

(5) A' bliadhna seo   thainig   geamhradh fuar   agus mòran sneachda,
     the+FEM year this come+PAST+IND   winter cold+MASC   and much snow+GEN

     le cur   is   cathadh
     with fall and drift
     'One year (there) came a cold winter and a lot of snow, in fall and drift'

(6) Oidhche   dhe na h-oidhcheannan,   bha   an iolaire
    night   of the+PLUR night+PLUR   be+PAST+IND   the+FEM eagle

    a' faireachdainn   an fhuachd.
    at feel+NOM   the+GEN cold+GEN
    '(On) one of the nights, the eagle was feeling the cold'

(7) 'Cha   do dh'fhairich   mi a lethid   de dh'fhuachd riamh'
    NEG+DECL DEP feel+PAST   I   its like   of cold+GEN   ever
    ' "I've never felt cold like this" '

(8) thuirt   i   rithe fhèin.
    say+PAST+IND   she   to-her self
    'She said to herself'

(9) 'Saoil'
    think+IMP
    ' "Think" '

(10) thuirt   i,
     say+PAST+IND   she
     'She said'

(11) 'an robh   oidhche   na b(u)'   fhuaire   na seo riamh   ann?'
     INT be+PAST+DEP night   REL be+PAST+IND cold+COMP than this ever   in-it
     ' "Was there ever a night colder than this?" '

(12) Bha   dreathan donn   a' fuireach   faisg oirre,
     be+PAST+IND   wren brown+MASC at live+NOM   near on-her
     'There was a wren living near her'

(13) is   chaidh   i
     and   go+PAST+IND she
     'And she went'

(14) far   an robh   an dreathan.
     where   REL be+PAST+DEP   the+MASC wren
     'Where the wren was.'

Abbreviation	Term	Explanation
DECL	declarative	expressing statements
INT	interrogative	expressing questions
IMP	imperative	expressing commands
PAST	past	past tense
FUT	future	future tense
DEP	dependent	in dependent (subordinate) clause
IND	independent	in independent (free) clause
REL	relative	links clause to preceding element
MASC	masculine	masculine gender (of nouns, articles, adjectives)
FEM	feminine	feminine gender (of nouns, articles, adjectives)
PLUR	plural	plural number
GEN	genitive	genitive (possessive) case
COMP	comparative	comparative form of adjective
NOM	nominal	nominal form of verb (gerund), verbal noun

In this case, the glossing was devised for exploring what is often called 'information flow' (see Chapter 11), and therefore the forms both of the verbs – which distinguish in Gaelic between what are technically known as 'dependent' and 'independent' forms as well as a number of different tenses – and also of the nouns – which have four different case forms – need to be indicated in detail. This glossing is basically designed for us to be able to 'follow' the different characters through the text, in other words, see how they are referred to differently at different stages in the narrative. If we take the main character, the eagle, we can see it (or 'she' in Gaelic – see discussion below) is referred to in a number of significantly distinctive ways:

(2)   *iolaire* 'eagle'
(3)   *i* 'she'
(6)   *an iolaire* 'the eagle'
(8)   *i* 'she'
(10) *i* 'she'
(13) *i* 'she'

What this seems to tell us is that there are three ways of referring to the eagle: by simply using the word itself, *iolaire*; by adding the 'definite article' *an* 'the'; or by using the 'pronoun' *i* 'she'. In fact, we need to do some further 'digging' to understand what the real contrasts here are. Gaelic, like English and many other European languages, distinguishes between 'indefinite' and 'definite' forms of the noun. But while English has two different 'articles' – indefinite *a / an* and definite *the* – Gaelic simply uses the noun by itself for the indefinite – thus, *iolaire* 'an eagle', and uses a definite article *a' / an / am* for the second – thus, *an iolaire* 'the eagle'. We can note what seems to be the same pattern later in the text with *dreathan* (*donn*) '(brown) wren – a wren' versus *an dreathan* 'the wren'.

If we look closely at the glosses, in *an iolaire*, the article *an* is glossed 'the+FEM', while in *an dreathan* it is glossed 'the+MASC'. How can the same form *an* have what seem to be two different meanings? Well, it turns out that a distinction between feminine and masculine **gender** runs right through the nominal classes of words (see Chapter 9) in Gaelic. In English, we have what is called 'natural gender', where entities are classified as male / female / inanimate, referred to with the pronouns *he / she / it*. However in Gaelic, as in many other European languages, there is a system of 'grammatical gender', where all nouns fall into either masculine or feminine, and are thus referred to either with *e* 'he' or *i* 'she'. This system to a certain extent conforms to natural gender, but there is no necessary connection, and of course all those entities that would be classified according to natural gender as inanimate (which often corresponds to 'not (fully) human' – note how we use *it* to refer to animals and small children in English) are perforce either masculine or feminine. However this system originally worked in the Indo-European family of languages to which Gaelic belongs, the function of grammatical gender in contemporary European languages that possess it, like Gaelic, is a **cohesive** one: in other words, it is used to link together certain linguistic expressions with related expressions.

So we can see now why it was crucial here, as it was not for the first text, to indicate the gender of each noun. Simply judging from the English glosses, we might think that the eagle was being personified as female, and the wren (referred to later in a part of the text not given here as *e* 'he') as male. In fact, the two nouns are simply feminine versus masculine gender, and a whole set of features are determined by the fact that *dreathann* 'wren' is masculine while *iolaire* 'eagle' is feminine: if we add an descriptive adjective, we have *dreathan donn* 'brown wren' versus *iolaire dhonn* 'brown eagle'; if we use a descriptor without the main noun we have *fear donn* 'the brown one' for the wren versus *tè dhonn* 'the brown one' for the eagle; if we vary the case of the nouns, we have *an dreathan / an dhreathain / an dreathan* 'the wren / of the wren / to the wren' versus *an iolaire / na h-iolaire / an iolaire* 'the eagle / of the eagle /

to the eagle'. And of course, we have already seen how the pronouns differ: *e* 'he' for the wren versus *i* 'she' for the eagle.

What is the significance of the differences in the glossing of these two Gaelic texts for glossing and parsing generally? First of all, it can be seen that glossing, like all description, is highly **contingent** on the purposes for which it is envisaged. We can note that, for certain purposes, it may be sufficient to use a type of glossing that is fairly close to the language of description: in other words, a glossing that uses as much as possible a 'one for one' approach. We used this type of glossing in the first text, where for the most part, with a bit of tweaking, one word of Gaelic was represented by one word of English. What this gives us is a type of telegraphese – like the 'what will-do we tonight then' of the first text – which makes the language under description sound like a quaintly distorted version of the language of description. The opposite of this approach is to use a highly technical type of glossing, with grammatical features being represented by technical terms, which has the advantage of more accurately representing the features of the language under description, but at the cost of making the text harder to interpret from the point of view of the language of description.

Secondly, all glossing is **contrastive**. Simply by representing one language in the words of another we are making a comparison between the two. Every language operates through a network of interlocking distinctions, and this network is never the same from one language to another. So if we are glossing – going between two different languages – we will need to make decisions as to which distinctions are going to be relevant for our purposes, and which are not. Thus glossing, as Becker argues, is in fact a crucial part of our description and so of our understanding of the text, because it highlights particular features of the original, and downplays or ignores certain other features. But no matter how detailed the glossing, we can never take the glossing for the text itself: we must always be aware that it is a representation, and thus a distortion, of the original. A text in the language under description is never simply either a telegraphically simplified or a technically complexified version of the language of description.

As Becker nicely sums it up, it is a condition of what he refers to as languaging that (1993: 61):

> …our understanding of another person's words is always approximate,
> always on the one hand exuberant, for we add much to what we hear or
> read, and, on the other hand, deficient, for there is much the sayer (or the
> writer) intended which we miss.

This problem of approximation versus exuberance is even more evident when we are going between languages, as we have done in the analyses above, and is thus something that we need to be very aware of in processing texts for analysis. We cannot *not* gloss: otherwise we are unable to make the text accessible to our own analysis, let alone to our readers' understanding; but we need to be aware that it is an inescapably distorting process.

Notes

1   Becker refers to this as 'parsing', a term more often reserved for the process of identifying words, as in Hockett's usage quoted in Chapter 1: this second stage of 'abstraction', in Becker's terms, is more normally referred to, again in line with Hockett's usage, as 'analysis'.

3   Linear sequence and structural order

As we saw in Chapter 1, one of the basic features of language is its **linearity**. The basic linguistic phenomenon is what the Swiss linguist Ferdinand de Saussure called the 'spoken chain' (Saussure 1916 / 1959: 104), a stream of sounds following each other through time. If we examine the nonsense poem *Jabberwocky* from Lewis Carroll's *Through the Looking Glass*, we will notice that many individual sections of this 'spoken chain' don't correspond to what we would recognise as ordinary English words.

Jabberwocky

'Twas brillig, and the slithy toves
Did gyre and gimble in the wabe;
All mimsy were the borogoves,
And the mome raths outgrabe.

'Beware the Jabberwock, my son!
The jaws that bite, the claws that catch!
Beware the Jubjub bird, and shun
The frumious Bandersnatch!'

He took his vorpal sword in hand:
Long time the manxome foe he sought –
So rested he by the Tumtum tree,
And stood awhile in thought.

And, as in uffish thought he stood,
The Jabberwock, with eyes of flame,
Came whiffling through the tulgey wood,
And burbled as it came!

One two! One two! And through and through
The vorpal blade went snicker-snack!
He left it dead, and with its head
He went galumphing back.

'And hast thou slain the Jabberwock?
Come to my arms, my beamish boy!
O frabjous day! Callooh! Callay!'
He chortled in his joy.

'Twas brillig, and the slithy toves
Did gyre and gimble in the wabe;
All mimsy were the borogoves,
And the mome raths outgrabe.

Lewis Carroll (1871) *Alice's Adventures through the Looking Glass*

As Alice remarks: 'Somehow it seems to fill my head with ideas – only I don't exactly know what they are!' How does Alice recognise the meaningfulness of this poem, even if she can't quite work out what it means?

Well, the organisation of language is not confined to relationships between immediately preceding and following elements: if it were, we'd have nothing much to talk about in this book. In fact, as the French linguist Lucien Tesnière pointed out, there is a difference between simple **linear sequence** and what he called **structural order**[1]. As he puts it (1959: 17–18):

> The spoken chain is of a single dimension, it appears in the form of a line. This is its essential characteristic…We can say that two words which follow each other in the spoken chain constitute a sequence.

However, in order to interpret the meaning relations between words, we have to 'place' them in a structural order (1959: 16), according to some sort of 'connection' between them, and this goes beyond their sequence:

> The structural order of words is that according to which their connections are established. Now the connections are multiple…the result being that structural order is of several dimensions.

Firth also made a similar point (1957 / 1968: 173):

> In [syntactic] structures, one recognizes the place and order of the
> categories. This, however, is very different from the successivity of bits
> and pieces in a unidirectional time sequence.

The process of producing and understanding speech, therefore, is one of going
between the structural order and the linear sequence, as explained by Tesnière
(1959: 18):

> …to speak a language is to transform its structural order into its linear
> sequence, and inversely, to understand a language is to transform its linear
> sequence into its structural order.

This phenomenon is what Hockett refers to as 'structure in depth' (Hockett
1987: 16): in other words, that we can recognise relationships between meaningful elements which are not simply a function of their relative sequence. So
what is the nature of this 'structure in depth'? To start with, we can identify
two aspects, two ways in which we perceive relationships that go beyond
the merely linear: to use what may seem like a paradoxical formulation, we
perceive relationships not only between the elements that are *actually present*
with each other, but also between the elements present and those that *aren't*
present but could have been.

Saussure was the first to formulate this distinction, and he did so in the
context of trying to determine how we identify linguistic units (Saussure 1916
/ 1959: 108) in other words, how do we know that we've said or heard the
same element on two different occasions? Saussure saw that this involved
two dimensions. On the one hand, there is a **horizontal** dimension by which
we distinguish a particular element from what precedes and follows it: these
are relationships *in praesentia* (actually present). But there is also a **vertical**
dimension by which we distinguish a particular element from what might have
been said at the same point: these are relationships *in absentia* (absent, but
potentially present) (Saussure 1916 / 1959: 123).

Let's see how this works with the third verse from the poem (nonsense
words italicised):

> He took his *vorpal* sword in hand,
> Long time the *manxome* foe he sought,
> Then rested he by the *Tum-Tum* tree,
> And stood awhile in thought.

How do we know what the nonsense words mean, or at least how do we
think we know what they mean? Well, from our knowledge of the horizontal

patterns of combination in English, we know that *vorpal* should refer to some sort of attribute or quality of the *sword* which follows it, likewise for *manxome* in relation to *foe*, while *Tum-Tum* must refer to a type of *tree*. From our knowledge of the vertical **possibilities of substitution** in English, we know of numbers of words that might have appeared as substitutes for these three nonsense words: so instead of *vorpal*, we could have had *voracious*, or *fatal*; while for *manxome* we could have had *manly* or *noisome*, and so on. In fact, as one of the characters, Humpty Dumpty, explains later to Alice in relation to the first stanza of this poem, many of these nonsense words are what he called 'portmanteau (suitcase)' words, 'two words packed up in one', and it is possible that Carroll had something like these possible alternatives in mind when he coined these expressions.

These two kinds of relations apply to all meaningful elements, and represent the basic mechanism by which words have meaning: **in combination with** other words, and **by substitution for** other words. The combination relations are commonly known as **syntagmatic** (from the Greek *syntagma*, 'joint arrangement'); while the substitution relations are called **paradigmatic** (from the Greek *paradigma* 'parallel display'). Firth extended this distinction into a claim that linguistic analysis generally needed to be based both on **structures**, i.e. combinations of elements, and **systems**, i.e. sets of options, and that, moreover, there was a basis for this distinction in our experience of the world (Firth 1956 / 1968: 90):

> The whole of our linguistic behaviour is best understood if it is seen
> as a network of relations between people, things and events, showing
> structures [of possible combinations EMcD] and systems [of alternative
> options EMcD], just as we notice in all our experience. The body itself is
> a set of structures and systems and the world in which we maintain life
> is also structural and systematic. This network of structures and systems
> we must abstract from the mush of general goings-on which, at first sight,
> may appear to be a chaos or flux.

These two patterns of organisation, therefore, can be seen as deeply rooted in how we are organised as physical beings, how we process the information that comes to us through our senses, as well as how we interpret aspects of that information in linguistic form.

The notion of structure is a rather complex one, which we will need to explore in depth in later chapters, but the notion of system can be easily shown. In the famous initial stanza from the poem, repeated at the end, at each of the italicised points a whole system of alternatives is possible (most of these are suggested by the character Humpty Dumpty in his later interpretation of the poem for Alice):

	broiling-time			lithe	badgers		
'Twas	*brillig*	and	the	*slithy*	*toves*		
	evening			slimy	corkscrews		
	gyrate			gambol			way-before
Did	*gyre*	and		*gimble*	in the	*wabe*	
	gyroscope			gimlet			way-behind
	miserable			birds			
All	*mimsy*	were the		*borogoves*			
	flimsy			mops			
	from-home	rats		grunted			
And the	*mome*	raths		*outgrabe.*			
	tame	laths		sneezed			

Relationships between words involve two further kinds of links, as was also pointed out by Firth. When we put together two words like *vorpal* and *sword*, as in the previous example, they are linked as **grammatical categories**: that is as adjective and noun, which in English normally appear in this order, and are interpreted in terms of attribute and thing, or quality and entity, and so on. For this sort of relationship, Firth coined the term **colligation**, from the Latin *colligare*, literally 'tie together'. As he explains (1956 / 1968: 181):

> Grammatical relations should not be regarded as between words as such…[but] as grammatical abstractions which state some of the relations between interrelated categories within a…sentence.

Besides the adjective-noun colligation in *vorpal sword* or *manxome foe*, we have a verb-pronoun colligation in *rested he* (in non-poetic English normally in the order pronoun-verb, i.e. *he rested*), a preposition-noun colligation in *in hand*, and so on. As we will see in a later chapter, these are not only combinations of particular grammatical categories, they also express particular syntactic relations.

Beside their relations as grammatical categories in a particular structure, words like *slithy* and *toves* are also linked as **lexical items**: that is, in Humpty Dumpty's universe at least, if we hear a mention of the word *toves*, we are likely to expect to also hear *slithy* somewhere in the context. This relationship is what Firth called **collocation**, from the Latin *collocare*, literally 'place together'. As he said pithily 'You shall know a word by the company it keeps!' (1957 / 1968: 179), or more technically (180–81):

> The habitual collocations in which words under study appear are quite simply the mere word accompaniment, the other word-material in which they are most commonly or most characteristically embedded…. The collocation of a word…is not to be regarded as mere juxtaposition, it is an order of mutual expectancy.

Other collocation relations in the poem, would be those between *vorpal* – meaning, say, something like 'sharp and dangerous' and *sword*, between *manxome* ('fierce'?) and *foe*; or between *took (take)*, *sword* and *hand*, or *sought (seek)* and *foe*.

All these different kinds of relations – syntagmatic (structure) vs paradigmatic (system), colligation (of grammatical categories) vs collocation (of lexical items) – begin to explain exactly how it is that we 'extract' the structural order, the structure-in-depth, from the linear sequence.

We can get some notion of how this works if we have a go at identifying the colligational and collocational relationships in the poem. Of course in many cases the same word will display *both* colligational (marked by ↳ ↵) *and* collocational (marked by ▶ ◀) relationships to neighbouring words. In order to show some of how Carroll's technique works, in the following analysis, for the nonsense words colligational relations only will be indicated – on the grounds that on first acquaintance with the poem we don't know really what these words mean (lexically) and only make a guess based on their colligational ties (grammatically). The separate lines of arrows also give some idea of Hockett's notion of 'structure in depth', with the same word often entering into more than one tie.

```
'T   was      brillig, and the slithy   toves
↳    ↵                      ↳            ↵
     ↳          ↵                ↳       ↵


Did   gyre  and  gimble  in   the  wabe;
↳     ↵                  ↳         ↵
↳                   ↵          ↳   ↵


All    mimsy   were    the   borogoves,
↳      ↵                ↳     ↵
       ↳          ↵  ↳        ↵


And   the mome    raths   outgrabe.
      ↳           ↵
          ↳          ↵  ↳     ↵
```

From this analysis we can see that in this first stanza (also repeated at the end of the poem) there are in fact no collocational ties of the ordinary sort: in other words all the lexical words are nonsense words, so any sense we make of it on a first reading is simply from the colligational ties.

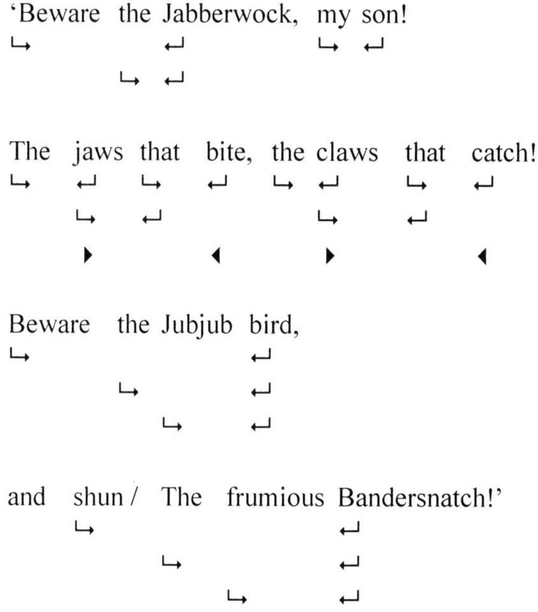

In the second stanza, although again there is a high proportion of nonsense lexical words, one whole line is perfectly normal English, with both colligational and collocational ties, which, significantly for the poem as a whole, indicates that what the hero will be dealing with is something dangerous that could hurt him.

So rested he by the Tumtum tree,

And stood awhile in thought.

In the third stanza, what we find is a more even mix of ordinary and nonsense lexical word, with in each case only the describing elements for *sword, foe,* and *tree* uninterpretable at first reading. We also note in the third and fourth line, a case whereby the same word *he*, relates to two other words, *rested* preceding it, and *stood* following it in the next line: this is a common case of two structures containing a common element which may be omitted the second time round.

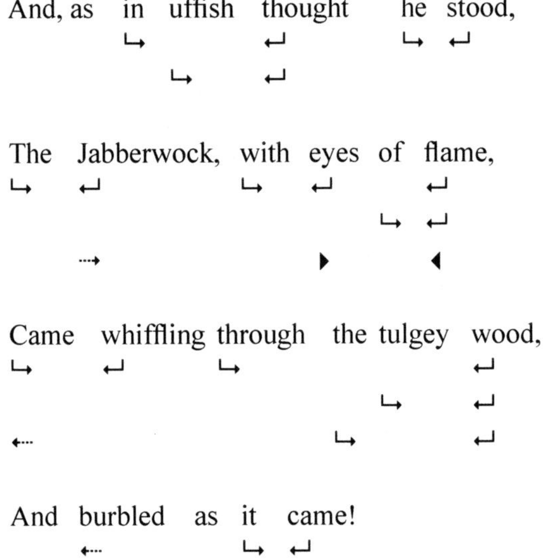

And, as in uffish thought he stood,

The Jabberwock, with eyes of flame,

Came whiffling through the tulgey wood,

And burbled as it came!

In the fourth stanza we have very little ordinary collocation, but a high degree of colligation, particularly between Jabberwock and the various actions which are linked with it: *came* (twice), *whiffling, burbled.*

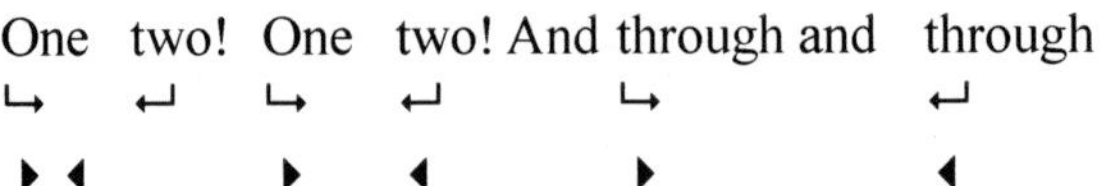

One two! One two! And through and through

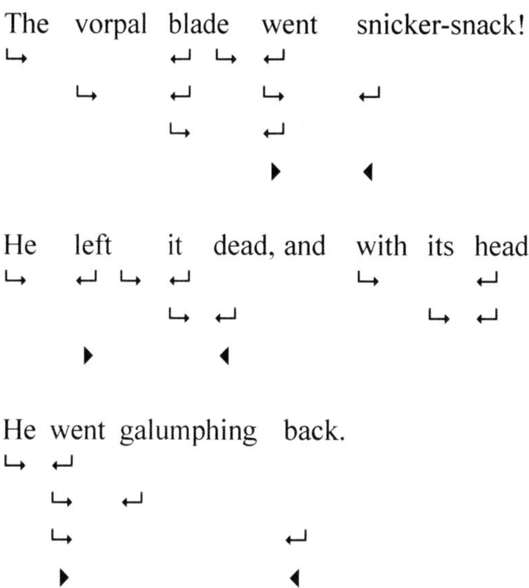

In the fifth stanza, there are some ordinary collocational links between actions and their results; I have also ventured to mark a collocational link between *went* and *snicker-snack* in the second line, since in combination with the verb *go* an alliterative pair like the latter is almost bound in English to indicate a sound (i.e. onomatopoeia) and would therefore be immediately interpretable.

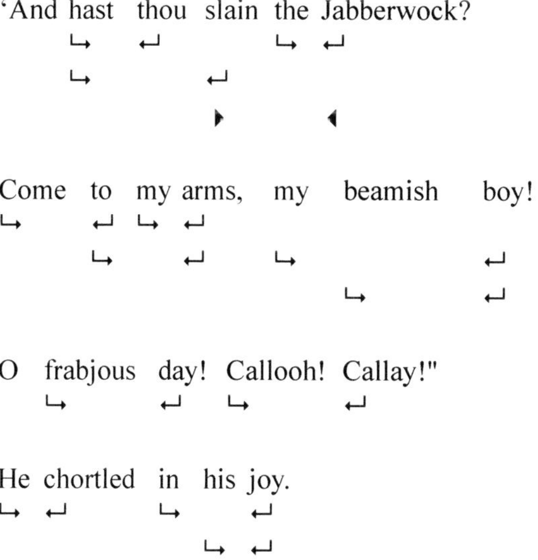

In the sixth stanza, there is little collocation, except arguably between *slain* and *Jabberwock*, since we are well aware by this point that it is some kind of vicious beast, of the kind that 'deserves' to be slain (compare a similar collocational link in normal English between *slay* and *dragon*).

Such an analysis can be only suggestive at this stage, since we are not yet in a position to characterise the colligational and collocational links in detail, but it does tell us a number of things. Firstly, it shows how much is going on 'beneath the surface', as it were, of the seemingly simple linear flow of language. It also shows how separation by one or more other words is no barrier to colligational or collocational links between words. And, as we saw with the poem cited in Chapter 1, literary artists are very sensitive to these 'hidden' relations: the above analysis shows very clearly how cleverly Carroll mixes the known and the unknown to tantalise but at the same time reassure the reader. In Part 2 of this book, we will see how we can describe colligational relations more specifically.

Notes

1   Tesnière's actual terms are 'ordre linéaire' and 'ordre structurale', but in line with Firth's usage, characterising the first as (concrete) 'sequence' as opposed to the (more abstract) 'order' brings out the distinction more clearly.

4   Identifying syntactic units

If we now understand in principle something about how to interpret the linear sequence in terms of its structure-in-depth, how do we go about revealing the patterns of this structure? In the next two chapters we're going to attempt to answer this question in relation to a particular language, Mandarin Chinese. As noted before, much syntactic analysis depends on identifying words, and the existence of words is often taken for granted, particularly in a writing system like that used for English that identifies words orthographically by leaving a blank space on either side. But the writing system used for Chinese, Chinese characters, does *not* distinguish words. Each character, as we will see below, corresponds to the sound unit of syllable, and in the majority of cases, though not all, to the minimal unit of wording, the morpheme. But readers have to work out for themselves where the word boundaries are. So deconstructing the reading process necessary for understanding a Chinese text gives us a good way of problematising the whole issue of identifying words in a language.

As a first step in identifying the units that will relevant for syntactic analysis – what we will call **syntactic words** – we can start from the information provided by the writing system of Chinese and see how far that takes us. Let's take a look at the text below, which is given first in Chinese characters. In this character version (Version A), as is normal in written Chinese, each character is evenly spaced from the others, and I have for the moment omitted any punctuation marks that would give clues about syntactic units. We are therefore forced, initially at least, to depend on other sorts of evidence to identify units.

Version A: original text in Chinese characters

从前有人在田里种地突然跑来了一只兔子一头撞在天边儿的大树上
兔子撞死了那个人非常高兴他把兔子拾起来带回家去从这天以后他
就放下锄头坐在大树下等着希望再有兔子跑来撞死在大树上他等了
很久兔子没有再来他的田地可荒芜了

What is the nature of the units identified by this writing system? We can start off simply by considering their **sound** features, i.e. what they would correspond to in a spoken version of the text. Version B below represents the text in a romanised form, i.e. using the letters of the Roman alphabet to represent the consonants and vowels, plus diacritics to represent the four lexical tones of Mandarin Chinese. In the first instance, each character – represented by a single **orthographic word**, that is, a collection of letters with a blank space on either side – is a **syllable**: the smallest unit of sound that can be pronounced in isolation. What is represented below, as a 'first run' of analysis indicated by the romanised form, is what someone would produce if just reading the characters one by one, like dictionary entries.

Version B: text transcribed into syllables

cóng qián yǒu rén zài tián lǐ zhòng dì tū rán pǎo lái liǎo yī zhī tù zǐ yī tóu zhuàng zài tián biān ér dì dà shù shàng tù zǐ zhuàng sǐ liǎo nà gè rén fēi cháng gāo xìng tā bǎ tù zǐ shí qǐ lái dài huí jiā qù cóng zhè tiān yǐ hòu tā jiù fàng xià chú tóu zuò zài dà shù xià děng zhuó xī wàng zài yǒu tù zǐ pǎo lái zhuàng sǐ zài dà shù shàng tā děng liǎo hěn jiǔ tù zǐ méi yǒu zài lái tā dì tián dì kě huāng wú liǎo

However, readers of a Chinese text do not simply pronounce syllable after syllable, any more than readers of English read word by word; they group some of these syllables into larger units according to a distinction between stressed and unstressed syllables – roughly, syllables articulated with greater versus lesser length and intensity. So if we modify our romanisation of the text according to these larger units, which we can call **stress groups** – a group of syllables containing one main stress, we get something like the Version C below, where each orthographic word contains a single stress:

Version C: text transcribed into stress groups

cóngqián yǒurén zàitián.li zhòngdì tūrán pǎo.lai.le yìzhītù.zi yìtóu zhuàng.zai tián.bian'r.de dàshù.shang tù.zi zhuàngsǐ.le nà.gerén fēicháng gāoxìng tā bǎtù.zi shí.qi.lai dài.huijiā.qu cóngzhètiān yǐhòu tā jiùfàng. xia chú.tou zuò.zai dàshù.xia děng.zhe xīwàng zàiyǒu tù.zi pǎo.lai zhuàngsǐ.zai dàshù.shang tā děng.le hěnjiǔ tù.zi méiyǒu zàilái tā.de tiándì kěhuāngwú.le

Apart from one instance where two syllables are 'squashed' into one – *biān* and *ér* into *biān'r* (pronounced *biār*) – the main differences from the 'one by one' version are as follows:

1. In most cases, syllables do not function in isolation but are pronounced in combination with other syllables, i.e. without a pause between them, and such combinations can thus written as a single orthographic word (this is not necessarily the same thing as a syntactic word, as we will see below);

2. Some of these syllables become atonic, in other words lose their lexical tone, indicated here by a preceding full-stop, and in a couple of cases also take a 'reduced' form – e.g. *de* for *dì*, *zhe* for *zhuó*, or *le* for *liǎo* – when pronounced in combination with other syllables. (As we will see below, these particular examples correspond to grammatical or function words, which add particular abstract meanings to the lexical or content words. It is quite common in languages around the world for such words to become unstressed and lose certain distinctive features of their pronunciation: cf. English *a, an* which are in origin unstressed forms of *one*).

Most speakers – except perhaps young children learning to read – would then group these stress groups into larger units, a combination of one or more stress groups joined by a single intonation contour which we can call **intonation groups**, separated by longer (potential) pauses, separated in the revised romanised Version D below by commas:

Version D: text transcribed into intonation groups

cóngqián yǒurén zàitián.li zhòngdì, tūrán pǎo.lai.le yìzhītù.zi, yìtóu zhuàng.zai tián.bian'r.de dàshù.shang, tù.zi zhuàngsǐ.le, nà.gerén fēicháng gāoxìng, tā bǎtù.zi shí.qi.lai, dài.huijiā.qu, cóngzhètiān yǐhòu, tā jiùfàng.xia chú.tou, zuò.zai dàshù.xia děng.zhe, xīwàng zàiyǒu tù.zi pǎo.lai, zhuàngsǐ.zai dàshù.shang, tā děng.le hěnjiǔ, tù.zi méiyǒu zàilái, tā.de tiándì kěhuāngwú.le

What we have done so far is carry out one part of the reading process that people who are literate in Chinese perform on Chinese texts – and which readers must perform in different ways for every writing system – matching the graphic forms to their spoken equivalents. This matching needs to be done not simply one by one, but according to certain sorts of groupings. The way we have done this is rather artificial, in that we have not at any stage referred to the other kind of evidence used in any reading process: the **meaning** of these units or their groupings. The sorts of sound patterns we have just identified are in fact highly significant, as we will see when we come to link them to meaningful units, but they do not by themselves give us exactly the units we need for syntactic analysis. For this we need to consider what Tesnière called the **connections** between meaningful elements: in a rough approximation, the syntactic relations which link **words**.

So how do we identify words? Well, this turns out to be a far from simple process. We saw above that the graph or written unit of Chinese writing represents the sound unit of syllable, but this is not the whole story: in fact, in most cases, it also represents the wording unit of **morpheme**. In other words, as a general rule, each graph in a written Chinese text represents a minimal significant unit of the language.

At this point, it might be useful to take a short historical excursus back to a stage of the Chinese language closer to that for which the writing system was originally devised. The original of which the above text is an adaptation is an anecdote about an inhabitant of the state of Song, in what is now north China, told as part of a political treatise by Chinese philosopher Hanfeizi (Master Han Fei) who wrote in the 3ʳᵈ century BC. The summary expression of this story – *shǒu zhū dài tù* 'guard a trunk waiting for a hare' – has become proverbial in Chinese for someone with unrealistic expectations. The text is in the standard written language of the time (unpunctuated in the version given here), now known as Classical Chinese (*wenyan*), which differs extensively from Modern Chinese in vocabulary and grammar (explanations of grammatical abbreviations are given below the text).

Sòng	rén	yǒu	géng	tián	zhě	tián	zhōng	yǒu	zhū	tù	zǒu
Song	person	exist	plough	field	NOM	field	in	exist	trunk	hare	run

chù	zhū	zhé	jǐng	ér	sǐ	yīn	shì	qí	lěi
strike	trunk	break	neck	CONJ	die	therefore	discard	3P.POSS	pitchfork

ér	shǒu	zhū	jì	fù	dé	tù	tù	bù	kě	fù	dé	ér
CONJ	guard	trunk	hope	again	get	hare	hare	not	able	again	get	CONJ

shēn	wéi	Sòng	guó	xiào
self	by	Song	state	laugh-at

Notes on glosses of grammatical morphemes

NOM   nominalizer: turns a preceding verb, adjective or clause into the equivalent of a noun, can be translated as 'the one who [does something]'.

CONJ   conjunction: a generalised conjunction that links verbs or clauses in a temporal or causal relation, can be translated as 'then, afterwards, therefore' according to context.

3P.POSS 3rd person possessive: a possessive pronoun referring back to some element in the text, which does not distinguish between one / many or male / female / inanimate, can be translated 'his, her, its, their' according to context.

In the written form of this stage of the language, variously called Old Chinese or Archaic Chinese, the majority of characters represented single morphemes, which in turn consisted of single syllables: thus the 'monosyllabic' tag often applied to Chinese (this is far from the case with modern Mandarin, as we will see below). Furthermore, each morpheme corresponded to a single word; or to put it another way, there was no distinction between morpheme and word – between the minimum meaningful unit and the minimum syntactic unit. Old Chinese was thus a paradigm example of a so-called 'isolating' type of language, where each word operates more or less independently in the clause. We can see how this works with the text above, by giving it a sort of informal word by word glossing:

> (Among the) people of Song there was a man who ploughed the fields, in his field there was a trunk, a hare ran (out), hit the trunk, broke its neck, and died; thereupon (the man) threw away his pitchfork and watched the trunk, hoping to again get a hare (in the same way); a hare couldn't again be got (i.e. he couldn't get another hare) and (the man) himself became the laughingstock of the (whole) State of Song.

Now despite some 'gaps' in the narrative when referring to entities – Old Chinese being one of those languages that tend to refer back to something by simply omitting it – it is not too difficult to follow through the narrative from word to word and make sense of the text as a whole. Indeed, to someone used to the extravagant inflectional patterns of Indo-European languages like Greek and Sanskrit, the Chinese may seem unnaturally bare. This is one of the contrasts that bred the myth that Chinese 'has no grammar', a misconception that shows the still common equation of syntactic relations with morphological marking – in other words, if there is no formal marker of a syntactic relation it does not exist. But certainly it is clear that for this stage of the language, a writing system that does not mark word boundaries works perfectly well

To come back to the modern Mandarin version of this story, the situation is far less clear-cut. From a syntactic point of view, some of the morphemes in this text can only enter into syntactic relations in combination with another morpheme: that is, they are what is called **bound**. Other morphemes are **free** – they can enter into syntactic relations by themselves – but just to complicate matters, they can't do so in all cases: a bound morpheme is always bound but a free morpheme is not always free (Chao 1968: 143–146). So we can't simply look up a dictionary and classify each morpheme as either bound – in which case we look for an adjoining morpheme to attach it to; or else free – in which case we just leave it as it is: and there we have our syntactic units. We need to consider morphemes in the context of the text itself in order to work out how they combine into syntactic words and thus into syntactic structures.

So what criteria can we use? Basically, there are three criteria which are useful for identifying words: independence, commutability, and identity. The easiest criterion to deal with is **independence**: in other words, whether a particular morpheme in context is free, and thus functioning as a word, or bound, and thus functioning as part of larger word. Now it a feature of Chinese that many bound morphemes, particularly those of the grammatical kind like the examples *dì~de*, *zhuó~zhe* and *liǎo ~le* that we saw above, follow the lexical morphemes to which they are attached, and are often atonic, that is do not have the lexical tone that is a feature of most words in Chinese. So simply on sound criteria, it is fairly easy to identify these and attach them to their respective lexical morphemes to form words. In the text above, these kinds of bound morphemes fall into two main subsets:

1. *tā.de* 'his', *děng.zhe* 'waiting' *děng.le* 'waited'; *tián.bian'r* 'field side ~ side of field', *shù.shang* 'tree top ~ on tree', *shù.xia* 'tree bottom ~ under tree'

The first subset consists of bound morphemes that also follow another morpheme and add some grammatical meaning to it: marking it as structurally subordinate to another element (*de*), or as an action that is continuing (*zhe*) or completed (*le*). Another group within this subset function to indicate the position of something and are derived from lexical words indicating a location of some kind: *bian'r* 'side~beside', *shang* 'top~on', *xia* 'bottom~under':

2. *tù.zi* 'rabbit', *chú.tou* 'hoe'

The second subset consists of bound morphemes like *zi* and *tou*, originally 'child' and 'head' respectively, which have now lost all their lexical meaning and simply mark a preceding morpheme as a noun – they are thus often called noun suffixes. The *ér~r* in *bian'r* 'side' was also originally a suffix of this kind, but now used much more widely, also with verbs, e.g. *wán'r* 'play', or expressions of manner, e.g. *mànmān'r* 'slowly'.

3. *jiù fàng(.xia)*, 'then put (down)', *zài lái* 'again come' *kě huāngwú* 'really desolate', *bǎ (tù.zi)* 'took (the rabbit)'.

The third subset of grammatical morphemes are a little different: they are bound, in the sense that they never appear by themselves, but they always precede, rather than follow, another morpheme, and usually preserve their full lexical tone. Here we have grammatical morphemes that add various meanings such as sequence (*jiù* 'then', *zài* 'again (in future)'), emphasis (*kě* 'really') and a rather complicated meaning Chinese linguists refer to as 'disposal' (*bǎ*). There are reasons for considering this third set as syntactic words by themselves, even though they don't satisfy the criterion of independence; we'll come back to them later.

Still using the criterion of independence, there is another set of morphemes which, although they may be free in other contexts, are bound here: we can simply list these in combination as words. Many of these were independent words in classical Chinese (the traditional written form we saw in the original version of the story above) but no longer function so in the modern language: for example, *rán* 'to be so', in modern Chinese attached to many expressions of manner, e.g. *tūrán* 'sudden, suddenly'; or *yǐ* 'to use, with', in modern Chinese appearing in many expressions of time or place, e.g. *yǐhòu* 'after, afterwards'. Here we can group *cóngqián* 'from front ~ before, previously', *tūrán* 'sudden so ~ suddenly', *fēicháng* 'not ordinary ~ extremely', *yǐhòu* 'with behind ~ afterwards'. Also in this group, but including one or more morphemes that can be independent words in the modern language but are not so in this context are *yìtóu* 'one head ~ headlong', *gāoxìng* 'high spirit ~ happy', *xīwàng* 'hope gaze ~ hope', *tiándì* 'field ground ~ fields', and *huāngwú* 'barren overgrown ~ desolate'.

So if we go back to the whole text now, by this criterion of independence we can tentatively group the major portion of the morphemes into 'words':

Version E: morphemes in text grouped by the criterion of independence

cóngqián	yǒu	rén	zài	tián.li		zhòng	dì	tūrán
formerly	exist	person	at	field in		plant	land	suddenly

pǎo.lai	.le	yì	zhī	tù.zi	yìtóu	zhuàng	.zai
run come	ASP:compl	one	MEAS	rabbit	headlong	bump	at

tián.bian'r	.de	dà	shù.shang,	tù.zi	zhuàng	sǐ	.le,
field side	SUB	big	tree on	rabbit	bump	die	ASP:compl

nà.ge rén		fēicháng	gāoxìng	tā	bǎ	tù.zi	shí.qi	.lai
that MEAS person		extremely	happy	he	DISP	rabbit	pick rise come	

dài	.hui	jiā	.qu	cóng	zhè	tiān	yǐhòu	tā	jiù	fàng.xia	chú.tou
take	back	home	go	from	this	day	after	he	then	put down	hoe

zuò	zài	dà	shù.xia	děng	.zhe	xīwàng	zài	yǒu	tù.zi
sit	at	big	tree under	wait	ASP:dur	hope	again	exist	rabbit

păo.lai	zhuàng sĭ	.zai dà	shù.shang	tā	dĕng.le	hĕn jiŭ
run come	bump die	at big	tree on	he	wait ASP:compl	very long

tù.zi	méi yŏu	zài lái	tā.de	tiándì	kĕ	huāngwú .le
rabbit	not have	again come	he SUB	fields	really	desolate ASP:compl

We can now call on the second criterion of **commutability**, that is, the possibility of a word being substituted by other words of similar meaning, to identify some further words. This criterion is based on the reasoning that the more likely an element is to be able to be 'taken out' of a particular structure and have something else put in its place, the more likely it is to be an independently functioning unit. So for example, *méiyŏu* 'haven't, didn't' can be substituted by the shorter form *méi* with the same meaning; *rén* 'person' can be substituted by *nánrén* 'man' or *nóngmín* 'farmer' without changing the meaning significantly. In some cases this substituted element may be not simply a word but a phrase, as in (*hĕn*) *jiŭ* '(very) long' which can be substituted by (*hĕn*) *cháng shíjiān* '(very) long time'. Some of the elements identified above as bound morphemes can also be substituted in this way, which suggests that they may have some of the features of a word: *shù dĭxià* literally 'tree bottom' for *shù.xia* 'under tree', *shù(.de) shàng.tou* 'tree('s) top' for *shù.shang* 'on tree'. This criterion is in effect another way of looking at independence, and though it is perhaps more suggestive than criterial, it does provide us with a useful extra yardstick for identifying words.

Our final criterion, which appeals much more directly to meaning, is that of semantic **identity**, that is finding another independent word of same or similar meaning – something that would suggest the morpheme we are examining may also be a word. Since it is in fact unlikely that a language will have two different words that are identical in meaning – or in what is really another way of saying the same thing, two different words that have identical functions – this criterion is the trickiest one to handle. For example, the morpheme *dì* 'land, ground' near the beginning of the text seems to mean much the same as *tiándì* 'field' towards the end; but whereas *tiándì* 'field' is plainly a word by the criteria of independence and commutability, *dì* is doubtful on both these counts. In terms of independence, *dì* usually only appears in combinations such as *zhòng dì*, literally 'plant land', or (with a slightly different meaning) *săo dì* 'sweep floor' and *dì.shang* 'on (the) ground'. Its near synonym *tián* 'field' is similar, appearing mostly as *tián.li* 'in field' as here, or in phrases like *yíkuài tián* 'one piece field – i.e. a field'. In terms of commutability, *dì* in *zhòng dì* 'plant field' is equivalent to *tiándì* 'field', but in *săo dì* 'sweep floor' it corresponds to *dìbăn* 'floor'; and in other collocations, to *tŭdì* 'soil, earth' or *dìqiú* 'earth' (i.e. the planet), or even, in the form *dì'r*, to *dì.fang* 'place'.

This suggests that what is going on here is a phenomenon more familiar from languages like Latin and Greek with complex word inflections: that the form of a word may in fact change depending on its syntactic function. This is a good argument *against* the common claim that 'Chinese has no morphology', as well as an argument *for* combining morphology with syntax in the analysis of texts – the principle we are following in this book. In certain combinations, most often when linked to particular verbs, a sort of basic, default form, *dì* 'ground', may be used whose specific meaning is determined by the verb; whereas in other contexts, a longer more explicit form such as *tiándì* 'field ground ~ field', *dìbǎn* 'ground plank ~ floor', or *tǔdì* 'soil ground ~ earth' is used. Thus it seems that the distinction between bound (morpheme) and free (word) in Chinese is by no means a straightforward one, but again must be determined in a particular textual context.

Similar examples where it is difficult to decide whether we are dealing with one word or two also abound in the text. One set involve the combination of a numeral and what is known as a 'measure word' or 'classifier', i.e. an element that assigns an object to a particular class and is used when the object is counted or specified. An example from the text is *zhī*, which can be glossed as 'classifier for animals' (the only close English equivalent would be *head* in phrases like *three head of cattle*.) For example is *yì zhī (tù.zi)* 'one [classifier] rabbit ~ a (rabbit)' one word or two? On the one hand, we can't say *yì (tù.zi)* without the classifier; on the other, we can substitute *zhī* with the 'general classifier' *.ge* seen elsewhere in the text with *rén* 'person' *nà .ge rén* 'that person', i.e. *yí .ge tù.zi* 'a rabbit', without changing the meaning too much.

Other examples involve the combination of two or more verbs. For example, how do we deal with *fàng .xia* 'place descend ~ put down'? On the one hand, *xià* can't appear by itself: it always comes either after a verb, e.g. *gē .xia* 'put down', *tuō .xia* 'take off (clothes); or before a noun, e.g. *xià chē* 'descend ~ get off bus', *xià kè* 'descend ~ finish class' On the other, it can be substituted, e.g. *fàng .xia .lai* 'put down (towards speaker), *fàng .jin .qu* 'put in (away from speaker)'. And what on earth do we do with *dài .hui jiā .qu*, which contains the four morphemes, in order, 'take', 'back', 'home', 'go'? It seems as if in terms of their ability to combine with each other, morphemes in Chinese have a quite high degree of flexibility; or from another point of view, making a distinction between a morpheme and a word may only be possible within a particular syntactic structure.

From these problems, we can see that the distinction between morpheme and word in Chinese is by no means a straightforward one. More broadly, the conclusion that can be drawn from the discussion above is that the unit we need to recognise for syntactic analysis, what was referred to above as the **syntactic word**, is by no means something that is given in advance. These basic syntactic units need to be worked out afresh for each language, and will normally involve some sort of descriptive compromise between different criteria, such as those of independence, commutability and identity suggested above. In fact, for Chinese it makes most sense to recognise a **cline** between morpheme and word which covers at least five different degrees of closeness between morphemes functioning in syntactic structures:

1. *cóngqián* 'formerly', *tù.zi* 'rabbit': this the greatest degree of closeness, such morpheme combinations always function as a single unit, and can be written orthographically as a single word.

2. *tián.li* 'in the field', *shù.shang* 'on the tree', *yìzhī (tù.zi)* 'one [animal classifier] (rabbit) ', *yìkē (shù)* 'one [plant classifier] (tree) ': this is the next greatest degree of closeness; the second element cannot be separated from the first, but it can be substituted with greater or lesser changes in meaning, e.g. *tián lǐ.bian 'r* 'inside the field', *shù shàng.mian 'r* 'on (or 'above') the tree', *yìmén kè* 'one class (as subject)' versus *yìjié kè* 'one class (as period)': these can also be written as a single orthographic word.

3. *zài lái* 'again come', *kě huāngwú* 'really desolate', *bǎ tù.zi* '(took) the rabbit': these represent the next degree of closeness; as with the previous subset the first elements here cannot appear by themselves, but on the other hand they are clearly distinct in meaning – and as we will see in the next chapter, in syntactic function – from the following words to which they are attached: they can therefore be written as separate orthographic words.

4. *fàng-xia* 'put down', *shí-qilai* 'pick up': these represent the next degree of closeness, and can be separated by a limited number of grammatical elements, such as the completed aspect particle *le*, e.g. *(yǐ.jing) fàng.le-xia* '(already) put down'; or in some cases by a noun, as in the text example *dài-hui jiā -qu* 'take back home go' where the noun *jiā* 'home' comes in the middle of the verb *dài-hui-qu* 'take back go (i.e. away from speaker)': they can be joined orthographically by hyphens.

5. *zhòng+dì* 'plant ground' or another example not in the text *shēng+qì* 'get angry' (literally 'produce steam'!): these represent the weakest degree of closeness; on the one hand, their particular meaning tends to be dependent on their combination – *dì* as 'field, ground' not 'floor' – but they may be separated by a number of different elements: e.g. *zhòng.le yìtiān dì* 'planted one day ground – i.e. spent a whole day working in the fields', *shēng wǒ.de qì* 'get my angry – get angry with me': these can be joined orthographically by a plus sign, to suggest they are the addition of two separate elements.

This may seem to be an enormous amount of trouble simply to identify a unit that most English-speakers would take for granted in their own language. However, not only does this show that nothing can be assumed as given in syntactic analysis, it also shows that such units must be explicitly identified, according to sets of specific – if sometimes conflicting – criteria. Just assuming the existence of a unit of syntactic word in a language – something many descriptions do without argument – incorporates a whole lot of unexamined assumptions into the analysis. The above discussion also shows how special graphic conventions such as spacing, and use of hyphens and other punctuation, can be used to make distinctions useful for syntactic analysis which would not necessarily be required for an ordinary orthography. In the case of ordinary Chinese texts written in characters, the whole question of syntactic words is simply ignored by the orthography; as it was, incidentally, in the earliest use of an alphabetic orthography by the Greeks, in which there were no spaces between words. So keeping in mind that the notion of 'syntactic word' in Chinese – and perhaps in many other languages – is a cline rather than a clear black and white distinction, we can now use these conventions to separate the whole text into words as in Version F below. It is now (almost) ready for syntactic analysis.

Version F: text divided into syntactic words

cóngqián   yǒu rén   zài tián.li   zhòng+dì   tūrán
formerly   exist person   at   field in   plant land suddenly

pǎo-lai.le   yìzhī   tù.zi yìtóu   zhuàng-zai
run come ASP:compl   one MEAS   rabbit headlong   bump at

tián.biān'r .de dà shù.shang,   tù.zi zhuàng-sǐ .le,
field side   SUB big tree on   rabbit bump die ASP:compl

nà.ge   rén   fēicháng gāoxìng, tā   bǎ   tù.zi shí-qilai,
that MEAS   person   extremely happy   he   DISP   rabbit pick up

dài-hui jiā -qu   cóng zhètiān yǐhòu   tā   jiù   fàng-xia chú.tou
take back home go from this day after   he   then   put down hoe

zuò-zai dà shù.xia   děng.zhe   xīwàng zài   yǒu   tù.zi
sit at   big tree under wait ASP:dur   hope   again exist rabbit

pǎo-lai   zhuàng-sǐ-zai dà shù.shang tā děng.le   hěn jiǔ
run come bump die at   big tree on   he wait ASP:compl very long

tù.zi méiyǒu zài   lái,   tā.de   tiándì   kě   huāngwú.le
rabbit didn't   again come he SUB   fields   really desolate ASP:compl

5   Bracketing and labelling

In the previous chapter, we used various techniques to work out the basic units for syntactic analysis, **words**, and saw that for Chinese at least there were at least five different kinds of syntactic words we needed to recognise in terms of the closeness between their component morphemes. Although this is an essential step in the analysis, we still don't have the units that we need in order to carry out syntactic analysis in the strict sense: for this we need to identify a unit usually called a **clause**.

The unit of clause is not one that is recognised by most traditional writing systems, whether the alphabetic orthography of English or the character orthography of Chinese. The reason for this is that a clause can only be identified by syntactic analysis, and most writing systems concentrate on identifying units that will be useful for reading purposes, such as syllable or word, leaving the readers to work out the syntactic units for themselves. Now just as with identifying words, the question of how to identify a clause is not one that we can determine in advance from general principles; it needs to be defined anew for each language. So what reasons do we have for thinking that we will need such a unit?

This goes back to this notion of what Hockett called 'structure-in-depth' or what Tesnière called 'connection': that is, the ways in which words are joined together beyond the simple sequence in which they appear. How do we know that words have such 'connections'? Well, for one thing, by the fact that a particular word is perfectly capable of being related to more than two other words at the same time, despite, as Tesnière points out, the 'impossibility of a word in the spoken chain being in immediate sequence with more than two neighbouring words' (1959: 21). Let's take an example from the text we analysed in the previous chapter, the word *rén* 'person':

cóngqián	yǒu	rén	zài	tián.	li	zhòng+dì
formerly	exist	person	at	field	in	plant land

Now in order to make sense of this sequence of words, we have to assume that *rén* 'person' relates not only to the preceding word *yǒu* 'exist' (it is the person who exists), and to the following word *zài* 'at' (it is the person who is at that particular place), but also to the word *zhòng+dì* 'plant the land' (it is the person who is doing the planting). So what sort of structure is it that we can recognise here?

The answer put forward by Tesnière is that there is a structure which consists of what he calls a **verbal node** (*noeud verbale*) which 'controls', in an abstract sense, a number of other elements. The particular reasons for this claim are discussed in detail in following chapters, but we can anticipate part of Tesnière's argument at this point by saying that one of the things that this structure does is represent a 'complete little drama', a sort of slice of experience, and the verbal node expresses what he called the 'process', or the action at the centre of this drama (1959: 102). The syntactic unit which contains a verbal node and expresses a complete 'drama' is what is normally called a clause.

So, as a basic rule of thumb, we should be able to go through a text, identify each verb, and the other elements which it relates to, and thus we will have our clauses. Let's see how this works with our Chinese text. In version G below, I have put each clause on a separate line, and numbered them for easy reference.

Version G: text divided into clauses

(1) Cóngqián   yǒu rén
     formerly   exist person
     'Once there was a person'

(2) zài tián.li   zhòng+dì,
     at   field in   plant land
     '(who was) working in the fields,'

(3) tūrán   pǎo-lai.le   yìzhī   tù.zi
     suddenly   run come ASP:compl   one MEAS   rabbit
     '(when) suddenly a rabbit came running out'

(4) yìtóu   zhuàng-zai   tiánbiān'r .de   dà   shù.shang.
     headlong   bump at   field side SUB   big   tree on
     '(and) ran headlong into a big tree on the side of the field.'

(5) Tù.zi   zhuàng-sǐ.le,
     rabbit   bump die ASP:compl
     'The rabbit was killed'

(6) nà.ge   rén   fēicháng gāoxìng,
    that MEAS person   extremely happy
    '(and so) the man was very happy'

(7) tā   bǎ tù.zi shí-qilai,
    he   DISP rabbit pick up
    'he picked up the rabbit'

(8) dài-hui   jiā   -qu
    take back home go
    '(and) took (it) back home.'

(9) Cóng   zhètiān yǐhòu tā jiù   fàng-xia chú.tou,
    from   this day after he then   put down hoe
    'From this day onwards he put down his hoe'

(10) zuò-zai dà shù.xia
     sit at   big tree under
     '(and) sat under the big tree'

(11) děng.zhe,
     wait   ASP:dur
     'waiting,'

(12) xīwàng
     hope
     'hoping'

(13) zài   yǒu tù.zi
     again exist rabbit
     '(that) there would be another rabbit'

(14) pǎo-lai
     run come
     '(which) would come running out'

(15) zhuàng-sǐ-zai dà shù.shang.
     bump die at   big tree on
     '(and) knock itself to death on the big tree.'

(16) Tā děng.le   hěn jiǔ,
     he wait ASP:compl very long
     'He waited a long time,'

(17) tù.zi   méiyǒu   zài   lái,
    rabbit didn't   again come
    '(but) another rabbit didn't come'

(18) tā.de   tiándì   kě   huāngwú.le.
    he SUB field   really desolate   ASP:compl
    '(and) his fields became quite overgrown.'

There are a couple of problems here that we need to deal with straight away. Firstly, any verbs which we have already identified as being part of a larger word, such as *pǎo* 'run' and *lái* 'come' in *pǎo-lai* 'came running (out)', or *zhuàng* 'bump' and *sǐ* 'die' in *zhuàng-sǐ* 'died by hitting itself (on the tree), count as a single syntactic word, and therefore a single verbal node. Secondly, some elements may seem to relate to more than one verbal node simultaneously: this is the case, for example with *rén* 'person' in *cóngqián yǒu rén / zài tián.li zhòng+dì* 'once there was a person / (who) was working in the fields'; or with *tù.zi* 'rabbit' in *zài yǒu tù.zi / pǎo-lai / zhuàng-sǐ-zai dà shù.shang* 'again would be a rabbit / (which) would run out / (and which) would kill itself on the big tree' – the 'relative' words *who* and *which* in the English translations show the connections very clearly. From a meaning point of view, we can explain this by saying that a particular entity, or what Tesnière called a 'participant' can take part in more than one 'process' in succession. Structurally, such examples are often analysed as 'pivot' clauses, with an element on which they pivot or share in common (Chao 1968: 124–29). There is one final point that applies particularly to languages like Chinese: the 'verb' in the final clause *huāngwú* 'desolate' is what would for English normally be translated by an 'adjective': in Chinese, as in neighbouring languages like Japanese, at the most general level there is no distinction between the two, so this still counts as a verbal node.

Having delimited the clauses, there are still a number of ways that we can identify their internal structure. The first thing to note is that not all elements in a clause are related equally closely. The differing closeness of different elements to each other can be shown by what is known as **bracketing**. Halliday (1994: 20) identifies two basic possibilities: **maximal** bracketing, 'put a bracket everywhere you can'; and **minimal** bracketing, 'put a bracket only where you have to'. Let's see how this works with clause 3 from the text:

```
(            (( ))          ((      )    ) )
tūrán        pǎo-lai.le      yìzhī  tù.zi
suddenly     run come ASP:compl    one MEAS rabbit
((     )     (            )     (         ) )
```

How do we interpret these different kinds of bracketing? Halliday points out that maximal bracketing (shown above the example) is a statement of 'the order of composition of the constituent parts', in other words the 'logical order in which the elements…are combined' (1994: 20, 23). In other words, what the use of maximal bracketing implies is: first combine *păo-lai* and *yìzhī* (which we pointed out in the previous chapter could be regarded as syntactic words), then combine *păo-lai* with *le*, and *yìzhī* with *tù.zi*, then take *păo-lai.le* and *yìzhī tù.zi* and combine them with *tūrán*. At each point you have what is called an **immediate constituent**, that is two elements which can be combined with each other in a meaningful way.

What exactly is this 'meaningful way'? In order to show this, we then need to **label** each element. As Halliday again points out, the sort of labelling that is most often associated with maximal bracketing is labeling each element for its syntactic category or **class**, that is, its 'general grammatical potential' (1994: 29). This is because one of the ways we recognise different classes of syntactic element in a language is by their possibility of combination, i.e. their syntagmatic potential. From this point of view, we can label our example as follows, changing the bracketing notation, for ease of comprehension, into what is called a structure 'tree', where each sideways-facing round bracket corresponds to a downward-facing square bracket:

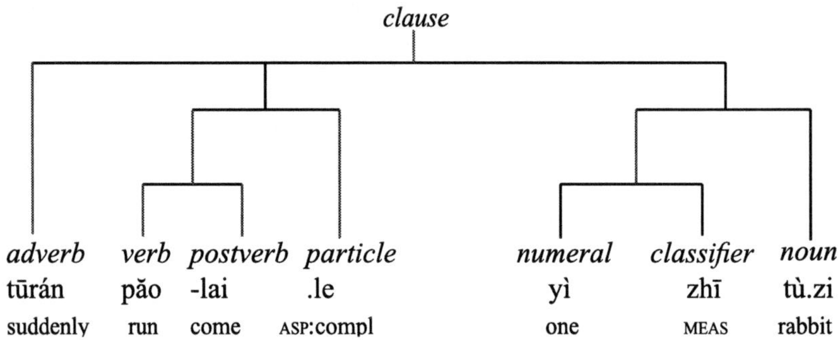

We need not go into the exact reasons for these particular labels at this stage, but the logic should be clear: a verb can combine with a postverb, and then their combination can combine with a particle; a numeral can combine with a classifier and then their combination with a noun; and then these two structures can combine with an adverb to form a clause. These sorts of relations correspond to Firth's colligational relations, i.e. the combination of different grammatical categories, and in theory, any words in the language that fell into these classes could be combined in the same way, for example, with the same structure (bracketing not shown):

adverb	*verb*	*postverb*	*particle*	*numeral*	*classifier*	*noun*
ránhòu	zŏu	.lai	.le	yí	.ge	nóngmín
afterwards	cross	go	ASP:compl	one	MEAS	farmer

'Afterwards a farmer walked over.'

Minimal bracketing, on the other hand, 'means putting together as constituents only those sequences that actually function as structural units in the item in question' (Halliday 1994: 24). What is this 'item' then?: in the first instance, the clause. So in effect this kind of bracketing works in the opposite direction, not from smallest to largest, but from largest to smallest. What this claims is that the clause as a whole divides into three elements, and then each of those elements may divide into further elements, and so on. This kind of bracketing depends on defining different levels of structure or what are called **ranks**, and so these kinds of constituents are called **ranked constituents**, that is constituents of the different ranks, or sizes of structure, in the clause as a whole. So how do we characterise the 'structural units'?: again, by labelling them, but in this case for function, in other words, by 'the part that the item is playing in the particular structure under consideration' (1994: 27). Thus we could label our minimally-bracketed example as follows:

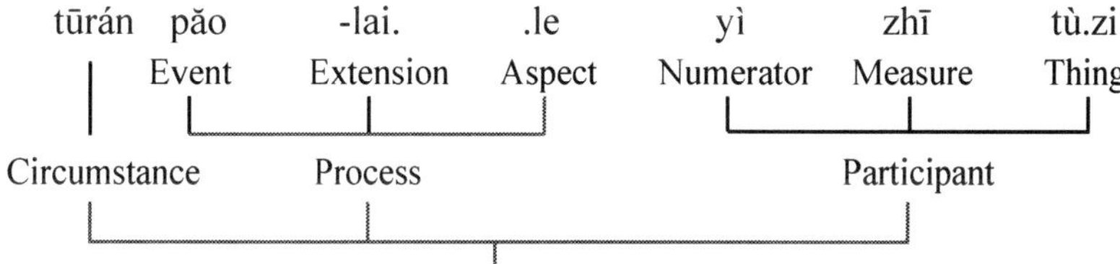

So, what this analysis tells us is that the clause breaks down first into three functional elements: a Circumstance, a Process, and a Participant, and then the Process and the Participant each break down into three elements: an Event (main action), Extension (indicating the direction of the action) and Aspect (indicating that the action is completed); a Numerator (counting the entity), a Measure (classifying the entity) and a Thing (the entity itself). Again we can 'invent' another example with exactly the same structure:

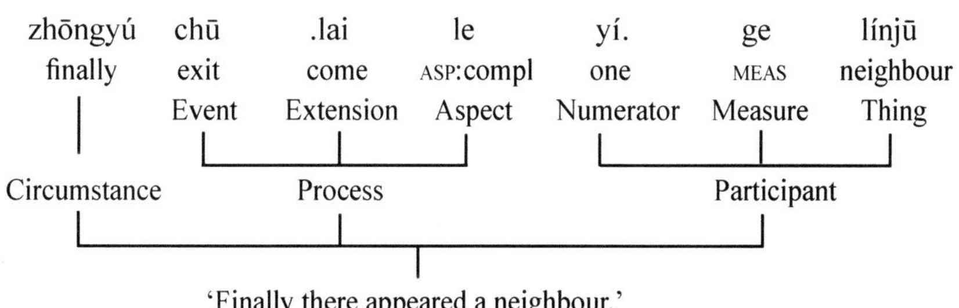

'Finally there appeared a neighbour.'

Presented above as finished products, these two kinds of analysis conceal an enormous number of assumptions about the structure of the clause. Each kind of bracketing and its associated labelling makes different claims about the sort of 'structure-in-depth' that we will recognise in a clause. Thus bracketing and labelling, like glossing, conceal a lot of descriptive 'work', and are not at all the simple 'first step' they are often made out to be. In fact, it would not be too much of an exaggeration to say that the core of syntactic description, the notion of syntactic structure and syntactic relations, is embodied in such analyses. In following chapters we will go on to discuss in more detail the sorts of notions of language structure that lie behind these different kinds of representation.

It is with the sort of analyses presented in this chapter that most syntactic descriptions usually start. In fact, as we have seen, an enormous amount of work must already have gone into processing the data before it is ready for such analyses to be carried out. But with the sort of isolated, often invented, sentences used in many accounts of syntax, where the examples are chosen specifically to illustrate or support a particular descriptive or theoretical claim, the processing work is done 'backstage', as it were. It is only in trying to deal with the complexities of actual texts that these issues come to the forefront, and that we can see how significant they are in shaping – and perhaps distorting – the description. So it is as well to remember from the minute we as analysts start to 'engage' with text data, we are bringing to bear a particular theoretical and descriptive model, a particular understanding of how language works, and we thus need to be as conscious and explicit as possible about the nature of that model.

Part 2
Description – analysing the clause

We are now at the point where we should be equipped to set forth into the 'tangled forest' of syntactic theories referred to earlier. What we have done so far, although often downplayed or even ignored in accounts of syntactic analysis, would in one form or other be accepted by pretty much all 'doers' of 'syntax' as the basic groundwork which underlies all subsequent analysis. From this point on, however, there is almost nothing on which a particular syntactic theory cannot, and does not, differ from another. As also noted earlier, the solution adopted here is to use two main 'guides': Lucien Tesnière and P.H. Matthews. Tesnière's valency theory will provide the basic framework that we will use to examine the theoretical and descriptive challenges that must be faced by any syntactic theory: laying down the basic path through the forest, as it were. Matthews will function as a kind of critical offsider, identifying the criteria and pointing out the implications of particular choices: asking 'Why did you choose that path? Mightn't this one be better?'.

We start in Chapter 6 by identifying the two main models for describing syntactic relations: constituency and dependency. In Chapters 7 and 8 we use Tesnière's framework to identify a set of clause functions, drawing on Matthews for an understanding of the reasons for identifying particular functions. We then go on to apply this framework to texts in our two main languages under description – Mandarin Chinese and Scottish Gaelic – ending up by translating each text into the other language, to compare how different languages represent the same experience, and how our developing descriptive framework deals with both. In Chapter 9 we look at the issue of whether it is necessary to recognise an intermediate unit between word and clause, and discuss some of the principles according to which words combine with each other. In Chapters 10 and 11, we go beyond our focus on the structure of individual clauses in order to examine the ways in which clauses may be joined to each other, and how particular pieces of information can be traced through a text. And finally in Chapter 12 we take a look at the so-called 'empty' or 'grammatical' words that express the interaction between speaker and addressee.

The emphasis throughout Part 2 will be on putting forward useful tools for analysis, using Tesnière's framework as critiqued by Matthews as a way of problematising the issues involved. A prominent sub-theme of this part of the book will be identifying the descriptive and theoretical traditions from which these tools emerge. A more specifically theoretical discussion of different themes and trends in syntactic study will be undertaken in Part 3.

6 Constituency and dependency

Given a text which we have divided into words and clauses, how do we then go about analysing the syntactic relationships between the elements of the clause? And what exactly *are* these elements? Let's first examine this question in relation to a short Gaelic text, a highly rhythmical song of the genre known as *puirt-a-beul* or 'mouth music' which tends to use a lot of word play and sound patterning.

(1) Fear   a bhitheas   fada   gun phòsadh
    man   REL be+FUT   long   without marrying
    'A man who goes long without getting married'

(2) fàsaidh   feur is fraoch is fireach   air;
    grow+FUT   grass and heather and moor   on-him
    'grass and heather and moor (= ill humor) grow on him;'

(3) fear   a bhitheas   fada   gun phòsadh
    man   REL be+FUT   long   without marrying
    'A man who goes long without getting married'

(4) fàsaidh   feusag mhòr   air.
    grow+ FUT   beard big+FEM   on-him
    'a great beard grows on him.'

Here we have two main types of clause. One, as represented by clauses 2 and 4, has what Tesnière would call the 'process' (the action) coming first – *fàsaidh* 'will grow, (usually) grows'; followed by a 'participant' (what is growing) – *feur* 'grass' etc; and a 'circumstance' (where it grows) – *air* 'on him'. Another, as represented by the identical clauses 1 and 3, has a 'participant' (the entity taking part in the action) – *fear* '(a) man' coming first; followed by a description of the man, introduced by the linking or 'relative' word *a* 'who, which, that', and containing a 'process' – *bhitheas* 'will be, (usually) is', and a couple of 'circumstances' – *fada* 'for a long time' and *gun phòsadh* 'without marrying'.

On the basis of the meanings of the individual clause elements, and how they relate to each other, we could use bracketing to give a preliminary analysis of their syntactic relationships as follows, with maximal bracketing above the clause and minimal bracketing below.

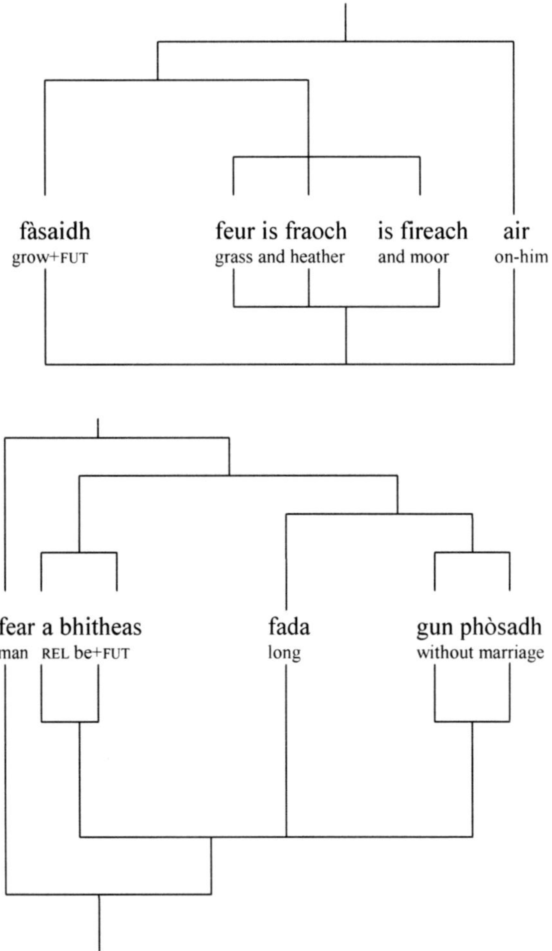

In the previous chapter, we identified two different kinds of labelling with which each kind of bracketing could be associated. Behind these combinations of bracketing/labelling lies a particular view of the organisation of meaningful elements in language, a particular model of syntactic structure known as **constituency**.

The constituency model derives from twentieth century theories of sound patterning or phonology, particularly those theories that depend heavily on the analytical method known as **distributionalism**. The distinctive sound units of language, phonemes, can be classified in two ways: according to how they **combine** with each other – Saussure's syntagmatic relations; and according to how they **substitute** for each other – Saussure's paradigmatic relations. Thus we can specify the distribution of a particular phoneme by exhaustively listing all its possible combinations and substitutions, and because phonemes have no meaning in themselves, we can do this in principle without referring to notions of meaning.

Having achieved great success characterising phonemes in this way, a group of American linguists, most conspicuously Zellig Harris (e.g. Harris 1951), decided that this would also be a good way of characterising the significant units of morphemes, words etc. By using the type of immediate constituent bracketing described in the previous chapter, combined with class labels for each of the elements, you could characterise the **distribution** of words in a clause (see Chapter 16) and thereby reveal its 'structure-in-depth', in Hockett's term. And moreover, although this is not a necessary concomitant of this model, you could do so without having to concern yourself with the meaning of these items: like phonemes, they were simply elements that fitted into certain slots in a structure.

Immediate constituent (maximal) bracketing tends to go together with class labels because the two are different ways of representing distributional relations: so for example you can define a 'noun', in English at least, as something that can be preceded by an article, by an adjective or by another noun etc. Furthermore, the combination of the two gives something that can be regarded simply as a formal structure: as a series of slots with elements filling those slots – each identified by its 'recognition criteria' in Hasan and Fries's terms (see discussion in next chapter). Function labels, in contrast, although they can also be defined in strictly formal terms, tend to involve more consideration of what they mean: of what Hasan & Fries would call their 'definition criteria'. For these reasons, class labels have tended to be seen as more basic, with some theories (see Chapter 13) referring to them simply as 'categories'.

As Halliday points out (1994: 24), there are good reasons why immediate constituents are normally labelled for class, and ranked constituents for function. In the case of immediate constituents and class, the part-whole relations are doing more of the descriptive work, in that they identify pair by pair how words are joined to each other; while the class labels simply indicate the distributional potential of the elements, i.e. what sorts of slots they can be fitted into. In the case of ranked constituents and function labels, the part-whole relations are simpler, and therefore doing less of the descriptive work, and more of the description is carried over by the function labels which specify exactly what that element is doing in the particular structure.

In languages like Latin, where there is a strict syntactic division of labour, so that particular classes tend to be associated with particular functions, the combination of immediate constituent bracketing and class labelling *is* probably sufficient to indicate most of the structural connections. However, in a language like Chinese, where the relationship between class and function is a much more flexible one, so that a particular functional role can be filled by a number of different classes, the combination of immediate constituent bracketing and class labelling is usually *not* sufficient to reveal the structural connections: thus analyses of Chinese that use immediate constituent analysis tend to combine this with function labelling. An example of this is given below labelled with translations of the Chinese terms usually used for clause functions (some of which, such as 'Complement' do not correspond to the terms used in this book). In this analysis, the clause first divides into a 'Subject' and a 'Predicate', and that these elements then divide into smaller elements.

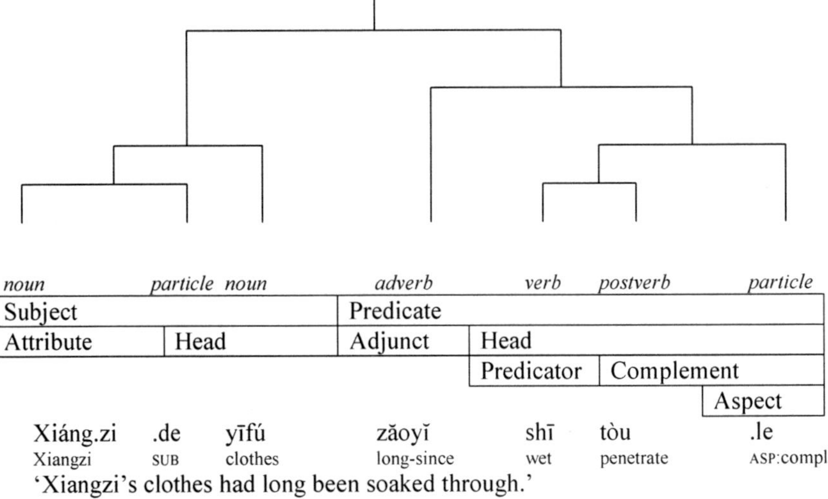

noun	*particle*	*noun*	*adverb*	*verb*	*postverb*	*particle*
Subject			Predicate			
Attribute		Head	Adjunct	Head		
				Predicator	Complement	
						Aspect
Xiáng.zi	.de	yīfú	zăoyĭ	shī	tòu	.le
Xiangzi	SUB	clothes	long-since	wet	penetrate	ASP:compl

'Xiangzi's clothes had long been soaked through.'

Traditionally, however, in the analysis of Latin a different model has tended to be used: the **dependency** model, based on theories of what was called **government**. The notion of government was a way of explaining the rich inflections of languages like Latin in terms of how particular words 'governed', that is, determined, the inflection of other words. In Saussure's terms, government explains the syntagmatic relations of the subtype Firth called colligation, i.e. relations between grammatical categories.

In order to understand how the government framework worked, we can take a Latin example used by Tesnière (1959: 20):

Tantae	molis	erat	Romānam
such+FEM+GEN+SG	labour+FEM+GEN+SG	be+IMPF+3SG	Roman+FEM+ACC+SG

condere	gentem
found+INF	people+FEM+ACC+SG

'Such a great labour it was to found the Roman nation.'

In this clause, the inflections immediately give us a lot of information about the relations between the different words. To start with, the form of the verb *erat* 'was' indicates its tense (past imperfect), person (third person) and number (singular). Since in Latin, as vestigially in English, the verb must be consistent ('agree' see below) with its **subject**, the only possible candidate for subject must also be third person and singular – in this case the infinitive (a sort of verbal noun), *condere*, 'to found' or 'founding'. From this point of view, we could say that the verb determines or **governs** its subject. The verb determines other connections in the clause as well. From the form of the noun *gentem* 'race, people' we can see that it is functioning here as the **complement** of the verb *condere*, thus 'to found the race'; and the form of *molis* indicates that it is functioning in the clause as an **adjunct**, 'of labour'. The terms used here will be explained in the following chapter, but all of these can be seen as relations of dependency. (In fact, as Mathews points out (1981: 18), including the subject here is an innovation of Tesnière's: for 'most earlier grammarians' the subject fell outside the government framework.)

We still need to explain, however, where *tantae* 'such, so great' and *Romānam* 'Roman' fit in. In these cases their marking indicates that they can be linked to two other elements in the clause. *Tantae* is technically genitive (also known as possessive) case, feminine gender, and thus is linked to *molis* which shares these same two features, thus 'with such great labor'; while *Romanam* is technically accusative (also known as objective) case, feminine gender, and so linked to *gentem* which again shares these features, thus 'the Roman nation'. Such secondary relationships are usually known, not as government, but as **agreement** (traditionally this is also how the subject-verb relationship is explained), and tend to be used in languages like Latin when particular clause elements are modified in some way; but these are also subsumed by Tesnière under the general framework of dependency.

In order to represent this structure, Tesnière draws what he calls a **stemma**, or in fact a series of connected stemmas, with the governing element or **controller** (*régissant*) on top, and the governed element or **dependant** (*subordonné*) on the bottom. Thus, to take the simplest example first, for the two nouns linked to their adjectives by agreement we have the following stemmas:

```
molis   gentem
  |        |
tantae  Romanam
```

For each clause, as we saw before, Tesnière identifies a main controller, the **verbal node**, which determines the relations of dependency in the clause: in this case, the verb *erat* 'was', while its subject *condere* 'to found' is then marked as dependent on it:

```
erat
 |
condere
```

At the same time, the verb *erat* also governs or controls the adjunct *molis* 'of labour':

```
erat
 |
molis
```

and *condere* 'to found', while the subject of, and thus the dependant of *erat* 'was', also controls a complement *gentem* ' the people':

```
condere
   |
gentem
```

This gives us a complete stemma for the whole clause as follows:

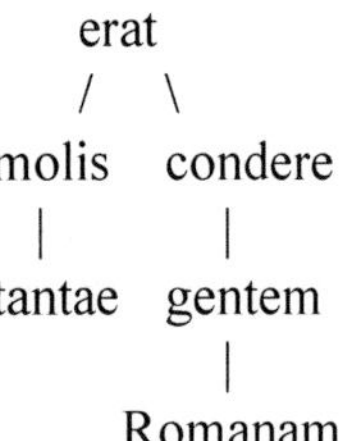

```
      erat
     /   \
  molis  condere
    |       |
  tantae  gentem
            |
         Romanam
```

Such a view of grammatical relations is harder to apply to languages like modern English or Chinese, in which there is little or none of the inflectional marking to identify these relationships. So in order to apply the theory more widely, Tesnière then reinterpreted dependency in **semantic** terms. As Matthews points out (1981: 124), this can also be regarded as extending the syntagmatic relations of the clause to include what Firth called collocational relations, i.e. links between lexical items. Tesniere framed his theory in terms of syntactic relations as expressing a model of experience (Tesnière 1959: 102, original emphasis, Tesnière's original terms indicated in parentheses):

> The verbal node, which is found at the center of most European languages, expresses a complete **little drama** *(tout un petit drame)*. Like a drama in actuality, it obligatorily consists of an **action** *(procès)*, and most often **actors** *(acteurs)* and **features of the setting** *(circonstances)*. Transposed from the plane of dramatic reality to that of structural syntax, the action, the actors and the features of the setting become respectively, the **verb** *(verbe)*, the **participants** *(actants)*, and the **circumstances** *(circonstants)*.

Such a model gives us a general framework for interpreting syntactic relations in all languages, in which the verbal node can be seen to express a **process**,[1] while subjects and complements express different kinds of **participants**, i.e. 'persons or things which, to whatever degree and in whatever way…participate in the process' (Tesnière 1959: 102), and adjuncts express different kinds of **circumstances** or features of the setting. This model also allows us to explain the significance of the difference between what we called above classes and functions – in Tesnière's terms, categories and functions – as well as their relationship to each other.

Tesnière first explains the **categories** of language as related to the categories of thought (Tesnière 1959: 48, original emphasis):

> Thought can only grasp the complexity of the external world by putting it into a framework of a system of ideas usually called **categories of thought**. Through the categories of thought, the human mind shapes the world in its own measure.
>
> Likewise, on the linguistic plane, language can only grasp thought by putting it in its turn into the framework of a system of notions usually called **grammatical categories**. Through grammatical categories language shapes thought in its own measure.

Tesnière stresses the similarities between these two types of categories – those of thought and those of language, but warns that the latter can vary considerably from language to language, as we have already seen above. (What he does not go into is the question of the extent to which the *former* also differ from language to language – something that has attracted great attention among linguists under the rather misleading title of the 'Sapir-Whorf hypothesis'.) He then goes on to stress that, in the analysis of syntactic relations, the emphasis should be placed, not on categories but on **functions** (Tesnière 1959: 49–50, original emphasis):

> Take for example the sentence, *Alfred frappe Bernard* 'Alfred hits Bernard'…if we envisage its **categories**, we are stating that *Alfred* and *Bernard* belong to the grammatical category of noun and *frappe* to that of verb…as long as we see it only from this point of view, we learn only that there was an entity 'Alfred', an entity 'Bernard', and an action of 'hitting': this tells us nothing about the organic tie that links these three isolated elements into a sentence.

> If by contrast we include the notion of **function**, we state that *Alfred* fills the function of subject, *Bernard* that of object, and *frappe* that of the verbal node. Thus everything becomes clear, the connections are established, the lifeless words become a living organism and the sentence takes on a meaning.

The notion of grammatical function is one of the most complex ones in the whole of syntactic study. Using Tesnière's semantic interpretation of the sentence (or rather, as we would say, clause) as a 'complete little drama', we will go on in the following chapter to see how at least two different languages represent this drama. Before we go on to explore this notion, however, it would be useful to see how a traditional government analysis – including relations of both government in the strict sense (relations with the verb) and agreement (relations between like elements) – would look for the type of language for which it was first devised.

The text below is a translation from Latin, an extract from the Old English version of Bede's original Latin *Historia Ecclesiastica Gentis Anglorum* (*History of the English Church and People*, written early 8th century), in which he tells the story of a famous illiterate poet, Caedmon, and how he first came to write poetry. Old English, like Latin, makes great use of inflections to indicate syntactic dependency relations. In the text below, government relations (between grammatical categories) are indicated by bent arrows (↪   ↩), while agreement relations (between lexical categories) are indicated by facing triangles (▶ ◀). In cases where two related elements, often two parts of a verb, are separated from each other by intervening clause elements, they are joined by broken arrows

(⋯→ ←⋯) e.g. *wæs…geseted* 'was set' in clause 1. If we follow the text through, we can get an idea of how both these kinds of dependency relations are expressed through the inflectional morphology. The exact details of the inflections themselves – the names of the cases and so on – are omitted, since the combination of the modern English glosses, and the dependency notation should be sufficient to indicate the meaning of each clause. Clause-joining elements (e.g. *ond* 'and' – see Chapter 10) have been omitted from the analysis.

(1) Wæs hē sē mon in weoruldhāde   geseted
     Was he that man in worldhood (secular life) set

(2) oð þā tīde þe hē wæs gelyfdre   ylde
     till the time that he was of-lived (advanced) of-age

(3) ond hē næfre nænig lēoð geleornode.
     and he never not-any song learned

(4a) Ond hē for þon oft in gebeorscipe,
     and he for that often in beership (drinking party)
     ↳(to 4b)   ↳(to 4b)

(5) þonne þær wæs blisse intinga gedēmed,
     when   there was of-bliss cause deemed (judged)

(6) þæt hēo ēalle sceoldon þurh endebyrdnesse be hearpan singan
     that they all should   through order   by harp   sing

(4b) þonne   hē   geseah   þā   hearpan   him   nēalacan
     when   he   saw   the   harp   to-him   come-near (approach)

    (to 4a)

(7) þonne   arās   hē   for   scōme   from   þæm   symble
    then   arose   he   for   shame   from   that   feast

(8) ond   hām   ēode   to   his   hūse.
    and   home   went   to   his   house

From the above analysis we can see that dependency relations hold between the following types of elements (in following examples where the dependency relation is indicated formally, a contrastive inflectional form is indicated below in parentheses, just to give an idea of what the particular form in the clause is in contrast with):

1. *Government*

a.   a verb controls its subject, which is in the nominative case, and can be either singular: e.g.

þonne   hē   geseah   þā   hearpan   him   nēalacan
when   he   saw   the   harp   to-him   come-near (approach)

[cf. hēo gesawon 'they saw']

or plural:

þæt   hēo ēalle   sceoldon   þurh endebyrdnesse   be hearpan   singan
that   they all   should   through order   by harp   sing

[cf. hē sceold 'he should']

b. a verb controls its complement (object), which is in the accusative case:

ond   hē   næfre   nænig   lēoð   geleornode.
and   he   never   not-any   song   learned

[cf. næniges lēoðes 'of any song']

c. a verb controls one or more adjuncts, expressed by either an adverb: e.g.

ond   hē   næfre   nænig lēoð   geleornode.
and   he   never   not-any song   learned

or by a noun: e.g.

ond   hām   ēode   to his hūse.
and   home   went   to his house

or by a preposition + noun (prepositional phrase): e.g.

þonne   arās   hē   for scōme   from   þæm   symble
then   arose   he   for shame   from   that   feast

d. an auxiliary (modal) verb controls another verb which is in the infinitive form: e.g.

þæt   hēo ēalle   sceoldon… singan
that   they all   should   sing

[cf. hē singeþ 'he sings']

e. a preposition controls its complement (object), either in the accusative case: e.g.

þæt   hēo ēalle sceoldon þurh   endebyrdnesse   be   hearpan   singan
that   they all   should   through order   by   harp   sing

(hearpa)

or in the dative case: e.g.

þonne arās hē for scōme from þæm symble
then   arose he for shame from that feast
            ↳   ↵   ↳   ↵
                  (scōm)   (symbel)

f.   a noun controls another noun, which is in the genitive case

þonne þær wæs blisse intinga gedēmed,
when   there was   of-bliss cause   deemed (judged)
                      ↳   ↵
                    (bliss)

2.   *Agreement*

g.   a participle (verbal adjective) agrees with its auxiliary verb in number and
     case: e.g.

Wæs hē sē   mon... geseted
was   he that   man   set
▸   ◂
3rd sg   nom. sg.

h.   an article agrees with its noun in number, gender, and case: e.g.

sē mon   þā hearpan   from   þæm symble
that man   the harp   from   that   feast
▸   ◂   ▸   ◂   ▸   ◂
masc. nom. sg   fem. acc. sg.   neut. dat. sg.
[þone mon]   [seo hearpa]   [þæt symbel]

i.   an adjective agrees with its noun in number, gender, and case: e.g.

gelyfdre   ylde
of-lived   of-age
▸   ◂
fem. gen. sg.
[gelyfode yldo]

From this sort of analysis, it is easy to see how the theory of government /
agreement – both dependency in Tesnière's framework – developed. In the
following chapters, we will explore Tesnière's dependency model further, and

see how it can be generalised across a range of different types of languages that do not show such clear inflectional markers of the dependency relations.

Notes

1   In order to avoid confusion between class labels (noun, adverb) and function labels (participant, circumstance), I have borrowed Tesnière's semantic term 'process' to render what he calls 'verb'.

7   Identifying clause functions

From this point onwards, we will be using a type of minimal bracketing –
ranked constituent analysis – where we divide the clause directly into its main
relational elements. So the question then becomes: how do we identify these
relations, or in Tesnière's formulation, the **functions** they play in the clause?
We can take a look at a short poem by English poet Edith Sitwell to see how we
might start going about this. Because it is in a style of verse where the sound
patterns are at least as important as the sense, it exhibits a rather convoluted
structure that takes some pulling apart – which makes it a good exercise for
our purposes.

> Sailors come
> To the drum
> Out of Babylon;
>   Hobby-horses
> Foam, the dumb
> Sky rhinoceros-glum
> Watched the courses of the breakers' rocking-horses and with Glaucis,
> Lady Venus on the settee of the horsehair sea!
> Where Lord Tennyson in laurels wrote a gloria free,
> In a borealic iceberg came Victoria; she
> Knew Prince Albert's tall memorial took the colours of the floreal
> And the borealic iceberg; floating on they see
> New-arisen Madam Venus for whose sake from far
> Came the fat and zebra'd emperor from Zanzibar
> Where like golden bouquets lay far Asia, Africa, Cathay,
> All laid before that shady lady by the fibroid Shah.
> Captain Fracasse stout as any water butt came stood
> With Sir Bacchus both a-drinking the black-tarred grapes' blood
> Plucked among the tartan leafage
> By the furry wind whose grief age
> Could not wither – like a squirrel with a gold star-nut
> Queen Victoria sitting shocked upon the rocking-horse

Of a wave said to the Laureate, 'This minx of course
Is as sharp as any lynx and blacker-deeper than the drinks
    and quite as
Hot as any hottentot, without remorse!'
      For the minx,'
           Said she,
    'And the drinks,
          You can see
Are hot as any hottentot and not the goods for me!'

Edith Sitwell, Hornpipe (*Collected Poems* 1930)

If we take the first part of the poem and divide it into clauses, we can tentatively identify the clause functions as follows (the reasons for identifying particular elements as performing particular functions will be discussed in this and the following chapter).

	Subject	Predicator	Adjunct	Adjunct
(1)	Sailors	come	to the drum	out of Babylon

	Subject	Predicator
(2)	Hobby-horses	foam

	Subject	Predicator	Complement
(3)	The dumb sky rhinoceros-glum	watched	the courses of the breakers' rocking-horses

	Adjunct	Complement
	and with Glaucis,	Lady Venus on the settee of the horsehair sea!

	Adjunct	Subject	Predicator	Complement
(4)	Where	Lord Tennyson in laurels	wrote	a gloria free,

	Adjunct	Predicator	Subject
(5)	In a borealic iceberg	came	Victoria;

	Subject	Predicator
(6)	She	knew

	Subject	Predicator	Complement
(7)	Prince Albert's tall memorial	took	the colours of the floreal and the borealic iceberg

This gives us the following set of patterns, simplified slightly by leaving out cases where a particular function is repeated twice in succession:

a. Subject   Predicator
    Hobby horses   foam

b. Subject   Predicator   Adjunct
    Sailors   come   out of Babylon

c. Adjunct   Predicator   Subject
    In an iceberg   came   Victoria

d. Subject   Predicator   Complement
    The sky   watched   the courses

e. Adjunct   Subject   Predicator   Complement
    Where   Lord Tennyson   wrote   a gloria

Now of course this is only seven clauses of the poem, and that poem only represents a fraction of the potential of the English language, but we can still sensibly ask the question: how representative are these patterns of the language as a whole? Or to put it another way, how can we generalise on the basis of the analysis given here so as to predict how likely we are to find similar patterns further afield? These are not peripheral or supplementary questions: they are inherently part of the process of doing syntactic analysis. As Halliday has said, to describe a linguistic feature is to relate it to other features in the language (Halliday 1996: 21), so whenever we identify a particular structure, say Subject plus Predicator, we are at the same time placing it in opposition to those other structures that are possible in the language – and those that are not.

The question that immediately raises itself on examining an analysis like that shown above is: on what basis exactly do we categorise something as, say, a Subject versus a Complement? This involves, as linguists Hasan and Fries (1985: xvi) point out, two complementary questions. First: what are the **recognition criteria** for the function: in other words, what are the observable characteristics – whether in terms of inflectional markings or word order or any other formal features – that allow us to recognise the presence of a particular function? And secondly: what are the **definition criteria** for the function: what does it mean for something to be a Subject in the clause rather than a Complement, how do we interpret the meaning of one function as opposed to another? Syntactic studies generally are very strong on recognition criteria, on working out what are the different characteristics – and there are usually more than one – that mark something as a Subject rather than a Complement; but they tend to be rather weaker on definition criteria, on identifying what is the implication of choosing something as a Subject. In fact, as we will see in Part

3 of this book, there is a large and influential school of thought which claims that the second question is basically irrelevant: that syntactic functions have no meaning in themselves, but are simply structural placeholders.

If we come back to the question of identifying clause functions, the usual answer given in the Western tradition, from the points of view of both recognition and definition, has to do with interpreting the case inflections. In the traditional government model of grammatical relations developed for Latin grammar, the verb governed most of the nouns of the clause, as shown by the inflectional patterns of case markings. However, in relation to case, as in most features of language, it is not easy to find a clear and unambiguous explanation for the meaning of any particular form. (See Chapter 14 for an account of different ways case has been theorised in the Western tradition.) For example in the following clauses, the so-called accusative or 'affected' case (commonly marked by *–m*) is used not only to indicate a complement (traditionally called 'direct object' – semantically something impacted by the action) of the predicator, but also an adjunct expressing goal or destination:

Aulus	Gaium	percussit.
Aulus+NOM	Gaius+ACC	strike+PERF+3SG

'Aulus struck Gaius.'

Aulus	Rōmam	revēnit.
Aulus+NOM	Rome+ACC	return+PERF+3SG

'Aulus returned to Rome'

Likewise the dative or 'giving' case (commonly marked by *–ō* or *–ae*) was used to indicate not only another kind of complement (traditionally the 'indirect object'), semantically someone or something affected by the action (either 'giving' or 'taking away'), but also an adjunct indicating location:

Aulus	Gaiō	librum	dedit.
Aulus+NOM+SG	Gaius+DAT+SG	book+ACC+SG	give+PERF+3SG

'Aulus gave Gaius the book.'

Aulus	Gaiō	librum	sustulit.
Aulus+NOM+SG	Gaius+DAT+SG	book+ACC+SG	remove+PERF+3SG

'Aulus took the book from Gaius.'

Aulus	Rōmae	habitat.
Aulus+NOM+SG	Rome+DAT+SG	live+PRES+3SG

'Aulus lives in Rome.'

And the ablative or 'taking away' case (commonly marked by –ō or –ā) was used not only to indicate the agent of the action (who or what an action was carried out by), but also an adjunct indicating the source of movement:

Domus	ventō	delēta	est.
house+NOM+SG	wind+ABL+SG	destroy+PT+NOM+SG+FEM	be+PRES+3SG

'The house was destroyed by the wind.'

Aulus	Rōmā	profectus	est.
Aulus+NOM	Rome+ABL	set-out+PT+NOM+SG+MASC	be+PRES+3SG

'Aulus set out from Rome.'

The theory scholars developed to explain this, first in the Byzantine Empire (originally the Eastern Roman Empire), then revived in European classical studies in the 19th century, was one based on a generalisation of the notion of **location**. It certainly seemed highly significant that there were regular alternations such as the following use of the preposition *in* either with the accusative case, where it meant 'into', i.e. towards a location, or with the ablative case, where it meant 'in', i.e. at a location:

Liberī	in hortum	cursunt.
child+NOM+PL	in garden+ACC+SG	run+PERF+3PL

'The children ran into the garden.'

Liberī	in hortō	ludēbant.
child+NOM+PL	in garden+ABL+SG	play+IMPF+3PL

'The children were playing in the garden'

On the basis of examples such as these, scholars saw the original meaning of the most of the cases of Latin as concerned with the motion of objects in space, originally literally so, but then applied metaphorically. On this basis, the three cases most directly associated with the verb in Latin could be explained as follows:

accusative	motion towards	Rōmam 'to Rome'
dative	location at	Rōmae 'in Rome'
ablative	motion away from	Rōmā 'from Rome'

As Latin evolved, the locative functions of these cases, which in classical Latin had already become restricted to certain words indicating place, became increasingly expressed by prepositions: so *ad* 'to' for 'motion towards'; *in* 'in' for 'motion into' or 'location at'; and *ā/ab* 'away from' or *ē/ex* 'out of' for 'motion away from' (see Chapter 9 for more discussion of this point in relation to Old English). But on the basis of this **locative** model, an explanation of the uses of these cases in non-motion contexts could also be given, as in the following examples:

accusative (metaphorical motion towards)
entity impacted on by action, goal, direct object

Hostis   habet   **murōs.**
enemy+NOM+SG   have+PRES+3SG   wall+ACC+PL
'The enemy have taken the walls'

dative (metaphorical location at)
entity affected by action, recipient, indirect object

Aulus   librum   **Gaiō**   dat.
Aulus+NOM   book+ACC+SG   Gaius+DAT   give+PRES+3SG
'Aulus is giving Gaius a book.'

ablative (metaphorical motion away from)
entity involved in action, agent/instrument

Naturam   expellas   **furcā**   tamen   usque   recurret.
nature+ACC+SG   drive-out+SUBJ+2SG   fork+ABL+SG   however   back   return+FUT+3SG
'You may drive Nature out with a pitchfork, but (she) will come back'

This type of theory lies behind the traditional designation of verbs as **transitive**, literally 'going through (to another entity)', or **intransitive**, 'not going through (to another entity)', where the potential presence of a noun in the accusative case is taken as criterial (see Chapter15 for an account of different theories of transitivity).

This sort of model, however, still leaves unexplained the meaning of another case, the 'nominative' or 'subject' case. One reason for this may be that every clause in Latin must have a subject, indicated by a particular marking on the verb, as well as optionally by a noun in the nominative case. When something is ubiquitous, there seems less need to explain it. But what exactly is this element that is marked both on the verb and on the noun? The following example, quoted from Matthews 1981: 105, shows the 'same' element in two different types of clauses:

Hostis   habet   murōs:
enemy+NOM+SG   have+PRES+3SG   wall+ACC+PL
'The enemy have taken the walls:'

ruit   altō   ā   culmine   **Troia**.
collapse+PRES+3SG   high+ABL+SG+MASC   from summit+ABL+SG   Troy+NOM+SG
'Troy collapses from its high summit.'

In the first clause the noun in nominative case, *hostis* 'the enemy' is the subject of a transitive verb, *habēre*, 'to have, possess'; while in the second clause, the nominative *Troia* 'Troy' is the subject of an intransitive verb *ruere* 'to collapse'. So what exactly is it here that is being marked as the same?

The explanation for Latin, and for other languages that have what is called a 'nominative-accusative' case-marking system, depends on the notion of transitivity explained above. That is, for such languages, an action can either take place with regard to a single entity, the **subject**, in which case the verb is intransitive, or be **extended** from the subject to another entity, the **object** or **complement**, in which case the verb is transitive. Because the subject is the essential element in either case, it is therefore marked with the same case ending, and additionally indicated on the verb.

This traditional explanation, as developed for English by modern linguists such as Quirk and Greenbaum (1973: 16), gives us a classification of three types of transitivity: **intransitive** 'not extended'; **(mono-)transitive** 'extended (once)'; and **ditransitive** 'extended twice'.

Type	Explanation	Complement functions
1. intransitive	action doesn't pass across	**Subject** only **Sailors** come.
2. (mono)transitive	action passes across to one other entity	**Subject** & *Direct Object* **The sky** watched *the courses.* **Tennyson** wrote *a gloria.*
3. ditransitive	action passes to one entity and then to another entity	**Subject** & <u>Indirect Object</u> & *Direct Object* **Queen Victoria** gave <u>the minx</u> *the drinks.*

The verb itself, whose function can be identified as **predicator**, is commonly specified as either intransitive, e.g. *come, stand*; transitive, e.g. *drink, eat*;

or ditransitive, e.g. *give, sell*. Strictly speaking it would be more accurate to characterise the **clause** itself as intransitive, or transitive etc., since especially in modern English, a particular verb can often be used in more than one way: e.g.

trans.   Subject   Predicator   Direct Object.
           Captain Fracasse   drank   the wine.

intrans.   Subject   Predicator   Adjunct
           This wine   drinks   very smoothly.

Tesnière's model of clause relations, already mentioned several times before, was slightly different. He borrowed the model of **valency** from chemistry, where it is used to describe the number of electrons controlled by the nucleus of a particular atom, to characterise the relationship between a verb and its accompanying nouns. This is basically a development of the traditional notion of government, with the nature of the verb determining the presence and number of nouns in the clause. As Matthews notes (1981: 103), '[i]n dependency grammar…the predicator is the only essential element [of the clause EMcD], and as such governs or controls a subject precisely as it controls the direct object and other elements that enter into valencies.'. In the French tradition, these elements are usually referred to as **complements** (*compléments*), including the subject, and what we are calling complements here (of both the direct and the indirect object kind). Furthermore, as was pointed out above, Tesnière interpreted these complements in semantic terms as **participants** (*actants*), which, using a terminology that has become widely used since Tesnière's time, might be characterised as follows:

syntactic term	*semantic interpretation*	*semantic label*
subject	performs the action	agent
direct object	undergoes the action	patient
indirect object	benefits from the action	beneficiary

Since Tesnière included the subject as a type of complement on par with the direct and indirect objects, his classification of clause types looks a little different from Quirk and Greenbaum's. So a clause with only a subject is classified as **monovalent** (one complement), one with a subject and an object as **bivalent** (two complements), and one with a subject, a direct object, and an indirect object as **trivalent** (three complements). But Tesnière's classification also recognises clauses which he called **avalent**: in effect, only an action with no participants, such as *il pleut* 'it is raining', where the *il* ('it' in English) doesn't refer to any entity but is simply a place marker, or what is often called 'dummy subject'. Thus Tesnière's framework includes four different types of valency:

Type	Explanation	Complement functions
1. avalent	action without participant	'dummy' **Subject** **It** is raining.
2. monovalent	action with only one participant	**Subject** only **The wind** was blowing.
3. bivalent	action with two participants	**Subject** & *Direct Object* **The wind** plucked *the leaves.*
4. trivalent	action with three participants	**Subject** & <u>Indirect Object</u> & *Direct Object* **Captain Fracasse** gave <u>Sir Bacchus</u> *some wine.*

What then is this 'subject' that appears in the avalent type, and why does it need to be there? In the traditional analysis inherited from logic, the clause as a whole divides into two parts, the **subject** and the **predicate**: the subject being 'that which lies under [focus]' (Latin *subiectum*), and the predicate 'that which is said about [the subject]' (Latin *prāedicātum*). Tesnière rejects this type of analysis as irrelevant for linguistic analysis, as we saw above (Tesnière 1959: 103–105), by reinterpreting the subject on par with other complements, all of these representing types of participants; and by distributing the traditional predicate among the different functions of predicator, complements and adjuncts. Again Matthews comments in this regard (1981: 101–2), '…all languages have some form of construction in which predicators are related to different classes of complement. A division of subject and predicate would be then no more than a secondary feature.' So why do we need the 'dummy' subject of the avalent type then? Well, in a language like Latin, we don't, since the marking on the verb is sufficient to indicate the type of subject without one being explicitly expressed: 'it is raining' in Latin is simply *pluit*, with the ending *–it* indicating 3rd person singular present tense. However, in languages like English and French, the subject not only in most cases represents a participant, it is also necessary for indicating the mood of the verb, i.e. for distinguishing between *il pleut* 'it is raining' (statement) and *pleut-il?* 'is it raining?' (question). Thus, even though in such cases it does not represent an actual entity, it still needs to be present in order to mark mood distinctions.

There is, however, another type of clause, known as the **copulative**, which falls outside both the transitivity and the valency classification altogether. If we look at the following example in Latin, both nouns are in the nominative case and they seem therefore to have the same relationship to the verb:

Aulus   consul   factus   est.
Aulus+NOM   consul+NOM+SG   make+PT+NOM+SG+MASC   be+PRES+3SG
'Aulus became consul'

What the case marking seems to be telling us here, therefore, is that there is no 'action' passing between the participants, and the verb is merely a 'linking element' (Latin *copula*) between two nouns. In many languages, such as sometimes in Latin and commonly in Russian when simply stating a fact, the copulative verb itself can be omitted:

Aulus   consul.
Aulus+NOM   consul+NOM+SG
'Aulus is consul'

In fact a number of the clauses or parts of clauses in the text appear in this predicator-less form:

Captain Fracasse [was] stout as any water butt

In analyses like that of Quirk and Greenbaum, the second nominal element in such clauses would be classified as a **complement**, as opposed to an **object** for the other kinds:

Subject   Complement
Captain Fracasse   [was] stout (as any water butt)

Complements, in this sense, can be realised not just by nouns, but also by adjectives or even prepositional phrases: e.g.

Subject   Complement
This minx   is   sharp   (as any lynx).

Subject   Complement
Queen Victoria was   upon the rocking horse.

So modifying Tesnière somewhat, our model of clause types for English could be summed up by classifying clauses in English as follows:

avalent	It was raining
monovalent	The wind was blowing
bivalent	The wind plucked the leaves
trivalent	Captain Fracasse gave Sir Bacchus some wine
copular	The minx is a lynx (noun complement)
	The drinks are hot (adjective complement)
	Lady Venus was on the settee (prepositional phrase compl.)

Both the transitivity and the valency model were initially developed on and for European languages. How might such a model be generalised to languages of quite a different type, such as Chinese? In this regard, the question of what sort of thing 'subject' might be in Chinese was the focus of spirited debate in (Mainland) Chinese linguistic circles in the 1950s (cf Lü 1958). One of the key points had to do with examples like some we will look at in the next chapter, where a place expression preceded the verb: e.g.

> Tái.shang   zuò.zhe   wěiyuánhuì.
> platform on   sit ASP:dur.   committee
> 'On the platform was seated the committee.'

Since Chinese has no morphological markers linking the 'subject' to the predicator – the type of marking which tells us that, for example in the English translation, *the committee* must be subject – the controversy had to do with what should be taken as primary: the semantic relationship of process to participant, with *wěiyuánhuì* 'committee' taken as subject since it is the committee that is doing the 'sitting'; or word order, with the place expression *tái. shang* 'on the platform' taken as subject since it is in the 'subject' position preceding the verb.

In fact, like many such debates which regard descriptive categories like 'subject' as having some sort of universal validity for all languages, the debate for Chinese was largely coming at these issues back to front. Some years earlier in his *Mandarin Primer*, American-based Chinese linguist Yuen Ren Chao had already pointed out that in Chinese the relationship of subject to predicate is one of 'subject matter…and something said about the subject matter'(Chao 1948: 35), a conception that in more recent work has been labeled a 'topic' as opposed to a 'comment' (Chao 1968: 69; Li & Thompson 1981: 4.1). Such a model, with what may seem from the point of view of European languages to be a 'looser fit' between the subject and its predicator (using those terms now as we have defined them in this book), does seem necessary to cover the range of relationships between clause functions in examples like the following, with the verb *shài* 'to shine (of the sun), to bask (of someone in the sun)':

Wǒ.men   shài   tàiyáng
I+PL   shine   sun
'We were sunbathing.'

Wǒ.men   dōu   gěi tàiyáng   shài-hēi   le.
I+PL   all   by sun   shine black   ASP:perf.
'We were all tanned by the sun.'

The sense of 'directionality' that seems so strong in European languages, with
the action 'passing on' from the subject to the complement(s) – the origin as
we saw above of the notion of 'transitivity' in the first place – seems almost
completely absent in Chinese, as with another famously ambiguous example
given by Chao, (1948: 35) where the noun *ji* 'chicken' may be interpreted as
either subject or complement:

Jī   chī   .le
chicken   eat   ASP:perf.
'The chicken has eaten (some grain)' or 'The chicken has been eaten
     (for dinner)'.

Here I have chosen to retain the term 'subject' to make comparison across
languages easier, but in the realisation that a more thorough-going analysis of
Chinese on its own terms would be very likely to redefine the notion or even
get rid of it altogether.

Nevertheless, just for the sake of comparison and to give some idea of
the extent of differences, we can see how Tesnière's classification of valency
types, which works pretty well for English and French, would look if we simply
translated the examples directly into Chinese:

'avalent'   (Tiān)   xià   yǔ.
                       sky   fall   rain
                       'It was raining.'

'monovalent'   Guā   fēng   .le.
                       blow   wind   ASP:perf.
                       'The wind was blowing.'

These two types are structurally almost identical, and are both often described
in grammars of Chinese as 'subjectless': they typically involve a predicator
and a single complement, which however follows rather than precedes the
predicator. In the first example, the possible candidate for subject, *tiān* 'sky',

may be omitted; it may also be translated 'weather' rather than 'sky', in which case the clause could be interpreted as a topic 'As for the weather' followed by a comment '(it) was raining.'

'bivalent'   Fēng   zhāi-kāi   .le   yèzi
                wind   pluck away   ASP:compl   leaf
                'The wind plucked the leaves.'

'trivalent'   F. jiànzhǎng gěi   .le   B. juéshì   yìdiǎn'r jiǔ.
                F. captain   give   ASP:compl   B. knight   a-little wine
                'Captain Fracasse gave Sir Bacchus some wine.'

These two clauses come closest to the familiar English patterns, in the familiar order of Subject Predicator Complement often taken to be typical of languages like English (often referred to in typological studies as SVO, i.e. Subject Verb Object), with the indirect object type of complement, like English, preceding the direct object type.

'copular'   Nèi.ge huàinǔ   shi   .ge   shānmāo
                that MEAS bad-woman be   MEAS   mountain-cat
                'The minx is a lynx.'

                Yǐnliào   hen   rè.
                drink   very   hot
                'The drinks are hot.'

                Yǐnliào   shi   rè.de
                drink   be   hot SUB
                'The drinks are hot ones.'

The copular with a noun complement is again very like the English pattern. But with what corresponds to the English adjective complement, Chinese shows two distinct patterns. In the first, the Predicator is the 'adjective' or 'stative verb' *rè* 'to be hot', which **describes** a state or quality of the Subject; while in the second, with the stative verb 'framed' by the verb *shi* 'be' preceding it and the 'nominalising' particle *de* following, the Predicator **classifies** the Subject, i.e. these are hot drinks as opposed to cold.

                V. fūrén   zài   shāfā.shang   (zuò.zhe).
                V. lady   be-at   sofa on   sit ASP:dur.
                'Lady Venus was (seated) on the settee.'

Finally, the copular type with a prepositional phrase can be expressed exactly as in English; alternatively, the prepositional phrase may function as an adjunct *zài shāfā.shang* 'on the settee' followed by a predicator like *zuò. zhe* 'sitting'.

The obvious next step at this point would be to go back and ask: what would a classification of valency types look like from the point of view of Chinese? We won't do this here; but the discussion above should be sufficient to counsel great caution in applying any sort of framework across different languages. So when we go on to apply the valency framework in more detail to Chinese and Gaelic in the following chapter, we will do it, as throughout this book, as a way of problematising the issues involved, rather than providing a fixed framework for analysis. Clause functions are one of the most complex aspects of language; but they are also one of the areas in which the greatest amount of 'imposing' of the patterns of one language onto another has taken place. Most European scholars up to the 18th century saw every language through the prism of Latin; while many modern-day accounts, explicitly or implicitly, take English as a baseline. This issue of the so-called 'universals of language' is one that already came up in Chapter 2, and will come up again and again in the course of this book. But before we explore these problems any further, let's first take a closer look at how we can argue for the analysis of clause structures in our main two languages under description.

8   Analysing function structures

As we saw in the previous chapter, a number of models have been put forward for describing clause functions. The one we will be using here to explore the description of clause structure is Tesnière's **valency** model, which operates in terms of a nuclear or nodal function, the **predicator**, which has the semantic role of **process**, and which, to a great or lesser extent controls the other functions in the clause. In many languages the clause function labelled **subject** has a special relationship to the predicator, which is often marked formally, and a clause containing a subject and a predicator (verb) tends to be regarded – by grammarians at least – as a 'basic' form of clause in the language. When we come to the other functions, Tesnière makes a semantic distinction between **participants**, realised by the subject and various kinds of **complements** (covering the two traditional types Quirk & Greenbaum (1973: 170) refer to as 'objects' and 'complements' proper), and **circumstances**, realised by various kinds of **adjuncts**.

The semantic distinction between participants and circumstances is very clear in principle, but when it comes to syntactic functions, different languages draw the line between complements and adjuncts in different places. Let's take a look at the following extract from a Chinese text, which problematises these issues very clearly. The syntactic functions are indicated above each clause using the general terms S(ubject), P(redicator), C(omplement) – including both objects and complements in the traditional sense – and A(djunct). Elements not relevant to the predication structure of the clause, in other words, not in any meaningful sense 'controlled' by the predicator, are not analysed here. I will go through the text in small chunks, explaining the reason for the functions assigned.

The first three clauses present essentially similar experiences, involving entities ('the ghosts') and their locations ('on earth', 'in our minds'), in different ways.

      S   P   C

(1) Dì.shang   méi yǒu   guǐ,
     earth-on   NEG -exist   ghost
     '(If) on earth there are no ghosts'

```
        S          P          C
(2)  guǐ        zài        nǎ'r?
     ghost      be-at      where
```
'(Then) where are the ghosts?'

```
        S              P        C
(3)  Guǐ       dōu   zài     rénxīn          lǐ.tou.
     ghost     all   be-at   people-mind     inside
```
'The ghosts are in people's minds.'

From an English point of view, analyses that may call for explanation are those such as in clause 1 of *dì.shang* 'on the earth' as subject or in clause 3 of *rénxīn lǐ.tou* 'in people's minds' as complement. Since expressions of place would tend to be understood as circumstances rather than participants, and thus expressed by adjuncts rather than complements, the first question is: why have they been assigned the functions of subject or complement here? As in all questions of predication, we need to start by looking at the verb. The verbs *yǒu* 'exist, have' and *zài* 'be located, be at' are almost exact opposites of each other in Chinese: they both control what semantically could be called an **existent**, i.e. an entity that exists (somewhere), and a **location**, where something exists; but appear in clause structures that are mirror images of each other, with *yǒu* having a location as subject and existent as complement, while *zài* has an existent as subject and location as complement. This semantic analysis implies, as Matthews points out (1981: 124) that there must be 'collocational restrictions' between process and participants. So syntactically speaking it is the relationship to the predicator in a particular clause which defines an element as subject or complement rather than adjunct: in another type of clause such elements could well be adjuncts.

Matthews further points out (1981: 125) that complements may also be 'optional' in a particular clause, in other words, may be omitted. In the examples above, whereas the existent element must normally be present in the clause, it is possible to omit the location element in both cases, as in the following conversational examples.

```
     P        C
     Yǒu      rén       .ma?
     exist    person    Q
```
'Is anyone there?'

```
     S              P
     Tā      bú     zài.
     s/he    NEG    be-at
```
'She's not in.'

However, as suggested by the English translations, the location element is always assumed, as some unspecified place, and is easily supplied:

```
S          P        C
Jiā.li     yǒu      rén      ma?
home in    exist    person   Q
'Is anyone at home?'
```

```
S          P        C
Tā    bú   zài      bàngōngshì.
s/he  NEG  be-at    office in
'She's not in the office.'
```

The location elements in such clauses, although structurally similar to place adjuncts in that they contain a noun often followed by a location marker, are therefore inherent to the meaning of the verb, in the sense that they are always understood as part of its meaning and can thus always be added. For these reasons, it seems to make more sense to analyse them as complements. As Matthews notes (1981: 125), 'a complement must be obligatory with at least some predicators', and we will use this as one of the criteria distinguishing complements (in the broad sense) from adjuncts.

Similarly to the two conversational examples above, the next two clauses of the text seem to be lacking something, clause 4 a complement and clause 5 a subject:

```
        S          P
(4)  Nǐ    bú      xìn?
     you   NEG     believe
     'You don't believe (me)?'
```

```
            P        C
(5)  Jiù   kàn      mèng.
     then  look     dream
     'Well, (you) take a look at dreams.'
```

However, again as suggested by the English translations, it is easy and natural to include these missing functions:

```
        S          P        C
(4')  Nǐ    bú      xìn      wǒ?
      you   NEG     believe  I
      'You don't believe me?'
```

```
         S           P    C
(5′) Nǐ    jiù   kàn   mèng.
      you   then  look  dream
```
'You consider dreams, then.'

In Chinese, under most circumstances, if the subject or complement have either been mentioned previously, or are implied from the general context, they may simply be omitted. They are thus what Matthews calls 'latent' (1981: 125–6) in the clause, in other words, will be 'understood' even if they are not explicitly there, and this potential is another feature that needs to be taken into account in distinguishing complement from adjunct.

The clauses in the next sequence each present two different experiences, and thus two separate predication structures, combined into one.

```
       S                          P     [| A    P |]   C
(6)  Mèng.li nà.me duō rén   dōu   .shi  nǎ'r   lái   .de?
      dream in so many person  all   be    where  come  SUB
```
'So many people in dreams, where do they all come from?'

```
       P     [| A                    P |]           C
(7)  Yǒu   hé nǐ zài yìqǐ          shēnghuó.guo   .de rén,
      exist  with you at together    live ASP: exp     SUB person
```
'There are people who have lived with you.'

```
        P     [| S      P               C |]           C
(8)  yě  yǒu   nǐ    zhǐ   tīngshuō.guo   míngzi .de rén:
      also exist  you    only  hear-tell ASP: exp  name   SUB person
```
'there are also people who you've only heard the names of'

The complement of each clause contains a further clause 'embedded' within it (function analysis indicated in double brackets – see Chapter 10 for further discussion), which functions as a kind of description of the main entity realised by the complement. In clauses 7 and 8, these correspond to what would traditionally be called 'relative clauses' – expressed in English by 'relative pronouns' such as *who, which, that*; in Chinese, such constructions are completely comparable to other simpler sorts of modifiers, as in the modified example below:

```
        P              [| P|]   C
(7')  Yǒu   hěn   qíguài  .de rén,
      exist  very  strange  SUB person
      'There are very strange people.'
```

The case of clause 6 is a little different. Firstly, the main entity supposedly represented by the complement is not actually present in the clause, though it could easily be supplied:

```
      S                           P     [| A    P |]      C
(6')  Mèng.li nà.me duō rén    dōu   .shi  nǎ'r   lái .de   rén?
      dream in  so many person   all   be    where  come SUB  person
      'So many people in dreams, are all people who come from where?'
```

However, this not only seems redundant, it is also forcing the interpretation somewhat. In fact, this is an example of a predication structure being utilised for other purposes: specifically, to give a certain element a particular information status (see Chapter 11). In this case, the verb *shi* 'be' directs the focus of information on to the immediately following element, i.e. the location element *nǎ'r* 'where'. Normally, speaking such circumstances in Chinese are realised as adjuncts preceding the predicator, as the following modified example, where the focus would most naturally fall on the final element, that is, the predicator itself:

```
      S      A                       P
      'Guǐ   zì    rénxīn     lǐ.tou   chū-lai.'
      ghost  from  people-mind inside  exit come
      'Ghosts *come* from people's minds.'
```

The structure of the original clause 6, often known in grammars of Chinese simply as the *shi...de* construction, moves the focus on to the adjunct, by 'dressing up' the clause as a simple S-P-C structure, where the focus naturally falls on the final element, here the complement, and thus the clause embedded within it:

```
      S                           P     [| A    P |]  C
(6)   Mèng.li  nà.me duō rén   dōu   .shi  nǎ'r   lái   de?
      dream in   so many person  all   be    where  come  SUB
      'So many people in dreams, *where* do they all come from?'
```

The next clause in the text is an example of a clause with only a subject, indicating a kind of state, where the predicator is realised by what in English would be an adjective, but in Chinese is most naturally classified as a subtype of verb, often known as a 'state verb' or 'stative verb':

```
     S             P
(9)  Zhè  dōu  bù   kěpà.
     this  all   NEG  frightening
     'None of this is frightening.'
```

Such clauses cannot contain a complement; on the other hand, the subject itself may contain an embedded clause, as shown in the modified example below:

```
      S    [| A      P                     C |]             P
(9')  Zài mèng.li  kàn  zhèyàng .de   rén    dōu  bù   kěpà.
      at dream in   look  this-type SUB   person  all   NEG  frightening
      'To see this kind of people in dreams isn't frightening.'
```

So, following Matthews (1981: 123–127), the basic criteria for distinguishing complements (in the broad sense, i.e. both subjects and complements proper) from adjuncts can be summed up as follows:

- there are **collocational restrictions** between particular predicators and their complements

- complements are an **obligatory** element of the meaning of the clause

- for this reason, they may sometimes be **optional**, i.e. not explicitly present in the clause

- as the other side of this, they may be **latent** in particular clauses, i.e. understood even though not present

- certain types of predicator may **exclude** particular types of complement, either colligationally (a monovalent clause cannot have a complement), or collocationally (a certain predicator will not normally be used with a certain complement).

Summing up now the overall clause structure of Chinese, what we might call its basic or default word order, that is, the order in which clause functions are likely to appear if there is no good reason otherwise, is SAPC. Variations on this may consist of putting an adjunct at the beginning of the clause, i.e. ASPC, or leaving out either subject or complement or both, i.e. (S)P(C). As we have also seen, with certain types of predicator, either the subject or the complement or both may have other clauses embedded inside them. The basic patterns may be exemplified as follows:

```
S           P
Zhè    bù    kěpà.
this   NEG   frightening
'This isn't frightening.'
```

```
S    A                      P
'Guǐ  zì    rénxīn       lǐ.tou    chū-lai.
ghost from  people-mind  inside    exit come
'Ghosts come from people's minds.'
```

```
S    A          P     C
Nǐ   zài mèng.li kàn   zhèyàng  .de rén
you  at dream in  look  this-type  SUB person
'You see this kind of people in dreams.'
```

```
S    P     C
guǐ   zài   rénxīn       lǐ.tou
ghost be-at people mind  inside
'The ghosts are in people's minds.'
```

```
S        P     (C)
Nǐ   bú   xìn   (wǒ)?
you  NEG  believe  I
'You don't believe (me).'
```

```
(S)          P     C
(Ni) jiù      kàn   mèng.
you then look  dream
'Consider dreams, then.'
```

The issues involved in determining basic clause functions can be thrown into relief by going through the same process in a completely unrelated and very different language: Scottish Gaelic. The following is an extract from a short narrative text in Gaelic, a traditional folktale already discussed in a different context in Chapter 2:

	A	P	S
(1)	Uair dha	robh	an saoghal
	time to-it	be+PAST+DEP	the+MASC world

'Once upon a time,'

	P	S	A			
(2)	bha	iolaire	anns na beanntan	a-muigh	taobh	Loch Tréig.
	be+PAST+IND	eagle	in the+PLUR mountain+PLUR	away	side	Loch Treig.

'there was an eagle in the mountains beside Loch Treig.'

The first contrast we notice is one of basic word order: the subject, rather than coming first as is normal in Chinese, always follows the predicator, as in clause 2. However, this basic order may be varied, for example by having an adjunct at the beginning of the clause, as in clause 1. For the next clause, clause 3, we need to recognise what we might call a 'split predicator', e.g. *bha...a' fuireach* '...was living'.

	P-	S	-P	A		A
(3)	Bha	i	a' fuireach	ann an	coire	an sin
	be+PAST+IND	she	at live+NOM	in	corry	there

'She was living in a corry [depression in the mountain side] there'

	A		P	S	C
(4)	ris	an	can	iad	An Coire Meadhain.
	to-it	REL	say+FUT+DEP	they	the corry middle+GEN

'which they call the Middle Corry.'

In certain situations in Gaelic, the verb splits into two parts: the lexical verb or predicator proper, and a **finite** element which indicates such things as tense and mood. Although there are arguments for recognising this finite as a separate clause function, for our present purposes, and in order to make the comparison with Chinese easier, we will simply indicate it as the first part of a complex predicator. Clause 4 is a type of embedded or relative clause (see Chapter 10), whereby the adjunct element, a so-called 'prepositional pronoun', e.g. *ris* 'to it' (in Gaelic 'to say a name to something' corresponds to English 'to call something a name'), is followed by the relative marker *a* or *an*. A non-relative form of the clause would look like the following, where the adjunct takes its normal position following the complement:

	P	S	C	A
(4')	can	iad	An Coire Meadhain	ris
	say+FUT+DEP	they	the corry middle+GEN	to-it

'They call it the Middle Corry.'

The following two clauses both put an adjunct element at the beginning of the clause for emphasis, in a very similar way to English, or for that matter, Chinese:

	A	P	S	
(5)	A' bhliadhna seo	thainig	geamhradh fuar	agus mòran sneachda,
	the+FEM year this	come+PAST+IND	winter cold+MASC	and much snow+GEN

A
le   cur   is   cathadh,
with   fall   and   drift
'One year (there) came a cold winter with much snow, in fall and drift,'

	A		P-	S
(6)	oidhche	dhe na h-oidhcheannan,	bha	an iolaire
	night	of the+PLUR night+PLUR	be+PAST+IND	the+FEM eagle

-P   C
a' faireachdainn   an fhuachd.
at feel+NOM   the+GEN cold+GEN
'one night, the eagle was feeling the cold.'

Clause 6 contains an interesting feature which shows very clearly the derivation of 'split predicator' structures such as *bha...a' fuireach* 'was living' in clause 3 or *bha...a' faireachdainn* 'was feeling' in this clause. Literally, this translates as '...was at feeling', where *faireachdainn* 'feeling' is a so-called 'verbal noun': that is, semantically a process but syntactically a noun; while *a'* or *ag* is derived from the preposition *aig* 'at', but here indicates something like 'continuing action'. When a complement is attached to the verbal noun *faireachdainn*, it takes the syntactic form of a noun modifying another noun, and is thus put in the so-called 'genitive' or 'possessive' case. Literally, then, *bha...a' faireachdainn an fhuachd* translates as '...was at the feeling of the cold'. (Compare a dialectal English example *you've been a working too hard*, where *a working* derives from an earlier 'on working' – there is reason to think that English here was influenced by neighbouring Celtic languages like Welsh, which is very like Gaelic in this respect.)

The next clause shows what we could regard as the 'default' order of clause functions in Gaelic, in other words, the order chosen unless there is some specific reason for doing otherwise, i.e. PSCA:

	P			S	C				A
(7)	'Cha do dh'fhairich			mi	a	lethid	de dh'fhuachd		riamh'
	NEG+DECL DEP feel+PAST			I	its	like	of cold+GEN		ever

' 'I have never felt cold like this' '

	P	S	A
(8)	thuirt	i	rithe fhèin.
	say+PAST+IND	she	to-her self

'she said to herself.'

The analysis of Clause 8 raises the important issue of the classes of elements that realise **complements** as against **adjuncts**: in other words the respective recognition criteria of the two kinds of functions. In this clause, the adjunct *rithe fhèin* 'to herself' could also be classified as a complement, since semantically, as the addressee of the speaking, it could be regarded as a participant rather than a circumstance. In the clearest cases, as assumed by Tesnière, complements in the broad sense are realised by nouns or collections of elements 'controlled' by a noun: so for example two French clauses cited by him which both have the same SPC structure:

S	P	C
Alfred	frappe	Bernard
Alfred	hits	Bernard

'Alfred is hitting Bernard.'

S	P	C
Les petits ruisseaux	font	les grandes rivières
The small streams	make	the big rivers

'Small streams make big rivers.'

Likewise, in the clearest cases, adjuncts are realised by adverbs:

A	S	P	C
Hier	Alfred	a oublié	son chapeau
yesterday	Alfred	has forgotten	his hat

'Yesterday Alfred forgot his hat.'

S	P	A	C
On	oublie	toujours	quelque chose
one	forgets	always	some thing

'People are always forgetting something.'

However, there is large set of adjuncts realised, not by adverbs, but by a combination of an adverb type of element, known traditionally as a 'preposition', e.g. *dans* 'in' or *à* 'at' in the following examples, plus a noun or collection of elements controlled by a noun (see Chapter 9 for a discussion of such structures, known normally as 'prepositional phrases'):

S	P	C	A
Alfred	a laissé	son chapeau	dans votre maison.
Alfred	has left	his hat	in your-pl house

'Alfred left his hat in your house.'

S	P	C	A
Alfred	a quitté	la maison	à neuf heures.
Alfred	has left	the house	at nine hours

'Alfred left the house at nine o'clock.'

The analytical problem then arises when such 'prepositional phrases' are used to realise what semantically seem like participants rather than circumstances, and should perhaps therefore be classified as complements rather than adjuncts:

S-	P	-S	A or C?
Ton père	habite-t-il		dans votre maison?
your-sg father	lives	he	in your-pl house

'Does your father live in your house?'

S	P	C	A or C?
Alfred	donne	un livre	à votre jeune cousine.
Alfred	gives	a book	to your-pl young female-cousin

'Alfred is giving a book to your young cousin.'

In terms of Matthew's notion of complements being 'obligatory' with their predicator, the location element *dans votre maison* 'in your house' would seem to be inherent to the meaning of the verb *habiter* 'live, dwell, inhabit', as would the recipient element *à votre jeune cousine* 'to your young cousin' to the meaning of the verb *donner* 'give'.

To come back to our Gaelic text, clauses like 8 present us with a similar problem:

	P	S	A or C?
(8)	thuirt	i	rithe fhèin.
	said	she	to-her self

'She said to herself.'

'Saying' would seem to be something that inherently involves an addressee, so on those grounds the 'prepositional pronoun' (a combination of a preposition and a pronoun) *rithe* 'to her' would be considered a complement rather than an adjunct. If we look at a range of similar verbs in Gaelic they turn out to have similar structures: e.g.

	P	S	A or C?
(8′)	dh'fhaighnich	i	dheth fhèin.
	asked	she	from-her self

'She asked herself.'

	P	S	A or C?
(8″)	dh'innis	i	dhi fhèin.
	told	she	to-her self

'She told herself.'

In English, such elements may be expressed either 'like complements' – as in *she told herself / she asked herself*, or 'like adjuncts' – *she said to herself*; and a similar double pattern is seen in the following Chinese examples, with the 'complement' types:

S	P	C		S	P	C
tā	wèn	zìjǐ		tā	gào.su	zìjǐ
s/he	ask	self'		s/he	tell	self'

'She asked herself.'   'She told herself.'

as opposed to the 'adjunct' types:

S	A or C?	P		S	A or C?	P
tā	gēn zìjǐ	shuō		tā	duì zìjǐ	shuō
s/he	with self	say		s/he	towards self	say

'She said to herself.'   'She said to herself.'

This is what is traditionally given the function label of 'indirect object', which as Matthews notes (19821: 128), '[n]otionally…is a participant…is also excluded by some predicators… [and] can also be latent'. We do not need to make a decision here as to whether such elements should be classed as complements or adjuncts, simply noting that in syntactic description there are always likely to be such 'in-between' cases, where different criteria point different ways.

Clause 9 consists simply of a predicator, with the subject omitted as is common in imperative mood, i.e. expressing a command: here there is no complement, but this clause is followed immediately by another clause, clause 10, which indicates that this is quoted speech.

P
(9) 'Saoil'
think+IMP
' 'Think' '

P	S
(10) thuirt	i,
say+PAST+IND	she

'she said'

Clause 11 contains a type of embedded or relative clause, which is how comparison is normally expressed in Gaelic:

P	S	[| S P	C	A |]
(11) 'an robh	oidhche	na b'	fhuaire	na seo
INT be+PAST+DEP	night	REL be+PAST+IND	cold+COMP	than this

A	A
riamh	ann?'
ever	in-it

' 'Was there ever a night colder than this?' '

The embedded clause *na b(u) fhuaire na seo*, literally 'which was colder than this', has a relative marker, in this case *na*, standing in the place of the subject, which here precedes rather than follows the verb, *bu*, a special form of the verb 'be'. In the corresponding non-relative clause, the subject would follow the verb, as normal:

P	S	C
(11')Bha	an oidhche	glè fhuar.
be+PAST+IND	the+FEM night	very cold

'The night was very cold.'

The final three clauses of this extract are all of types we have discussed above:

	P-	S	-P	A
(12)	Bha	dreathan donn	a' fuireach	faisg oirre,
	be+PAST+IND	wren brown+MASC	at live+NOM	near on-her

'There was a wren living near her'

	P	S
(13)	is	chaidh	i
	and	go+PAST+IND	she

'and she went'

	A	P	S
(14)	far an	robh	an dreathan.
	where REL	be+PAST+DEP	the+MASC wren

'where the wren was.'

So to sum up, what we could identify as the default order of clause functions in Gaelic may be summarised as PSCA, as in Clause 7, with the common variant with 'split predicator' P-S-PCA as in Clause 12. A common alternative is to move the adjunct to the beginning of the clause for emphasis, viz. APSC as in Clauses 5 and 6; and there is also the 'relative clause' form where a particular function is moved to the front of the clause with a relative marker *a / an / na* (symbolised in the following formulas by a small r), either an adjunct as in Clauses 4 or 14, i.e. ArPSC; or a subject / complement as in the embedded comparative in clause 11, i.e. SrPCA. The basic patterns may be exemplified as follows:

P	S
Chaidh	i.
go+PAST+IND	she

'She went.'

P	S	A
Bha	iolaire	anns na beanntan.
be+PAST+IND	eagle	in the+PLUR mountain+PLUR

'There was an eagle in the mountains.'

P-	S	-P	A
Bha	i	a' fuireach	ann an coire.
be+PAST+IND	she	at live+NOM	in corry

'She was living in a corry.'

A	P	S
A' bhliadhna seo	thainig	geamhradh fuar.
the+FEM year this	come+PAST+IND	winter cold+MASC

'One year (there) came a cold winter.'

A	P-	S	-P
An oidhche seo	bha	an iolaire	a' faireachdainn
the+FEM night this	be+PAST+IND	the+FEM eagle	at feel+NOM

C
an fhuachd.
the+GEN cold+GEN

'One night, the eagle was feeling the cold.'

P		S	C		A
Cha	do dh'fhairich	mi	a lethid	de dh'fhuachd	riamh.
NEG+DECL	DEP feel+PAST	I	its like	of cold+GEN	ever

'I have never felt cold like this.'

Ar		P	S	C
ris	an	can	iad	An Coire Meadhain.
with-it	REL	say+FUT+DEP	they	the corry middle+GEN

'which they call the Middle Corry.'

Sr	P	C	A
na	bu	fhuaire	na seo
REL	be+PAST+IND	cold+COMP	than this

'which was colder than this'

Such brief analyses, based on such small segments of text, cannot hope to give us a comprehensive picture of clause functions in either language. Rather than introducing further text data, or attempting to make broader generalisations on the basis of data not shown here, what I will do now is extend this comparative approach by *cross-translating* each text into the other language. Seeing how the other language represents the same experiences should give us some useful insights into the range of variation in syntactic functions that exists across languages. (Note that, as above, parts of the sentence which are not part of the predication structure are again omitted from the analysis.)

To start with the Chinese 'Ghosts' text, the first three clauses translated into Gaelic show a PSA structure, in contrast to the SPC structure of the Chinese original:

	P	S	A	
(1)	Mur eil	taibhsean	air	an	talamh
	if-not be+DEP+PRES	ghost+PL	on	the+DAT+MASC	earth+DAT

'If on earth there are no ghosts'

	Ar	P	S
(2)	Càit'	a bheil	na taibhsean?
	where	REL be+DEP+PRES	the+PL ghost+PL

'where are the ghosts?'

	P	S	A	
(3)	Tha	taibhsean	ann an	inntinnean	dhaoine
	be+IND+PRES	ghost+PL	in	mind+PL	person+GEN+PL

'Ghosts are in people's minds.'

The verb *bi* 'be' plays a number of functions in Gaelic. Where it realises the predicator in a clause asserting the existence of something, as in these examples, it normally appears with a place adjunct, as in all three clauses here, or with a 'dummy' adjunct *ann* 'in it', as in the following modified example:

	P	S	A
(1′)	Tha	taibhsean	ann
	be+IND+PRES	ghost+PL	in-it

'There are ghosts, ghosts exist.'

The fact that an adjunct, even in dummy form, seems to be obligatory in such clauses might lead us to argue that these place elements are in fact complements rather than adjuncts, just as in Chinese; but since the verb *bi* 'be' appears in a number of other clause types in which an adjunct is *not* obligatory, we will provisionally retain the adjunct analysis here. In clause 2, the relative clause structure is that required for certain types of questions: literally it could be translated 'Where (is it) that the ghosts are?'.

Clause 4 shows the same configuration of functions as the original Chinese, albeit in a different order, and with the familiar Gaelic 'split predicator'.

	P-		S	-P	C
(4)	Nach	eil	thu	a' creidsinn	seo?
	NEG+INT	be+DEP+PRES	you	at believe+NOM	this

'Don't you believe this?'

In relation to the predicator, we can note that all verbs in Gaelic obligatorily express their present tense in this split way, whereas in English it tends to be confined to verbs expressing actions or behaviour, e.g. *I'm walking, I'm talking*, but not of thoughts or feelings, e.g. *I think, I hope*. The following clause, similar to clause 8 of the eagle text, likewise raises the problem of whether what follows the verb should be analysed as a complement or as an adjunct:

```
      P                 A or C?
(5)   Smaoinich        air aislingean    ma-tha
      think            on dream+PL       then
      '(Well) consider dreams, then.'
```

The following clause shows a similar structure to the original Chinese. It does not use the special 'focussing' structure of the Chinese, but rather splits the subject into two, a sort of 'topic-like' phrase at the very beginning of the clause, and then a 'resumptive' pronoun *iad* 'they', which picks up the same information, in the subject position following the (first part of the) predicator:

```
      S-                                   Ar        P-
(6)   Daoine gu leòr    ann an aislingean,  cò às      a tha
      person+PL enough   in dream+PL         what from  REL be+IND+PRES

      -S         -P
      iad uile   a' tighinn?
      they all   at come+ NOM
      'So many people in dreams, where do they all come from?'
```

The adjunct, since it is a question word, is again expressed as a type of relative clause, which puts it at the beginning of the main clause structure: literally 'what from-it (is it) that (they are coming)', *cò* being a sort of all-purpose question word 'who, what'. In both immediately following clauses, 7 and 8, the word *ann* acts as a sort of 'dummy' adjunct, indicating the existential meaning of the verb *bi* 'be'. However, the descriptive embedded clauses, both marked in the original Chinese by the subordinating particle *de*, are expressed in interestingly different ways. The first, clause 7, is indicated by the familiar relative clause type, introduced by the relative marker *a* (also appearing according to context as *an*, *am* or *na*) and which functions as the subject of the embedded clause.

```
      P           S          A     [| Sr  P            C       A              |]
(7)   Bidh        daoine     ann    a    bha          beò     cuide riut
      be+IND+FUT   person+PL   in-it  REL   be+IND+PAST   alive   together with-you
      'There are people who have lived with you.'
```

However in clause 8, rather than a relative clause, there is simply another clause 'joined on' by the linking word *is* 'and':

```
         P            S         A
(8a) Bidh         daoin'    ann   cuideachd
     be+IND+FUT   person+PL in-it also
     'there are also people'
```

```
                   P          S          C
(8b) is   cha    chuala      tu    ach  na h-ainmean   aca
     and  NEG+DECL hear+IND+PAST you  but   the+PL name+PL  at-them
     'who you've only heard the names of'
```

The relative meaning, in other words, the fact that this clause is referring back to the subject of the main clause *daoine* 'people', is indicated by the resumptive expression at the very end of the second clause *aca*, literally 'at them' or 'their'. The whole clause could thus be literally translated 'There are also people and you've not heard but their names'.

The final clause is more like the SPC structure of its English equivalent than the original Chinese SP in which the quality expression functions directly as a predicator, without the need for a copular verb:

```
             P          S    C
(9)  Chan    eil       seo  eagallach  idir
     NEG+DECL be+DEP+PRES this frightening at-all
     'None of this is frightening.'
```

Now going the other way, we can see how the structures of the original Gaelic text translate into Chinese. The first difference, as we see in Clause 1, is that existential meanings in Chinese are expressed, not by the verb *shi* 'be' but by a special existential verb *yǒu* 'exist', which we saw in the original Chinese texts and which in other contexts is equivalent to the English *have* (compare the French *il a* 'it has' and *il y a* 'it there has – there is'):

```
     A            P      C
(1)  Cóngqián    yǒu    yì  shìdài
     formerly    exist  one age
     'Once upon a time'
```

This same existential structure appears again in clause 2, this time with a place element as subject:

	S		P	C
(2)	T. húbian'r	de shān.shang	yǒu	yìzhī yīng.
	T. lake-side	SUB mountains on	exist	one MEAS eagle

'there was an eagle in the mountains beside Loch Treig.'

In clause 3, allowing for the difference in word order, we have exactly the same configuration of functions as the original Gaelic:

	S	A		P
(3)	Tā	zài nèi.bian'r de	shāngōu.shang	qīxī
	s/he	at there SUB	mountain-gully on	nest

'She was living in a gully there'

The following clause, expressed as a relative clause in the Gaelic original, has in fact two possibilities in Chinese: one is the form shown here, where it is simply 'tacked on' to the end of the previous clause, i.e. 'She was living in a mountain gully there, (and its) name is the Middle Gully':

	S	P	C
(4)	míng.zi	jiào	zhōnggōu.
	name	call-as	middle-gully

'(whose) name is called the Middle Gully.'

The other possibility would be to embed it in the previous clause: e.g.

	S	A	[| S	P	C |]		P
(3′)	Tā	zài	míng.zi	jiào	zhōnggōu .de shāngōu.shang		qīxī
	s/he	at	name	call-as	middle-gully SUB mountain-gully on		nest

'She was living in a gully there called the Middle Gully'

The difference between these two versions is one of information status (see Chapter 11): in the first, the gully is presented as an unknown one which happens to have this name; in the second, as a known and determinate place.

In the immediately following part of the text, what was a single clause with multiple adjuncts in Gaelic is most naturally translated in Chinese into a succession of clauses:

	A	S	P
(5a)	yǒu yìnián,	dōngtiān	hěn lěng,
	exist one year	winter	very cold

```
         S     P              A
(5b) xuě    xià.le         hěn dà,
       snow   fall ASP:perf    very great


         P                    C
(5c) xià-cheng   le          xuěduī.
       fall become   ASP:perf    snow-pile
```
'One year there came a cold winter with much snow, in fall and drift'

This kind of what is known as a 'serial verb construction' is common in Chinese when expressing the manner or extent of the process. Chinese provides a number of different constructions for realising manner / extent / result, all with slightly differing meanings. For example clause 5b above, which emphasises the manner of the snow's falling, could also have been expressed using the 'extent construction', which structurally is another clause embedded in the predicator:

```
       S     P      [| P |]
(5′) xuě    xià de  hěn dà,
       snow   fall EXT  very great
```
'The snow fell very heavily (the extent to which the snow fell was great).'

or using the 'resultative construction' (see Chapter 18), which structurally forms a verb compound together with the main verb, and here carries a connotation of change of state:

```
        S        P
(5″) xuě      xià-dà     .le.
       snow      fall great    ASP:perf
```
'The snow fell more heavily (than before), the snow fell too heavily.'

A similar compound construction appears in clause 5c, where what is semantically the 'product' of the falling, *xuěduī* 'snow pile', is linked to the verb *xià* 'fall' by the postverb *chéng* 'become, (change) into'.

It may also be noted that in clause 5a, as in clause 6, the 'existential' verb *yǒu* 'exist', appears at the very beginning of the clause: here it is not functioning as a full process in its own right, but rather informationally (see Chapter 11), marking the time adjunct as indefinite, as again in the following clause:

	A	S	P	C
(6)	yǒu yìtiān wǎn.shang,	nèizhī yīng	gǎn-dao	hěn lěng
	exist one day evening	that MEAS eagle	feel reach	very cold

'(there was) one night (that) the eagle was feeling the cold.'

In both clause 6 and clause 7, the verb is the compound type noted above in clause 5", where the postverb *dao* 'reach' links the verb *gǎn(jué)* 'feel' to the following complement:

	S	A	P	C
(7)	'Wo	cónglái	méiyǒu	gǎn-dao	zè.me lěng.'
	I	hitherto	NEG:perf	feel reach	thus cold

' 'I've never felt cold like this' '

Clause 8 is exactly the same as the Gaelic, except that the (self-) addressee *rithe fhein* 'with herself' of the Gaelic would be more idiomatically expressed in Chinese by the adjunct *xin.li* 'in (her) mind':

	S	A	P
(8)	Tā	xīn.li	shuō.
	s/he	mind in	say

'she said to herself.'

An alternative possibility would be to use *duì zìjǐ* 'towards self', which would then raise the same problem of analysing it as complement or adjunct as we had for the Gaelic:

	S	A or C?	P
(8')	Tā	duì zìjǐ	shuō.
	s/he	towards self	say

'she said to herself.'

Clause 9 exhibits a characteristically Chinese structure where the verb is repeated, with or without the numeral *yī* 'one', in order to indicate a meaning of short duration or attempt, similar to the English *have a think (about it)*:

	P
(9)	'Xiǎng.yi.xiang'
	think one think

' 'Think' '

Clause 10 exhibits exactly the same functions, in the opposite order, as the Gaelic original:

```
    S    P
(10) tā   shuō
    she  said
    'she said'
```

Clause 11a and b show a similar structure to clauses 3 and 4, which are simply joined together with no explicit link:

```
     P                  C                          A              P
(11a) 'Yǒu méiyǒu   yí.ge wǎn.shang    (11b)  bǐ zhèi.ge      hái yào lěng?'
     exist not exist    one MEAS evening          compare this MEAS  still will   cold
     ' 'Was there ever a night colder than this?' '
```

Again there would be the possibility of embedding the second clause in the first, with similar informational differences as before:

```
     P                  [| A                   P |]            C
(11') 'Yǒu méiyǒu    bǐ zhèi.ge        hái yào lěng .de    yí.ge wǎn.shang?'
     exist not exist     compare this one   still will cold SUB    one MEAS evening
     ' 'Was there ever a night colder than this?' '
```

Clause 12 shows an identical structure to clause 2, again with the existential verb *yǒu* marking the Subject *jiāoliáo* 'wren' as new information:

```
     S                       P            C
(12) yǒu yìzhī jiāoliáo    zhù-zai     tā fùjìn,
     exist one MEAS wren      live at  she   nearby
     '(There was) a wren (that) was living near her'
```

In clause 12, however, the verb is again a compound, this time with the locative postverb *zai* 'at'. Finally the original clauses 13 and 14 of the Gaelic original are telescoped into one in the Chinese, with the expression 'where the wren was' indicated in Chinese simply by the adjunct structure *dào jiāoliáo nèi. bian'r* 'to (the) wren there':

	S	A		P
(13/14) ér	yīng	dào jiāoliáo	nèi.bian'r	qù.le
	and eagle	to wren	there	go ASP:perf

'and she went where the wren was.'

There are several lessons we can draw from this sort of comparative exercise. The first is a general point about how languages represent the world. As can be seen from these analyses, languages differ not just **lexically** – so for example, Gaelic *coire* 'depression in a mountain side' or Chinese *xīn* 'heart / mind' cannot be translated directly into the other language nor into English – but also **grammatically**. When we 'render', to use an interesting metaphor, the Gaelic adjunct *le cur is cathadh* 'with fall and drift' into two separate Chinese clauses *xuě xià.le hěn dà* 'the snow fell very great', and *xià-cheng.le xuěduī* 'fell into piles', we are in fact transforming the experience being represented. The point here, from the point of view of language analysis at least, is that there is no one 'real world' out there that we can appeal to as an independent criterion for determining which rendering is the 'right' one: we always only have access to experience through the lexical and grammatical categories of a particular language. In these terms, it can be said that each language gives us its own **model** of the world of experience.

The second point has to do with our descriptive framework, the 'predicator – subject – complement – adjunct' **meta-model**, that is, our general model we used to analyse the individual model that is each language. In order to make comparison easier, I have assumed that the same meta-model is in fact applicable to both languages, not to mention to English. This, however, is a rather dangerous assumption which should not be accepted unthinkingly. Despite the presence of a large and influential school of linguistics (see Chapters 13 and 14) which has based much of its legitimacy on the claim that such categories – so-called 'universals of language' – can be applied across all languages, once you try to account for a language **on its own terms** rather than through the distorting lens of another language, such claims come to seem increasingly untenable. In the following chapter, we will explore in more detail what are often regarded as the basic 'grammatical categories' – known traditionally as the 'parts of speech' (itself a mistranslation – see Chapter 14) – and see how they in fact developed out of a very specific and historically constrained descriptive tradition.

9   Words and phrases

So far we have operated under the assumption (argued for in Chapters 4 and 5) that every text may be divided into clauses and words. Nevertheless, in many of our analyses we have in fact assumed the existence of an intermediate unit between these two – equivalent to the 'phrase' or 'group' of many accounts. However, we have not yet explicitly discussed the necessity for recognising such a unit. For this purpose it is useful to look at a language like Old English which, as opposed to modern English, makes great use of different forms of words, particularly endings, to indicate relations between them in clauses. Below we examine a short text, a famous parable on the nature of life as opposed to what comes before and after it, reported to have been told to an English king by the missionary Augustine, and appearing in the same Old English translation of Bede's Latin *History of the English Church and People* used in Chapter 6. (The text is divided into clauses, some of which, e.g. clauses 3 and 4, have multiple predicators joined by *and* 'and' – this doesn't affect the current analysis.)

(1) Tō wiðmetenesse   þēre   tīde   þe ūs
    to   comparison+DAT+SG   that+DAT+SG+FEM   time+DAT+SG   REL we+DAT

    uncūð   is
    unknown   be+IND+3+SG
    'In comparison with that time that is unknown to us'

(2) swylce þū   æt swæsendum   sitte
    such   thou   at feast+DAT+PLUR   sit+SUBJ+3+SG

    mid þīnum ealdor-mannum   on winter-tīde
    with thy+DAT+PL elder-man+DAT+PL   on winter-time+DAT+SG
    '(It is) as if you should be sitting at feast with your elders in winter time'

(3) and   sīe   fyr   onæled   and   þīn
    and   be+SUBJ+3+SG   fire+NOM+SG   kindle+PST+PRT   and   thy+NOM+SG

    heall   gewyrmed
    hall+NOM+SG   warm+PST+PRT
    'and there is a fire kindled and your hall warmed'

(4) and hit rīne   and snīðe   and styrme   ūte
     and it   rain+SUBJ+3+SG   and snow+SUBJ+3+SG   and storm+SUBJ+3+SG   out+DAT
     'and it is raining and snowing and storming outside'

(5) cume   ān   spearwe
     come+SUBJ+3+SG   one+MASC+SG   sparrow+NOM+SG
     'There comes a sparrow'

(6) and   hrædlīce þæt   hūs   þurhflēo
     and   quick+DAT that+ACC+SG +NEUT   house+ACC+SG   through-fly+SUBJ+3+SG
     'and quickly flies through the house'

(7) cume   þurh ōðre   duru   in
     come+SUBJ+3+SG   through one-of-two+ACC+SG   door+ACC+SG   in
     'He comes in through one door'

(8) and   þurh   ōðre   ūt   gewite.
     and   through   one-of-two+ACC+SG   out   depart+SUBJ+3+SG
     'and departs out through the other '

(9) Hwæt, hē on þā   tīd   þe he inne bið,
     lo   he on that+DAT+SG+FEM   time+DAT+SG   REL he in+DAT be+IND+3+SG
     'Lo, in the time that he is inside '

(10) ne bið   hrinen   mid þy   storme
     NEG be+IND+3+SG   touched   with that+INSTR+SG   storm+INSTR+SG

     þæs   wintres
     that+GEN+SG+MAS   winter+GEN+SG
     '(he) is not touched by the winter's storm'

(11) ac þæt   bið   ān   ēagan   bryhtm
     but that   be+IND+3+SG one+NOM+SG+MAS   eye+GEN+SG   flash+NOM+SG

     and   þæt   læste   fæc
     and   that+NOM+SG+NEUT   least+NOM+SG+NEUT   time+NOM+SG
     'but that is a twinkling of an eye and the least time'

(12) ac hē sōna   of wintre   on þone
     but he   straightway   from winter+DAT+SG on that+ACC+SG+MAS

     winter   eft   cymeð
     winter+ACC+SG   back   come+IND+3+SG
     'but he straightway from winter comes back into winter'

(13) hwæt   þær   foregange,
   what   there   forgo+SUBJ+3+SG
   'What may precede that'

(14) oððe   hwæt þær   fylige
   or   what   there   follow+SUBJ+3+SG
   'or what may follow that'

(15) wē   ne   cunnen.
   we   NEG   known+PRES+IND+PL
   'we do not know'

We can throw this issue into focus if we concentrate on how the different clause functions are realised. If we start by picking out the **predicators** from each clause, we see the majority of them are realised by a single inflected verb, e.g. 1. *is* 'is', 2. *sitte* 'should be sitting', 4. *rine* 'should be raining'; while in a small number of cases with a passive meaning, the predicator is realised by a double structure, e.g. 3. *sīe onǣled* 'should be kindled', 10. *bið hrinen* 'is touched'. We can also note a clear distinction between the majority of verbs in the text, which are in the so-called 'subjunctive' mood – translated here somewhat awkwardly by 'should be …ing, 'might …', or 'may…' – which is used to represent a situation as hypothetical; and the so-called 'indicative' mood, which presents a situation as real. In a couple of cases also, we can note what seems like internal structure within the lexical verb, where a verb indicating manner is preceded by an element indicating direction: e.g. 6. *þurhflēo* 'through-flew – flew through', 13. *foregange* 'fore-go – go before, precede'.

Comparing the realisation of the predicators in the Old English text with their translations into modern English, we can note two main differences. Firstly, typologically speaking, verbs in Old English are largely **synthetic**, that is their different functions are realised by a single inflected word, which can be broken down into a **stem,** or number of different stems, and an **ending**: so for example, *cum+e* 'should come' (where the ending indicates 3rd person singular present subjunctive) versus *cym+eð* 'comes' (where the ending indicates 3rd person singular present indicative). The verb in Modern English, by contrast, is largely **analytic**, with the different functions realised by a number of different words, which may or may not be inflected for different endings, with each word adding a certain meaning: e.g. *should be sitting*, where *should* indicates the hypothetical nature of the situation, *be* + the ending *-ing* on the following verb continuous action, and the lexical verb stem *sit-* the action itself.

In terms of the analysis, therefore, for Old English we can mostly get away with the descriptive statement that the predicator is realised by a single word, i.e. a verb with the appropriate inflection, or at most two words. However in Modern English, there would be strong reasons for recognising what we could call a **verbal group**: that is, a group of words containing a lexical verb joined to various grammatical or 'auxiliary' verbs (see discussion below), and which together realise the function of predicator.

There are various reasons for recognising such an intermediate unit between the units of word and clause we have operated with so far. Even in Old English, there were a number of elements that normally 'went together' with the verb. On the one hand are forms of the verb that, like the verbal noun in Gaelic, are joined to another verb form expressing tense and other verbal categories: the so-called 'participle' form we find in passive expressions like *sīe onæled* 'should be kindled' or *bið hrinen* 'is touched', which in terms of its class could be classified as a verb inflected as an adjective (in effect, a verbal noun); as well as the 'infinitive' form which follows an auxiliary verb in an example like *sceoldon…singan* 'must sing' from the Caedmon text discussed in Chapter 6. Such combinations of verbal elements are even more complex and widely used in Modern English, with long forms, particularly in the spoken language, like *was going to have done* or *should have been done*. On the other hand are elements that are strictly speaking non-verbal, but are normally linked to a verb, such as the negative *ne* 'not' that we find in clause 10 *ne bið hrinen* 'is not touched' and clause 13 *wē ne cunnen* 'we do not know'. The situation in modern English is comparable, with the difference that a negative *not* is always attached to an 'auxiliary verb', often in abbreviated form, e.g. *cannot / can't, do not / don't*, and so on.

In our analyses so far in previous chapters we have simply ignored such complexities, concentrating on identifying at least a lexical verb that could function as predicator, and not worrying too much about other meanings that might be being expressed (note the complex verbal group!) alongside that. And as we have seen, in languages like Latin or Old English, since the majority of such meanings were expressed as inflections on the lexical verb stem, the issue of recognising a larger unit than the word didn't really come up. But in languages like Modern English – and Chinese as we will see below – recognising such a unit considerably simplifies our analysis.

Moving on now to the realisation of **complements** – including subject and complement proper – in the old English text, we see a similar pattern of variation between single words and groups of words. First of all, in this text, we have a number of complements realised by pronouns: e.g. *þū* 'thou, you' in clause 2, *hit* 'it' in clause 3, *hē* 'he' in clause 9, all of which operate in very similar ways to their modern English counterparts. We also have one example of a single noun by itself in clause 3, i.e. *fyr* 'fire'. But for the most part nouns are preceded by an 'article', often also known as a 'determiner', as in clause 5, *ān spearwe* 'a sparrow'; or by a possessive pronoun (in origin the genitive case of the personal pronoun), as in clause 3, *þīn heall* 'thy hall'; by the combination of an article and an adjective, as in clause 11, *þæt læste fæc* 'the least time'; or by (an article and) a noun in the genitive case, as in clause 11, *ān ēagan bryhtm*, literally 'one eye's flash – a flash of an eye'. In all of these cases, the inflectional endings show very clearly the relationship of the noun or pronoun to the rest of the sentence, as well as the relationship of other elements to the noun. Thus again for this stage of the language, a concept of 'group' is not really necessary.

When we compare the situation in Old English with that of Modern English, superficially they look very similar, with most of the examples above translating more or less directly into their modern English counterparts. The main exception is the 'noun in the genitive case + noun' structure, whose modern counterpart, 'noun's noun' is largely restricted to human or at least animate possessors: e.g. *my brother's name, the sparrow's wing*, in other cases being replaced by the 'noun of (article) noun' construction, e.g. *the twinkling of an eye*. However in Modern English, with a few exceptions such as the number agreement between demonstrative pronoun and following noun in expressions like *this book* vs *these books*, there is almost none of the extensive inflectional marking of Old English to show the links between such elements. And if we cannot show that those links exist, it may cause difficulties for recognising what exactly are the elements realising particular clause functions.

There are two solutions to this descriptive dilemma. The first, taken by Tesnière, is to recognise the same sort of dependency relations existing between nouns and other elements like articles and adjectives as between the central verb and its accompanying nouns. The description of the clause thus becomes, as it were 'layered', with the top two layers representing the valency relations, and succeeding lower layers other dependency relations. So for example we could analyse clause 11 of the text as follows (omitting for the moment the conjunction *ac* which links this clause to the preceding ones, and simplifying the glossing to save space):

```
                biþ
         /   is    \                      \
þæt                  bryhtm    and      fæc
that                / flash \    and    / time \
                 ān    ēagan      þæt    læste
                  a     eye's     that   least
       '(but) that is the twinkling of an eye and the least time'
```

The other alternative, on the analogy of the verbal group, is to recognise a unit we could call the **nominal group**: that is, a unit which may be realised by a single noun or pronoun (the latter traditionally understood, as its name suggests, as a 'pro-noun' or noun substitute), or by what is normally called a **head** noun accompanied by various other elements which relate to that head in different ways. So we could analyse the same clause as follows, using either an immediate constituent analysis with class labels (shown above the example), or a ranked constituent analysis with functional labels (shown below):

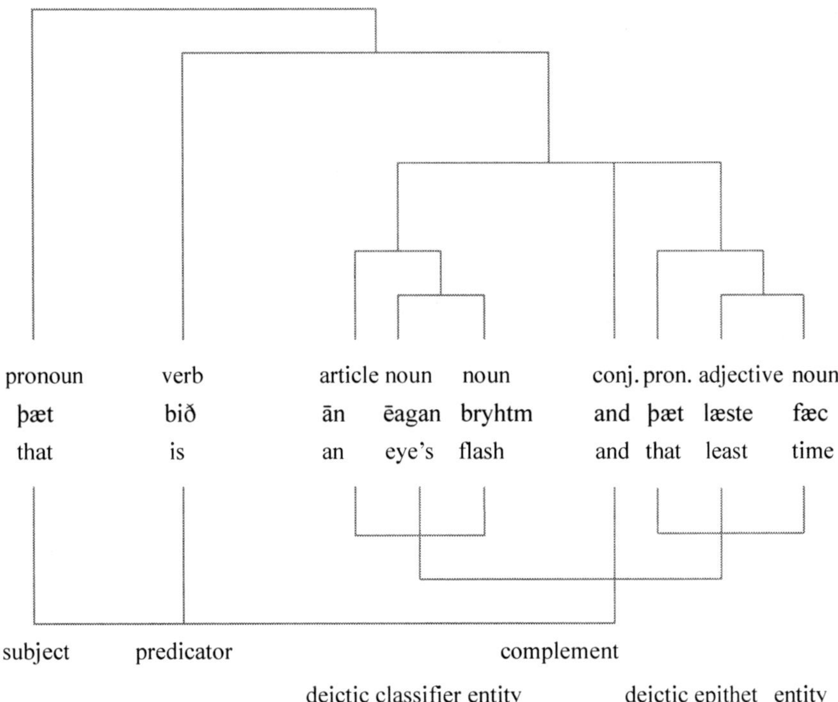

Moving on now to the realisation of **adjuncts**, we find here two main patterns: one a single word of the adverb class:

(4)   *ūte* 'outside'   (6) *hrædlīce* 'quickly'   (12) *eft* 'back'

or alternatively a complex structure of preposition plus nominal group, the latter including the range of elements already identified above:

(2)   *mid þīnum ealdormannum* 'with your elders' *on wintertīde* 'in winter time'

(7)   *þurh ōðre duru* 'through one door'   (10) *mid þy storme* 'by the storm'

In order to understand the realisation of adjuncts in Old English, and indeed that of complements as well, we need to take a historical excursus back to an earlier period before the differentiation of the language from its Germanic forebears. Old English reflects an intermediate stage of development from a common Indo-European syntactic pattern based on single inflected or uninflected words which has been reconstructed as something like the following (Lehmann 1993):

Function	**Class**	**Morpho-syntactic features**
process	verb	inflected for tense, mood, person, number
participant	noun	inflected for gender, number, case, with cases indicating both participant valencies (agent, patient, beneficiary) and circumstantial relations (goal, location, source)
circumstance	adverb	a small set of uninflected elements indicating position, direction etc.

By the Old English period (roughly 800–1000 AD in terms of the greatest number of surviving texts), this neat system had become a little messier. First of all, the verbs had developed various analytic forms, mostly incorporating verbs like *wesan* 'be', and *habban* 'have', whose descendents, as we saw above, have become even more prominent in Modern English. Certain lexical verbs had also developed specialised grammaticalised meanings in conjunction with other verbs: so for example, the verb *cennan* 'know' gave rise to the form *can* 'know how to' which became modern English *can* indicating ability or possibility. These two types of what are now normally known as **auxiliary** verbs, have taken on an enormous range of functions in Modern English including, as we also saw above, taking part in the expression of the negative forms of verbs.

Equally radical changes were underway in the division of labour between complements and adjuncts. As we have already seen in the case of Latin, noun inflections in Old English not only realised participant valencies such as agent, patient and beneficiary, but various other circumstantial relations such as goal and source. One example we saw in the Caedmon text in Chapter 6 is *hām* 'to home', which has indeed survived into modern English *home* in exactly the same function. But already in the Old English period, as again in Classical Latin, this system had become confined to certain lexical items indicating place, and more generally the language was moving towards a pattern whereby a preposition indicated the specific circumstantial meaning, in conjunction with an inflected noun. The following example from the Caedmon text indeed shows these two patterns side by side:

ond	**hām**	ēode	**tō**	his	**hūse.**
and	home	went	to	his	house

These 'prepositions', so-called because in Latin at least, they were normally 'placed before' (*prāepositus*) the noun they were joined to, were a development of the Indo-European adverbs. In the earliest texts we have, from languages like Greek and Sanskrit, these adverbs are moveable elements, either independently realising circumstantial meanings in the clause: e.g.

(4) and   hit rīne   and snīðe   and styrme   **ūte**
     and it rain+SUBJ+3+SG   and snow+SUBJ+3+SG   and storm+SUBJ+3+SG   out+DAT
     'and it is raining and snowing and storming **outside**'

or directly attached to the verb:

(6) and   hrædlīce   þæt hūs   **þurhflēo**
     and   quick+DAT   that+NEUT   through-fly+SUBJ+3+SG
     'and quickly **through**-flies ~ flies through the house'

As noun inflections increasingly became specialised for indicating participant functions, it was a short step from this latter form to the Modern English pattern where the 'adverb' is directly attached to an appropriate noun, rather than the verb, a pattern which indeed appears in the very next clause:

(7) cume   **þurh**   **ōðre**   **duru**   in
     come+SUBJ+3+SG   through   one-of-two+ACC+SG   door+ACC+SG   in
     'He comes in **through one door**'

At the Old English stage, although already moving towards the pattern whereby the circumstantial meaning was wholly expressed by the adverb / preposition, an older distinction still existed between a meaning of 'motion towards' expressed by the accusative case of the noun versus a meaning of 'location at' expressed by the dative case, where the same preposition could mean two different things depending on the case of the noun which followed it: e.g.

(12) **on** þone   winter   (2) **on** winter-tīde
       on   that+ACC+SG+MAS   winter+ACC+SG   on   winter-time+DAT+SG
       '**into** the winter'   '**in** winter time'

A distinction between 'motion to' and 'location at' could also be seen in adverbs, with the latter usually expressed by a dative-like *–e* inflection:

(8) and... **ūt** gewite
    and   out depart+SUBJ+3+SG
    'and departs **out**...'

(4) and hit rīne...   **ūte**
    and it   rain+SUBJ+3+SG out+DAT
    'and it is raining...**outside**'

(7) cume...   **in**
    come+SUBJ+3+SG in
    'He comes **in**...'

(9) ... he   **inne**   bið
    he   in+DAT be+IND+3+SG
    '... he is **inside**'

In certain cases realising non-locational meanings, another distinction could be recognised between the dative case and another case, the instrumental, which only was marked distinctly in the demonstrative pronoun:

(2) **mid** þīnum ealdor-mannum
    with thy+DAT+PL elder-man+DAT+PL
    '**with** your elders'

(10) **mid** þy   storme
    with that+INSTR+SG storm+DAT+SG
    '**by** the storm'

But the majority of prepositions 'controlled' just a single case, which had no particular relation to the meaning of the preposition: e.g.

(1) **tō** wiðmetenesse
    to comparison+DAT+SG
    '**as** / **in** /**by** comparison'

(2) **æt** swæsendum
    at feast+DAT+PLUR
    '**at** feast'

(7) **þurh** ōðre   duru
    through one-of-two+ACC+SG door+ACC+SG
    '**through** one door'

(12) **of** wintre
    from winter+DAT+SG
    '**from** winter'

For expressing circumstances of manner, another form which has become the most common way of indicating adverbs in Modern English involved the grammaticalisation of the noun *līc* 'body'. Attached to a noun or verb, it formed an adjective, e.g. *hrædlīc* 'quick'. Since adjectives in Old English, as in most Indo-European languages, were a subspecies of noun (reflected in the older terminology of 'noun substantive' versus 'noun adjective'), they could be inflected; and the dative case of *līc*, *līce*, became specialised in a circumstantial meaning 'with a...body': thus *hrædlīce* 'with a quick body – quickly'. This termination *–līce* is the origin of Modern English *–ly* (cf the comparable adverbial termination in Romance languages *-mente* / *-miente* / *-ment* etc. which derives from the Latin *-mente* 'with a...mind').

So if we look at the overall situation of adjuncts in Old English, again in the majority of cases we have clear inflectional markers of the relationships of elements to each other, with inflected nouns related either directly to the verb, or to a preposition. Such structures could again be analysed, à la Tesnière, in terms of multiple layers of dependencies, as in the following example (again simplifying glossing and omitting irrelevant elements):

(2)

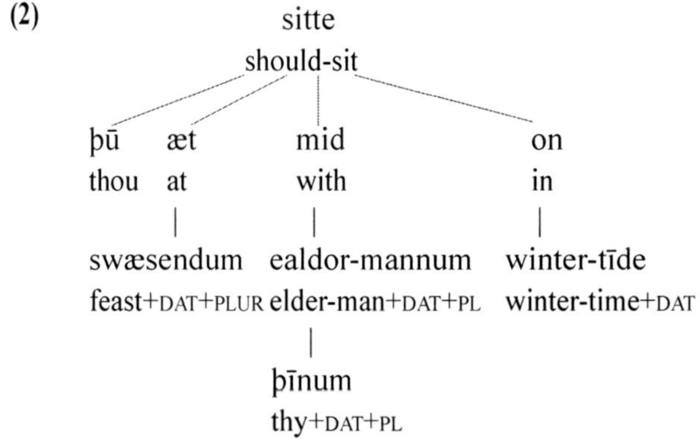

'(It is) as if you should be sitting at feast with your elders in winter time'

For modern English, in contrast, we might again be drawn to recognising an intermediate unit covering the combination of a preposition + nominal group. However the case of such a unit would be different from that of the verbal group and the nominal group we have discussed so far. Structurally speaking such groups always have a head: that is, a single word (verb, noun / pronoun) to which the whole group can be reduced. So for example, although of course in context there is a clear difference between a form such as *onæle* 'should kindle' and *sīe onæled* 'should-be kindled', structurally speaking they are equivalent in that they both realise the clause function of predicator. However, in the case of a structure such as *æt swæsendum* 'at feast', there is no single word form to which it could be reduced without changing its clause function (apart from the 'relic' forms of a case-inflected noun functioning as an adjunct). Thus while we can justifiably consider a verbal group as an expansion of a verb, we cannot do the same for a structure such as *æt swæsendum* 'at feast'. In fact, both the inflectional markings and the dependency analysis seem to suggest that such structures are analogous to predicator + complement structures. As Matthews remarks (1981: 151), '[a]lthough its construction is not predicative, and its notional role is not that of a participant, the complement of a preposition is similar to the direct object of a verb, with valencies determining when it is obligatory, optional and excluded'.

For this reason, it seems useful to borrow a terminological distinction introduced by Halliday (1985 / 1994: Section 6.5) between nominal, verbal (and also adverbial) **groups**, and the **prepositional phrase**. The group, as suggested by its Chinese equivalent *cizu* 'word combination', is an **expansion** of a word; while a phrase, again as suggested by the Chinese term *duanyu* 'short phrase' is a **contraction** of a clause. In terms of their relationship to clause functions, the predicator is realised by a verbal group, complements (including subject) by nominal groups, and adjuncts by adverbial groups or prepositional phrases.

As we have seen, these sorts of issues do not really come up in the sorts of languages, like Latin and Old English, for which the dependency framework was originally developed. In such languages, the inflections of verbs and nouns, the latter extending also to adjectives and even some adverbs, show clearly the government relations between verbs or prepositions and the nouns they govern, and the agreement relations between the nouns and the articles and adjectives which agree with them. Only a small number of words in such languages are *un*inflected – mostly adverbs like *eft* 'back', *þær* 'there', *sōna* 'straightaway' – and they are usually explained as having a direct relationship with the verb itself (hence the term 'ad-verb' or '(connected) to the verb'). So for this type of language, positing only the two syntactic units of **word** and **clause** (traditionally 'sentence'), mostly works very well. Any word, with the exception of the adverbs just mentioned, can be clearly linked through its inflections either directly to the verb as the nucleus of the clause, or indirectly by being linked to another word dependent on the verb.

However, for a language like Chinese that has none of these inflections, such a model does not seem so obviously applicable. That is not to say that it was *not* applied: it was so extensively in the first half of the twentieth century, as for example in the highly influential grammar by Li Jinxi called *Xinzhu Guoyu Wenfa* (A New Grammar of the National Language), which came out first in 1924. Li's description of clause relations takes the form of dependency analyses very much à la Tesnière, such as of the following clause (function labels are translations of the originals – the double vertical lines indicate the traditional break between 'subject' and 'predicate' that we are not recognising here):

Xŭ duō   qiángzhuàng .de gōngrén zào yízuò   cháng .de tiě qiáo
very many strong   SUB worker   build one MEAS long SUB   iron bridge
'Many strong workers are building a long iron bridge.'

	Subject	‖	Predicator	Object
	gōngrén	‖	zào	qiáo
	worker	‖	build	bridge

xŭ duō   qiángzhuàng .de ‖   yízuò   cháng.de   tiě
very many   strong SUB   one MEAS   long SUB   iron

However, in the late 1940s new models came into China which drew directly on the Immediate Constituent Analysis introduced by Bloomfield, of which one of the most influential was the grammatical sketch by Yuen Ren Chao in his 1948 textbook *Mandarin Primer*, which was quickly translated into Chinese (Li 1952). In this model, alongside the basic units of word (*ci*) and clause / sentence (*xiaoju* / *juzi*), an intermediate unit of group / phrase (*cizu* or *duanyu* in Chinese) was also recognised, defined by immediate constituent relations. In fact traditional Chinese scholarship had long worked with the three units *zi*, *dou* and *ju*, corresponding roughly to word, group / phrase and clause, so such a unit was straightaway recognised as very useful for the description of Chinese. Although Chao's 1948 constituency model was in fact weakly equivalent to Li's 1924 dependency model, in later work based on constituency analysis, the focus of analysis moved towards describing the internal structure of such groups. Indeed in the work of a later generation of linguists like Zhu Dexi (1982), it is groups rather than clauses that are seen as defining the basic syntactic structures of Chinese, in what became known as the *cizu benwei* or 'group (as) basic unit' model. Let's see how such an analysis works, and what might be some of its advantages, using an extract from a short story, describing a little boy called Tommy doing a writing exam:

(1) Yí.ge   [| jiào Tángmǐ |]   .de nánhái   zài jìnxíng
     one MEAS   call   Tommy   SUB male-child   ASP:prog undergo

     tā. de   zuòwén kǎoshì
     s/he SUB   composition exam
     'A boy called Tommy was doing his writing exam,'

(2) tímù .shi wǒ.de gǒu.
     topic be I SUB   dog
     'the topic was: my dog.'

(3) Zhìshǎo   yào   xiě   150   zì.
     At-least   must   write   150   word
     '(He) had to write at least 150 words.'

(4) Tángmǐ   xiǎng .le   .xiang,
     Tommy   think ASP:compl   think
     'Tommy thought a bit,'

(5) kāishǐ xiě:
     begin   write
     '(and) began writing:'

(6) 'Wǒ yǒu yìtiáo   gǒu,
    I   exist one MEAS   dog
  ' 'I have a dog,'

(7) wǒ jiào tā Bàobǐ,
    I   call   it   Bobby
  'I call it Bobby,'

(8) wǒ ài   wǒ.de gǒu,
    I   love I SUB   dog
  'I love my dog,'

(9) tā quánshēn dōu.shi hēisè   .de,
    it whole-body all be   black-colour SUB
  'it's black all over,'

(10) zhǐ   yǒu   bí.zi .shi bái   .de.'
    only   exist nose be white SUB
  'except for (its) nose (which) is white.' '

(11) Tángmǐ   tíng-xialai,
    Tommy   stop down
  'Tommy stopped,'

(12) 21 .ge   zì.
    21   MEAS   character
  '21 words.'

(13) Tā jìxù   xiě:
    he continue   write
  'He continued writing:'

(14) 'měi tiān, wǒ dōu dài   Bàobǐ qù gōngyuán   sànbù,
    each day I all   take Bobby go park   stroll
  ' 'every day I take Bobby to the park for a walk,'

(15) dàn rúguǒ tiān xià   yǔ,
    but if   sky   fall   rain
  'but if it's raining,'

(16) wǒ jiù   bú   dài   tā   qù sànbù.'
    I   then NEG take s/he go stroll
  'I don't take him for a walk.' '

(17) Yòu   .shi 24 .ge   zì,
further   be 24 MEAS character
'another 24 words,'

(18) tā shǔ .le   .shu,
he   count ASP:compl. count
'he counted (them)'

(19) yígòng   45 .ge   zì.
altogether 45 MEAS character
'altogether 45 words.'

First let's recall the IC analysis by which such groups were determined, with each immediate constituent, and thus each group, being labelled for function. We can do this with the first clause of the text. What this analysis reveals is a type of recursive 'embedding' of different groups within each other, which could be characterised as follows, going from the largest ICs to the smallest, again using translations of the function labels most commonly used in the Chinese tradition.

1. Subject Yí.ge [| jiào Tángmǐ |] .de nánhái 'A boy called Tommy'		Predicate zài jìnxíng tā.de zuòwén kǎoshì 'was doing his writing exam'	
2. Modifier Yí.ge [| jiào Tángmǐ |] .de 'a…called Tommy'	Head nánhái 'boy'	6. Adjunct zài 'at' (progressive aspect)	Head jìnxíng tā.de zuòwén kǎoshì 'undergo his writing exam'
3. Numeral yí 'one'	Classifier .ge (measure word)	7. Predicator jìnxíng 'undergo'	Object tā.de zuòwén kǎoshì 'his writing exam'
4. ? jiào Tángmǐ? 'called Tommy'	? .de (subordinating particle)	8. Modifier ta.de 'his'	Head zuòwén kǎoshì 'writing exam'
5. Predicator jiào 'be called'	Object Tángmǐ 'Tommy'	9. Modifier zuòwén 'writing'	Head kaoshi 'exam'
		10. ? ta 's/he'	? .de 'subordinating particle'

The sorts of structures seen here present quite a different picture from those we saw in the Old English text. Apart from the subordinating particle *de*, which links a modifier to a following head, there are **no** explicit structural signals, apart from relative order, showing how the different parts of the text fit together. It is no doubt the great reliance of Chinese syntax on word order that explains a large part of the success of this kind of immediate constituent analysis among Chinese linguists. Numbers of different kinds of relationships can be fairly unequivocally delimited and assigned functional labels; ironically with the exception of those immediate constituents joined by *de*, which such analyses typically ignore, or else – which amounts to the same thing – simply label as '*de* constructions' (*'de' zi jiegou*). Given this situation, it is easy to understand how Chinese linguists enthusiastically embraced IC analysis and the groups defined by it. Here at last was a simple and objective way of identifying syntactic relationships in Chinese in terms of the order in which syntactic units combine with each other.

The fact that such analyses saw no essential difference between a Subject-Predicate 'group' (*zhu-wei cizu*) that effectively identified a complete clause, and a Numeral-Classifier group (*shu-liang cizu*) that only identified one small part of a nominal group, was very much in the spirit of IC analyses like those of Zellig Harris, which used the same distributional principles to build up syntactic structures from the combinations of individual morphemes all the way to the complete clause. However, as already noted in Chapter 6, there was one major difference between the way such analysis was carried out on Chinese: the immediate constituents were given function, rather than class, labels, because otherwise with the rather sparse (from an Indo-European point of view) structural marking of Chinese, there would have been no way to unambiguously identify the different groups.

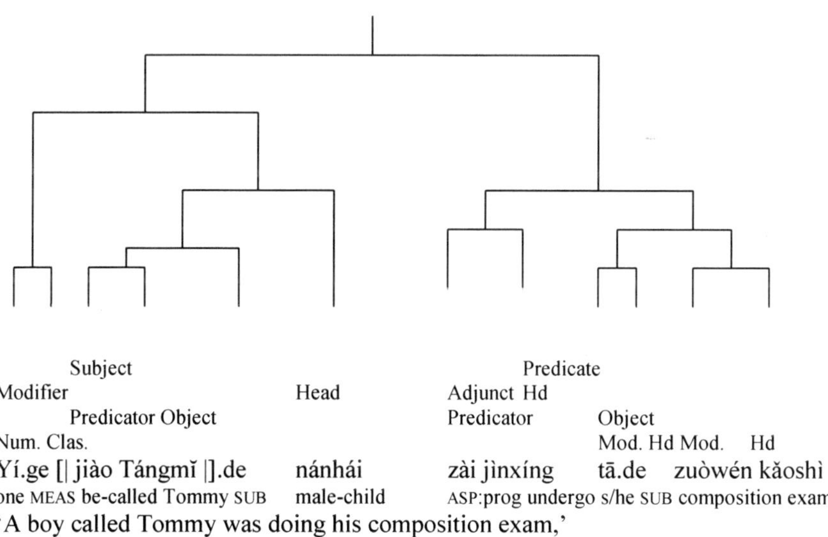

Yí.ge [| jiào Tángmǐ |].de   nánhái   zài jìnxíng   tā.de   zuòwén kǎoshì
one MEAS be-called Tommy SUB   male-child   ASP:prog undergo s/he SUB composition exam
'A boy called Tommy was doing his composition exam,'

Even so, certain of these functionally-labelled groups were used to cover a wide range of elements with a range of different functions in the clause. This was particularly the case with the Adjunct-Head group (*zhuang-zhong cizu*) which covered not only instances where an adverb directly modifies a verb: e.g. *hěn xǐ.huān* 'very like – really like', but also those where an adverb modifies other elements in the clause, or even the clause as a whole. For example, clause 15 of the text has two groups that would be labelled Adjunct-Head:

Adjunct   Head
           Subject Predicate
           Adjunct   Head

(15) 'měi tiān,   wǒ   dōu   dài   Bàobǐ   qù   gōngyuán   sànbù,
     each   day   I   all   take   Bobby   go   park   stroll
   ' 'every day I take Bobby to the park for a walk,'

In the first group, the adjunct *měi tiān* 'every day' modifies the rest of the clause by setting the time in which the action takes place. In the second group *dōu dài*, literally 'all take', where the adjunct *dōu* 'all', although directly preceding the verb, and thus structurally at least most closely related to it, in fact in terms of its meaning relates most directly to the time phrase *měi tiān* 'every day', and could thus be translated something like 'in all cases'. In terms of its class, the adjunct *měi tiān* 'every day' is a numeral plus measure group – which can be seen as a type of nominal group – realising the clause function of adjunct (in the sense in which we have been using that term in this book), while *dōu* 'all' is an adverb of scope, another example being *yě* 'also' which though always attached to a following verb in fact refer back to a preceding nominal group.

Such problems suggest that it may in fact be more useful for Chinese to distinguish the units that make up clause structure – in functional terms the process, participants and adjuncts – from the units that form the internal structure of groups. In other words, a **ranked constituent** analysis may be more useful for Chinese than an **immediate constituent** analysis. Such an analysis, however, would still leave us with the challenge of delimiting group structure from clause structure, something which in Chinese, just like that of identifying words, turns out not to be all that simple. Let's take a look at some of the problems below. We will leave the realisation of the predicator till last, since it is the most complicated.

Let's look first at the realisation of **complements**. Here we have a number of different patterns. The simplest is a noun or pronoun by itself:

(2) *tímù* 'topic'   (14) *gōngyuán* 'park'   (7)   *tā* 'it'

A similar pattern is shown with proper nouns, i.e. names:

(1) *Tángmǐ* 'Tommy'   (7)   *Bàobǐ* 'Bobby'

In certain cases, two nominal elements can appear side by side, in the equivalent of a possessive structure in English:

(9) *tā quánshēn* 'it whole-body – its whole body'

A slightly more complex pattern has a number plus measure word (also known as a 'classifier') preceding the head noun:

(6) *yìtiáo gŏu* 'one dog'   (12) *21 .ge zì* '21 words'

There is also an example of an embedded clause (see Chapter 10) describing the head noun, which is itself joined to a numeral + classifier structure, with the relationship marked by the subordinating particle *de*:

(1) *yí.ge* [|*jiào Tángmĭ* |] *.de nánhái* 'one called Tommy *de* boy – a boy called Tommy'

And finally we have a couple of examples of a structure we saw in Chapter 8 above, where the complement is 'framed' by *shi* 'be' and the subordinating particle *de*, in which the 'framed element' classifies the subject of the clause:

(9) (*tā quánshén dōu .shi*) *hēisè .de* '(its whole body is) black / a black one.'

(10) (*zhĭyŏu bí.zi .shi*) *bái .de* '(except for (its) nose which is) white / a white one.' '

Moving on to the realisation of **adjuncts**, we have two main patterns attested here, nouns or nominal groups and adverbs. The nominal kind are often time expressions such as the following:

(14) *mĕi tiān* 'every day'

The adverbial kind may be adverbs directly followed by the verb:

(11) *zhĭ* (*yŏu*) '(there) only (is)'   (14) *dōu* (*dài*) 'in all cases (take)

(17) *yòu* (*.shi*) 'again (is)'

In some cases where the clause is of a copular kind, like *.shi* 'be' or *yŏu* 'exist' the adverb may appear without an accompanying verb:

(19) *yígòng* [*yŏu*] (*45 .ge zì*) 'altogether [there were] (45 words)'

Sometimes two adverbs may occur in succession:

(16) *jiù bù* (*dài*) 'then don't (take)'

Finally, we may have a complex structure of adverb + (stative) verb, which here functions as a unit:

(3) *zhìshǎo* 'most few – at least'

The other main realisation of adjuncts, which does not occur in this particular text but which we have seen in previous analyses, is analogous to the English prepositional phrase type. The preposition element is often known as a **coverb** in the Chinese grammatical tradition, since in many cases the same element functions both as predicator (main verb) and as part of an adjunct (coverb), as in the following example we discussed in Chapter 7:

V. fūrén   zài   shāfā.shang   (zuò.zhe).
V. lady   be-at   sofa on   sit ASP:dur.
'Lady Venus was (seated) on the settee.'

There are two possible Chinese renderings of the original English clause. In the shorter version without the verbal group in brackets, the verb *zài* 'be at' functions as the predicator; while in the longer version it functions as what we could call a **minor predicator** in the coverbial phrase *zài shāfā.shang* 'on the sofa'. This coverbal phrase itself exhibits what is a common structure for place expressions, whereby the coverb indicates the general meaning of location or direction, and the postnoun *shang*, literally 'top', indicates the specific place in relation to the object (we had a similar example in the text we examined in Chapters 4 & 5 *zài tián.li* 'at field inside – in the field'). We will return to a discussion of such elements below.

Determining the types of element that realise the **predicator**, or what amounts to the same thing, working out how to distinguish the predicator from the other parts of the clause, is a highly complex task in Chinese. Not only do we have elements like *zai* 'at' which, depending on context, may function either as (main) predicator or as the minor predicator in a coverbial phrase, there are also numerous cases where we have what may seem like a succession of predicators with no structural marking as to which should be taken as the 'main' one. If we start with the first two clauses of the text, there is no doubt which element should be identified as predicator:

(1) Yí.ge   [| jiào Tángmǐ |] .de   nánhái   **zài jìnxíng**
     one MEAS be-called Tommy SUB   male-child   ASP:prog undergo

tā.de   zuòwén kǎoshì
s/he SUB   writing exam
'A boy called Tommy was doing his composition exam,'

In the first clause, we can note an element immediately preceding the predicator which is in fact etymologically the same form as the *zài* 'at' we have just been discussing; however in this case, like the form *a' / ag* of similar meaning and function in Gaelic, it is indicating that the action is ongoing: *zài jìnxíng* 'was (in the process of) doing'. In the second clause, the verb *shi* 'be' is the only possible candidate for predicator in this copulative clause:

(2) tímù .**shi** wǒ.de gǒu.
     topic be   I SUB   dog
     'the topic was: my dog.'

However, in the following clause from later in the text, there are at least three candidates for predicator (indicated in bold):

(14) 'měi tiān, wǒ dōu **dài** Bàobǐ **qù** gōngyuán **sànbù**,
     each day I all   take Bobby go park   stroll
     ' 'every day I take Bobby to the park for a walk,'

Such structures, often known in the literature as 'serial verb constructions' (Li & Thompson 1981: Ch.21), cause problems not only for determining the predicator itself, but also, looking at the same problem from the opposite angle, for drawing the boundaries between one clause and the next. It would, for example have been perfectly possible, calling on the principle of 'one verb per clause' we used in Chapter 5, to recognise here not one clause, but three:

(14') 'měi tiān, wǒ dōu **dài** Bàobǐ
      each day I all   take Bobby
      ' 'every day I take Bobby'

(14″) **qù** gōngyuán
      go   park
      'go to the park'

(14‴) **sànbù**
      stroll
      '(and) have a walk'

The fact that in the original English translation of clauses 14" and 14'" the verbs are 'transformed' into prepositional phrases, although interesting in suggesting at least a semantic correlation between verbs and prepositions in English, is of course irrelevant for deciding the status of these elements in Chinese.

There are also other verbal forms whose relation to the predicator may not always be immediately clear. One of the less complicated examples, which also came up in the Chinese translation of the Gaelic 'Eagle' text in Chapter 8, is a simple repetition of the lexical verb to indicate short duration or tentativeness, with the first verb potentially marked for aspect, as in the examples in this text:

(4) xiǎng   .le   .xiang   (18) shǔ   .le   .shu
     think   ASP:compl   think   count ASP:compl   count
     'thought a bit,'   'counted (them) over'

Another type has two verbs placed side by side, the first indicating the state of progression of the action expressed by the second:

(5) kāishǐ xiě   (13) jìxù   xiě
     begin   write   continue   write
     'began writing'   'went on writing'

Something that is in effect the opposite, both structurally and semantically, of this type is expressed by a structure consisting of the main verb followed by a so-called **postverb**, which is structurally dependent on it, and expresses a metaphorical directional meaning (compare similar English examples like *slow down* and *speed up*):

(11) tíng-xialai
     stop down
     'stopped,'

Finally, we have another example with two separate verbs, but in this case the first verb indicates an obligation or possibility applying to the process expressed by the second verb:

(3) yào xiě
     must write
     'had to write'

The solution to the descriptive problem of the verbal group in Chinese relates, as I mentioned before, to that of the clause. What is referred to as the 'serial verb construction' in Chinese is not in fact a typical or paradigmatic example of that structure (for an example of one such language, see Pawley 1993), where there is really no principled way to distinguish between the structure of the verbal group, or perhaps better in Tesnière's terms 'verbal node', and that of the clause. Examples like 14 above are closest to this type, and it could indeed be analysed as three separate clauses: from another point of view it could be viewed as what has been called a 'topic chain': that is, the same 'topic' with three different 'comments' (see discussion in Chapter 11 below). On the other hand, examples like 5 or 13 are more efficiently analysed as a single complex verbal group, with the first verb often characterised as an **auxiliary** to the second, main verb.

So a description of Chinese in ranked constituent terms would posit clause functions – predicator, complement, adjunct, realised by group / phrase classes – verbal, nominal, adverbial, coverbial. Each group / phrase would be characterised in turn by group functions – event, entity, scope – realised by the major word classes – verb, noun, adverb – and subsidiary word classes pronoun, demonstrative, postnoun, measure, particle (nominal), and auxiliary verb and postverb (verbal) – as well as the 'mixed type' of prepositional phrase, realised by a coverb and a nominal group. This kind of analysis is summarised below (see also Halliday & McDonald 2004).

The verbal group contains the central or nodal function of **event**. We can identify the following group function structures with their class realisations (detailed arguments for this analysis can be found in McDonald 2004):

Event alone:
main verb   *.shi* 'be'

Event, Aspect
main verb, particle   *shŭ le* 'counted'
auxiliary, main verb   *zài jìnxíng* 'in (the process of) counting'

Event reduplicated
(with optional Aspect)
main verb, (particle), verb   *shŭ .le .shu* 'had a count of'

Phase, Event
auxiliary, main verb   *kāishĭ xiě* 'began writing'

Event, Extension
main verb, postverb   *tíng-xialai* 'stopped writing'

This covers the principle types of verbal group in Chinese. A couple of other structures involving verbs can better be analysed as part of clause structure: so for example the 'classifying' *shi...de* construction found in 9 and 10 is really to do with the type of predication / valency (see Chapter 8); while the 'auxiliary' *yào* 'must' in 3 is a type of interactional 'modality' element (of the kind analysed in Chapter 12 below): both of these cases are better analysed as directly part of clause structure.

Moving on to the nominal group, we can give the nodal noun or pronoun the functional label of **entity**, and identify the following function structures and their class realisations:

Entity alone:
noun   *tímù* 'the topic'
pronoun   *tā* 'it'
proper noun   *Tángmǐ* 'Tommy'

Conjoined entities:
pronoun, noun   *tā quánshēn* 'its whole body'

Numeral Classifier
number, measure   *měi tiān* 'every day'

Numeral Classifier Entity
number, measure, noun: *yìtiáo gǒu* 'one [measure for long thin things] dog'

Modifier Entity
embedded clause, noun: [|| *jiào Tángmǐ* ||] *.de nánhái* 'a boy called Tommy'

Quality (Entity)
adjective, particle, (noun):   *bái .de* 'a white one', *bái .de bí.zi* 'a white nose'

The adverbial group can be analysed as having the nodal function of **scope**, with the following class realisations:

Scope
adverb: *zhǐ* 'only'   *dōu* 'all, in all cases'
               zhìshǎo 'at least' *yígòng* 'altogether'
               jiù 'then'

There are also some more complex structures that don't appear in this particular text, but can be identified as follows:

Scope Range
adverb, verb: *zuì hǎo* 'best' (literally 'most good')
                  gèng hǎo 'better ('even-more good')'

Range Scope
verb, adverb: *hǎo yìdiǎn'r* 'better' ('good (by) a little')'

The coverbial phrase, which as noted above is a combination of two different elements that cannot be reduced to either one or the other, has the nodal functions of **minor predicator** and **minor complement**, and has the following class realisations:

Minor predicator, minor complement
coverb, noun: *gēn Tángmǐ* 'with Tommy
coverb, pronoun: *gēn wǒ* 'with me'
coverb, noun, postnoun: *zài shāfā.shang* 'on the sofa'

Finally, there are a couple of elements that fall outside these classifications, realising not clause-internal functions, but clause-linking functions, such as we will look at in the next chapter: for example, *dàn(.shi)* 'but', *rúguǒ* 'if'.

The point of giving a description such as that of the Chinese text above, or the Old English text earlier in the chapter, is not that there is any one 'correct' analysis: on the contrary, several different analyses are possible depending on whether one is concentrating on the representational meanings expressed, as in Tesnière's process – participant – circumstance model; or on the links between processes (see discussion in the following chapter); or on tracing pieces of information through the text (see Chapter 11). In some languages, like English for the most part, all those three types of analysis will pretty much depend on identifying the 'same' clause unit; while in Chinese, they may well require three separate units. Such indeterminacy is not simply a quirk of individual languages like Chinese, but an inherent feature of all syntactic analysis. And as we have seen throughout this book, any analysis is necessarily **contingent** in that it depends on a particular configuration of descriptive, theoretical and applicational variables. The form taken by any one description will be determined by a compromise between these different variables, and the nature of that compromise cannot be separated from the purpose for which the description is envisaged.

Up to this point, in our exploration of the various relationships between words, we have been using the term 'clause' rather than the more traditional term 'sentence'. One of the reasons for this is that the term 'sentence' is ambiguous between what we would here call a single clause, a 'simple sentence', and a combination of clauses, a 'compound / complex sentence'. In the following chapter, we will examine how clauses are joined to each other in running text, and what sorts of descriptive categories are needed to capture such combinations.

10 Combining clauses

In the previous chapters of Part 2, we have been looking at the relationships *within* clauses, and have assumed that a text can most directly be divided into the individual clauses which make it up. If we're dealing with conversational texts, where clauses tend to be shared out among the speakers, and the relationship between clauses is often a *dialogic* one, in terms of so-called speech functions like question and answer, or statement and challenge, then that assumption is in many cases a workable one. However when we come to look at *monologic* texts, i.e. those produced by a single speaker, or a single writer, as is the case with most written texts, then we need to recognise other kinds of relationships between clauses. Let's look at an extract from the following Gaelic text, an oral narrative (taken from Lamb 2001: 97–101):

(1) Agus   sin   a rinn   e
     and   that   REL did   he
     'And that (was what) he did'

(2) thug   e   a-mach   ceann an t-sìomain leis
     took   he   out   head of-the of-rope   with-him
     'he took the end of the rope out with him.'

(3) agus cho luath 's   a fhuair   e   a-mach   air an doras
     and   so fast and   REL got   he   outside   on the door
     'And as soon as he got outside the door'

(4) cheangail   e   an sìoman   leis an tughadh
     tied   he   the rope   to the thatch
     'he tied the rope on to the thatch.'

(5) a   bh' air barr   na h-airidhe,
     REL was on top   of-the of-sheiling (a hut for keeping animals)
     'that was on top of the sheiling,'

(6) 's   dh'fheuch   e   air falbh   dhan a'bhaile
    and tried   he on leaving   to the town
    'and he set off for the town'

(7) cho luath 's   a   bh' aige,   e fhèin 's   an cù
    so fast and   REL was at-him   he self   and   the dog
    'as fast as he could, himself and the dog'

Here the speaker is narrating a local legend from North Uist, an island in the Hebrides off northwest Scotland. The previous section of the story has told of an old man and seven young men who go off into a deserted place to repair a sheiling, a shed for keeping cattle. In response to a rash wish by one of the young men while they are sitting in the hut at night, seven young women appear, accompanied by an old woman. The young women and young men go off together and are not seen again, leaving the old man together with the old woman. On the pretext of checking the sky for the next day's weather, the old man then goes outside, holding a rope with the old woman at the other end, so that she can be sure he won't run off.

The first clause of the extract resumes the old woman's instruction – 'and that's what he did' – but the following clauses show how he tricks the old woman by tying the rope on to the thatch of the roof, and then running off to town with his dog. If we want to sum up the meaning relations between these clauses, we could add some expressions to relate each clause to the next (using the English translations just for convenience):

and so	'that (was what) he did'
that is	'he took the end of the rope out with him.'
at that time	'as soon as he got outside the door'
then	'he tied the rope on to the thatch'
that /which	'was on top of the sheiling,'
and then	'he set off for the town'
in this manner	'as fast as he could, himself and the dog'

Of course the original text does also have some of these clause joiners, or **conjunctions**, the most common ones in Gaelic being *agus* or its shortened version *'s* 'and', or what is often called a relative marker, *a* 'that, which'; or more complex combinations of these such as *cho luath 's a*, literally 'so fast and that', i.e. 'as soon as', or 'as fast as'. However some of the clauses don't have any explicit marker but are merely placed next to each other.

So it is just not the presence or absence of conjunctions, but the **ordering** of clauses that is highly significant. In some cases different orderings are possible:

e.g. in the case of the clauses linked by *cho luath 's a* 'as soon / quick as'. In the first case, the clause with *cho luath 's a* **precedes** the clause it is linked to;

(3) agus   cho luath 's   a fhuair   e   a-mach   air an doras
     and   so fast   and   REL got   he   outside   on the door
     'And as soon as he got outside the door'

(4) cheangail   e   an sìoman   leis an tughadh.
     tied   he   the rope   with the thatch
     'he tied the rope on to the thatch.'

While in the latter case the clause with *cho luath 's a* **follows** the other clause.

(6) 's   dh'fheuch   e   air falbh   dhan a'bhaile
     and   tried   he   on leaving   to the town
     'and he set off for the town'

(7) cho luath 's   a bh'   aige,   e fhèin 's   an cù
     so fast and   REL was   at-him   he self   and the dog
     'as fast as he could, himself and the dog'

In other situations, such as with the relative marker *a* 'that, which', only one order is possible or meaningful:

(4) cheangail   e   an sìoman   leis an tughadh.
     tied   he   the rope   with the thatch
     'he tied the rope on to the thatch'

(5) a bh'   air barr   na h-airidhe,
     REL was   on top   of-the of-sheiling (a hut for keeping animals)
     'that was on top of the sheiling,'

This wouldn't make sense in any other order.

How do we explain such patterns? Traditionally, a distinction is made of two kinds of relationship between clauses: coordination and subordination (Matthews 1981: Chapters 8 & 9). Because these terms have a wide range of meanings, and because subordination in particular may also be used for relations of the dependency kind, I am going to replace these Latinate terms with their Greek equivalents: **parataxis**, literally 'arrangement beside' (coordination) and **hypotaxis**, 'arrangement underneath' (subordination), and use the general term **taxis** for structural linkage between clauses. In the first type, parataxis, clauses are linked mainly by ordering, and each clause is more or less **free**, that is, it can usually stand by itself. Compare the next two clauses of the text:

(6) agus ach co-dhiubh an ceann uine   thug e suil   às a dhèidh.
    and   but anyway   the head of-time   gave he eye   from his behind
    'And but anyway, in a little while he gave a glance behind him.'

(7) 's ò   bha   an t-each mòr geal
    and oh   was   the horse big white
    'and there was this big white horse'

Here, although clause 8 is linked to clause 9 by the conjunction *'s* 'and', each clause remains an independent structural entity, and could be used by itself without any problem. In a closely following portion of the text, the two clauses linked by parataxis are, indeed, merely rephrasings of each other:

(11) 's   thuirt e,
    and said   he
    'and he said'

(12) ò   ars'   esan
    oh   quoth he-EMPH
    ' said he'

In contrast, with clauses related by hypotaxis, one of the clauses, normally the one that has an explicit conjunction, is structurally **bound** to the other, in other words, it can only be fully interpreted in conjunction with the other clause, and cannot appear without it, for example with the second pair of clauses related by *cho luath 's* 'as soon as':

(6) 's dh'fheuch e   air falbh   dhan a'bhaile
    and tried   he   on leaving   to the town
    'and he set off for the town'

(7) cho luath 's   a   bh' aige,   e fhèin 's an cù
    so fast and   REL was at-him   he self   and the dog
    'as fast as he could, himself and the dog'

Similarly, in the opposite order, with the two clauses from the text following the two 'quoting' clauses 11 and 12:

(13) 'A chù Mhic a Phì   mur   an do rinn   thu   a-riamh   e
     o dog of-Mac Phee   if-not PAST did   you   ever   it
     ' 'O Mac Phee's dog, if you've never done it (before),'

(14) 'nì   thu   a-nochd   e.'
     will-do   you   tonight   it
     ' 'you'll do it tonight.' '

As well as the two relations of parataxis and hypotaxis, there is a third kind we need to recognise, that of **embedding**. As the name suggests, when one clause is embedded in another clause, it is structurally part of it or contained within it. For example in clauses 4 and 5:

(4) cheangail   e   an sìoman   leis an tughadh.
    tied   he   the rope   with the thatch
    'he tied the rope on to the thatch.'

(5) a bh'   air barr   na h-airidhe,
    REL was   on top   of-the of-sheiling (a hut for keeping animals)
    'that was on top of the sheiling,'

the second clause, linked by the relative marker *a* 'that, which' is structurally part of the nominal group *an tughadh* 'the thatch', and semantically specifies the particular thatch that is meant, the thatch 'on top of the sheiling'. Embedded clauses like this, also often called **relative** clauses, are often structurally different from independent clauses. For example an independent clause of a similar meaning, 'the thatch was on top of the sheiling', would take the following form in Gaelic, with the subject following the predicator, as normal:

(5') Bha   an tughadh   air barr   na h-airidhe.
    was   the thatch   on top   of-the of-sheiling
    'The thatch was on top of the sheiling'

In an embedded clause, however, what would normally be the subject is omitted, and the relative marker which precedes the verb, i.e. comes at the very beginning of the clause like most conjunctions, in some sense takes the place of the subject, as in the other example from the text:

(7) 's   ò   bha   an t-each mòr geal
    and oh was   the horse big white
    'and there was this big white horse'

(8) a bha   an-seo a'tighinn   aca   tarsainn na monaidh
    REL was   here   at coming   at-them   across the moor

    aig astar   eagallach   às a dhèidh
    at speed   frightful   from his behind
    'that was here coming at them across the moor at a frightful speed behind
    him'

A final point that needs to be made is the question of recognising clause boundaries, i.e. where one clause ends and another begins. As we saw in Chapter 5,
we normally take the presence of a single verbal node and its dependents as
criterial for recognising a single clause. We need to modify this definition to
account for at least two exceptions:

    a.   there are two verbs in a single clause, but one of them is joined to the
        other as a modification of it, for example, *dh'fheuch* 'tried' and *falbh*
        'leaving' in clause 6:

(6) 's   dh'fheuch e   air falbh   dhan a'bhaile
    and tried   he   on leaving   to the town
    'and he set off for the town'

In the case of languages like Gaelic, and English, as suggested by the translations, there is often a structural difference between the two types of verbs,
where *dh'fheuch* is what is called **finite** – roughly, 'with tense' i.e. indicating
a particular time, here past – while *falbh* is **non-finite**, i.e. not indicating a
particular time but rather the action of leaving in general.

    b.   there is no verb at all in the clause, but there seem to be predication
        relations, such as the following clause from the text:

(15) Agus   siud an cù   am bad   an eich,
    and   yon   the dog in place   of-the of-horse
    'And there (went) the dog at the horse'

This clause literally indicates simply that the dog and the horse are in the same place, in other words it is a kind of copulative clause, a clause type in which, as we saw in Chapter 8 above, the verb may often be omitted.

In order to mark the relationships between clauses, we can use a very simple notation introduced by Halliday (1985 / 1994: Section 7.2) which identifies the three different types of taxis – parataxis, hypotaxis, and embedding – as follows:

type of taxis	parataxis		hypotaxis		embedding	
relations between clauses	initial	1	free	α	independent	//
	continuing	2, 3, 4	bound	β,γ,δ	embedded	[|

An analysis of the whole text with this notation is shown below, with the notation indicated at the beginning of each clause. We can note here that this gives us a different sort of 'numbering' than if we just numbered the clauses by order. If a clause is hypotactially bound to or embedded in another clause, then according to this analysis it counts as a single unit with it. Furthermore, one clause may have a relation both to the clause preceding it and the clause following it: so for example, the third clause relates paratactically to the preceding clause, but is hypotactically bound to the following clause; while the fourth clause is both hypotactically bound to the third clause and has the fifth clause hypotactically bound to it. This can be taken as another example, at a larger scale, of the sort of 'structure-in-depth' feature of language noted by Hockett: i.e. that linguistic units can be and often are related to each other in ways that go beyond simple linear sequence.

1   Agus   sin   a rinn   e
   and   that   REL did   he
   'And that (was what) he did'

2   thug   e   a-mach   ceann an t-sìomain   leis
   took   he   out   head of-the of-rope   with-him
   'he took the end of the rope out with him.'

3   β   agus cho luath 's   a fhuair   e   a-mach   air an doras
        and   so fast and   REL got   he   outside   on the door
        'And as soon as he got outside the door'

    α // cheangail e   an sìoman   leis an tughadh.
        tied   he   the rope   with the thatch
        'he tied the rope on to the thatch.'

    [| a   bh' air barr   na h-airidhe,
         REL was on top   of-the of-sheiling
         'that was on top of the sheiling,'

4   α   's dh'fheuch e   air falbh   dhan a'bhaile
        and tried   he   on   leaving   to the town
        'and he set off for the town'

    β   cho luath 's   a bh'   aige,   e fhèin 's an cù
        so fast and   REL was   at-him   he self   and the dog
        'as fast as he could, himself and the dog'

5   agus ach co-dhiubh an ceann uine   thug e   suil   às a dhèidh.
    and but   anyway   the head of-time   gave he   eye   from his behind
    'And but anyway, in a little while he gave a glance behind him.'

6   //   's ò   bha   an t-each mòr geal
         and oh   was   the horse big white
         'and there was this big white horse'

    [| a bha   an-seo a'tighinn aca   tarsainn na monaidh
         REL was   here at   coming   at-them   across the moor

         aig astar eagallach   às a dhèidh
         at speed   frightful   from his behind
         'that was here coming at them across the moor at a frightful speed
         behind him'

7   's   thuirt e,
    and said   he
    'and he said'

8   ò   ars' esan
    oh   quoth he-EMPH
    'oh said he'

9 β 'A chù Mhic a Phi   mur   an do rinn   thu   a-riamh   e
     o dog   of-Mac Phee   if-not PAST did   you   ever   it
     ' 'O Mac Phee's dog, if you've never done it (before),'

   α 'nì   thu   a-nochd   e.'
     will-do you   tonight   it
     ' 'you'll do it tonight.' '

10 Agus siud   an cù   am bad   an eich,
    and   yon   the dog in place   of-the of-horse
    'And there (went) the dog at the horse'

Now let's look at a Chinese text, where the relationships between clauses are
expressed in what may seem like a much looser way. The following text is
an extract from a monologue, where the speaker, a Chinese man in his 20s,
is discussing the originally positive view he had of America and how that
has changed. The topic was one brought up in previous discussion which he
was then asked to elaborate on. The speaker occasionally includes English
words and phrases in his discussion (here indicated in italics), which have been
analysed as part of the Chinese text.

1 1 Yīnwèi   wǒ   yìzhí   jué.de
     because   I   all-along   feel
     'Because I always thought'

  2 shuō, rúguǒ, wǒ   gāngcái gēn nǐ   jiǎng .de,
     say   if   I   just   with you   talk SUB
     '(I) mean, if, (as) I just told you'

2 1 *there is only country* [zhǐ   yǒu   yí.ge   guójiā]
                  only   exist   one MEAS   country
     'There is only one country'

  2 bǐrú,   xiàng   zhè.me   yí.ge guójiā
     for-instance resemble such   one MEAS country
     'for instance (that) is like such a country'

  3 α yǒu yítào   wánzhěng.de fǎlù.de xìtǒng – *legal system* – shì.ma,
     exist one set complete SUB   law SUB system   be Q
     '(which) has a complete legal system – 'legal system', isn't it?'

   β lái   bǎozhàng   tā .de   gōngpíng.de jìngzhēng
     come   protect   it SUB   fair SUB   compete
     'to protect its fair competition,'

4 dàn.shi quán shì.jiè.de *race and cultures and* suǒyǒu.de   sīxiǎng
   but   whole world SUB   all SUB   ideology

   dōu   nénggòu zìyóu .de   zài nèi.bian   jìngzhēng
   all   can   free MAN   at there   compete
   'but the whole world's races and cultures and all ideologies can freely
   compete there,'

5 α nà.me, zhèi.ge guójiā,   zhǐ yǒu   yí.ge guójiā.
      well   this MEAS country only exist one MEAS country
      'well, this country, there's only one country.'

   β jiù   .shi Měiguó
      just be   America
      'and (that)'s America.

This text shows a more complex pattern of multiple relations between clauses
than the Gaelic text, albeit one expressed mainly through parataxis rather than
through hypotaxis. If we think about the differences in the purpose of each
text, the reason for this seems clear. The Gaelic text is a **narrative**: that is, it is
concerned with presenting a series of actions as they happened, and describing
the characters and the setting. Thus in most cases, the semantic relationship
between clauses will be one of time – this happened, and then this happened;
or of detail – this particular action or character was like this. In contrast, the
Chinese text is an **exposition**: that is, it lays out not an account of what happened, but an argument about why something is the case, and how a particular
state of affairs should be interpreted.

We can see this more complex structure very clearly from the notation.
Basically the whole text we have here, an extract from a much longer discussion, is one large opinion, expressed through the first clause, where the speaker
identifies himself as the source of the opinion, and then the third clause, where
he sums up what his opinion is, the two being linked paratactically, i.e. simply
by ordering:

1 Yīnwèi   wǒ yìzhí   jué.de
   because   I all-along feel
   'Because I always thought'   …

2 *there is only country* [zhǐ yǒu yí.ge   guójiā]
                                only exist one MEAS country
   'There is only one country'

The text starts with the conjunction *yīnwèi* 'because', which here harks back to the earlier request made to the speaker to elaborate on his previous comments about America, i.e. '(why I'm saying this is) because…' (this clause may thus be regarded as hypotactically linked to the previous part of the text not given here). He then emphasises this background by explicitly adding a comment, paratactically linked to the first clause:

1 Yīnwèi   wǒ   yìzhí   jué.de
   because   I   all-along   feel
   'Because I always thought'

2 shuō, rúguǒ, wǒ gāngcái gēn nǐ   jiǎng .de,
   say   if   I   just   with you   talk SUB
   'I mean, if, (as) I just told you'

Because the speaker is putting together this argument 'on the hop', he has a couple of tries at linking the second clause to the first: starting off with the verb *shuō* 'say', which has the effect of 'let's say', or 'I mean' in English; then trying a conditional conjunction *rúguǒ* 'if'; but finally simply stating the fact of the previous discussion 'I mentioned this before'(it is for this reason that the relation is marked as paratactic, not hypotactic, despite the presence of the conjunction).

What follows is an extended elaboration of how he sees America, and in what sense it is 'the only country'. This takes the form of a series of paratactically related clauses, which add different kinds of detail to this basic claim, with the final clause restating the first with the addition of the 'summing up' conjunction *nà.me* 'well then, and so':

1 *there is only country* [zhǐ yǒu yí.ge   guójiā]
                             only exist one MEAS   country

2 bǐrú,   xiàng   zhè.me yí.ge guójiā
   for-instance resemble   such   one MEAS country
   'for instance (that) is like such a country'

3 yǒu yítào   wánzhěng.de   fǎlǜ.de xìtǒng – *legal system* – shì.ma,
   exist one set complete SUB   law SUB system   be Q
   '(which) has a complete legal system – 'legal system', isn't it?' …

4 dàn.shi quán shì.jiè.de *race and cultures and* suǒyǒu.de   sīxiǎng
   but   whole world SUB   all SUB   ideology

   dōu   nénggòu zìyóu .de zài nèi.bian   jìngzhēng
   all   can   free MAN   at there   compete
   'but the whole world's races and cultures and all ideologies can freely
       compete there,'

5   nà.me,   zhèi.ge guójiā,   zhǐ yǒu   yí.ge   guójiā,
    well   this MEAS country   only exist   one MEAS   country
    'well, this country, there's only one country.   …

If we look at the translations of the three elaborating clauses in the middle of this passage, it can be seen that the most natural way to express such relations in English is by means of relative clauses, headed by 'relative pronouns' like *that, which, where* (modifying the original rendering somewhat):

> 'There is only one country, **that** is like this country, **which** has a complete legal system, **where** the whole world's races and cultures and all ideologies can freely compete…'

This tells us two things about these clauses that are perhaps not so clear from the original Chinese. Firstly, these following clauses relate to the first not as wholes, but by each clause picking up a particular aspect of 'this country' to elaborate on:

> '(There is only)   **one country,**
>   **that** (is like) **this country,**
>   **which** (has a complete legal system),
>   **where** the whole world's races and cultures
>   can freely compete…'

The other thing to note is that the Chinese clauses in this instance correspond to only one type of relative clause in English. English has two types of such clauses: what are traditionally called 'defining' or 'restrictive' relatives, which **identify** the entity realised by a preceding noun: e.g. *My colleague who comes from London* (I have other colleagues from different places, but this is the only one from London); and 'non-defining' relatives, which simply **describe** an entity already identifiable in other ways: e.g. *My brother, who lives in London* (I only have one brother, who happens to live in London). In these terms, all the Chinese examples here are of the latter type, and the way this is expressed structurally in Chinese is by simple paratactic ordering. The equivalent of the former identifying type is expressed in Chinese by the sort of embedded clause we have already seen in a couple of the previous texts and which forms a single unit with a noun, in this case following the embedded clause and joined to it by the subordinating particle *de*:

yí.ge [| jiào Tángmǐ |] .de   nánhái…
one MEAS be-called Tommy SUB   male-child
'a boy (who was) called Tommy…

… [| hé nǐ zài yìqǐ   shēnghuó.guo |]   .de rén,
with you at together   live ASP:exp   SUB person
'…people who have lived with you.'

Two of the clauses in this series of elaborations have further hypotactic links
to other clauses. In one case, it is a hypotactic clause of purpose, introduced
by the verb *lái*, literally 'come', which like its exact opposite *qù* 'go' is often
used in Chinese to introduce an expression of purpose:

α   yǒu   yítào   wánzhěng.de fǎlǜ.de xìtǒng – *legal system* –   shì.ma,
     exist   one set   complete SUB   law SUB system   be Q
     '(which) has a complete legal system – 'legal system', isn't it?'

β   lái   bǎozhàng   tā .de   gōngpíng.de   jìngzhēng
     come   protect   it SUB   fair SUB   compete
     'to protect its fair competition,'

The other case, the final clause of this extract, is the conclusion of this whole
series of reasoning, with the identification of the specific country being talked
about, introduced by the adverb *jiù* 'then' or 'precisely':

α   nà.me, zhèi.ge guójiā,   zhǐ yǒu   yí.ge guójiā,
     well   this MEAS country   only exist   one MEAS country
     'well, this country, there's only one country.'

β   jiù   .shi Měiguó
     then   be   America
     'and (that)'s America.

These analyses of taxis in the Gaelic and Chinese texts give some idea of
sorts of notions needed to deal with the range of clause combinations found
in languages, although the specific types will of course differ from language
to language. Despite the seemingly greater 'looseness' of the way Chinese
joins clauses compared to Gaelic or English, there is a sense in which for
all languages the ways in which clauses are combined is more open-ended
that the ways clause-internal functions are joined together. For example, it
is not at all unusual in many languages, particularly in 'unplanned' spoken
texts, to have two clauses simply said one after the other without any clear
marker of the relationship between them; although it is usually not too

much of a stretch to find some semantic relationship between the two. In the internal structure of the clause, by contrast, the order of elements will normally have some explicit functional meaning, such as predicator plus complement, and there tends to be less leeway for leaving the structural relations unmarked.

The impression of greater 'looseness' of **inter**-clause as opposed to **intra**-clause relations may also come from the model adopted here, which is largely that of Halliday 1985/1994. In the traditional analysis of clause combinations, as summed up by Matthews (1981: 168–70), relationships **between** clauses are assimilated to the model of relationships **within** clauses. There is a 'main clause', very much akin to the nuclear 'predicator', which in effect 'controls' the 'subordinate clauses' attached to it. These latter are of three kinds, each with their intra-clause analogues: 'peripheral', corresponding to adjuncts; 'complement', corresponding obviously to complements; and 'modifying', corresponding to the group- or phrase-internal descriptive elements known as 'attributives'. These are distinguished by the 'familiar criteria of valency': as to whether they are 'obligatory', 'latent', or 'excluded' in relation to their main clause (Tesniere (1959: Part 2, Chapters 134–150) provides a similar description under the heading of *jonction*, i.e. 'junction'). Here Halliday's model has been used on the grounds that inter-clause relationships, as noted above, are more open-ended than intra-clausal ones; but this must be recognised as a theoretical claim which must stand or fall by its usefulness for description; as well as by the recognition that, applicationally, it was developed to deal not with written texts, the object of most traditional descriptions, but rather with spoken texts like the two analysed above, which tend to display much more complex inter-clausal relationships than most written texts.

Nevertheless, when looking at clause combinations, we are still analysing words: that is, more or less discrete 'packages' of sound which have reasonably discrete meanings. For languages with a written form, some unit like *word* in English, or *facal* 'word' in Gaelic, or *zi* 'character / word' in Chinese, can be called upon by ordinary users of the language in order to describe what they are doing; and so most writing systems make a point of identifying such a unit. But there are other meaningful characteristics of language, not expressed by discrete units such as consonants and vowels and tones, but rather by 'washes' of sound, particular pitch levels or contours that characterise whole chunks of word-like units. In the following chapter, we will see the sorts of meanings such features tend to realise, and argue that these significant uses of sound also need to be brought within the purview of syntactic studies.

11 Information flow

Once we start looking at clauses in the context of a whole text, apart from the relationships between the clauses themselves that we looked at in the last chapter, there is another type of organisation we need to take into account: something that is often called 'information structure', or more metaphorically **information flow**. First of all we need to be clear about what we mean by 'information' in this context. The sorts of meanings we have been considering in previous chapters could be said to be concerned with the aspect of linguistic expressions as **representation**: that is, how language represents the world of experience – the action, actors and settings of Tesnière's little 'drama'; plus the ways in which each 'drama' relates to those around it – in syntactic terms, how each clause is linked to the next. In contrast, when we examine linguistic expressions as **information**, we are looking at how these representations are 'packaged' or presented as messages.

We can get a preliminary idea of how this works by examining a text of a particular and unusual kind. The following is an extract from the genre of Chinese stand-up comedy known as *xiangsheng* or 'cross-talk' (Hou & Guo 1980). In its classic form, as represented here, it is performed by two speakers, the *dougen* 'provoke laughter' or main speaker, and the *penggen* 'support laughter' or feed. Basically all the information is provided by the main speaker, while the role of the feed is to ensure that the crucial pieces of information are clear to the audience. If we examine the opening of this extract, from a longer dialogue about drunks and their antics, we can see some of the ways in which this works (in the following A indicates the main speaker, B the feed; numbering is by clauses):

(1)A Zhēn.de   hē-zuì   .le,
      really   drink drunk   ASP:perf
      '(If someone) is really drunk'

(2)   nǐ   kàn-de-chūlái.
      you   look POT out
      'you can tell'

(3)B   O,   zhēn   hē-zuì   .le,
    oh   really   drink drunk   ASP:perf
    'Oh (if someone) is really drunk'

(4)   nǐ   qiáo-de-chūlái.
    you   look POT out
    'you can tell'

The main speaker delivers his overall analysis of how people act when they are drunk (a theme that has already been explored in the previous segments of the text) and his feed's strategy here is a simple one: to repeat, using the same or similar words, the key pieces of information: *zhēn*(*.de*) 'really', *hē-zuì.le* 'drunk', *kàn-de-chūlái* 'can tell'.

Repetition, however, is not the whole story. This extract follows on immediately from a previous story told by the main speaker about a man who pretended to be drunk and lay down on the road daring all traffic to 'come at him', but who got up as soon as something really big and dangerous came at him. This is why the main speaker emphasises the word *zhēn*(*.de*) 'really'; in fact, he emphasises it not only by putting it at the beginning of the clause, a phenomenon we will look at in more detail below, but also by *emphasising* it, that is by using **intonational** prominence.

Questions of intonation are often seen as peripheral to syntax proper, concerned merely with 'stylistic' features of language. However, there are good reasons for thinking that this attitude is misguided. Firstly, there is no spoken utterance that does *not* have an intonation contour, i.e. a movement in pitch from beginning to end, and so this would seem on the face of it to be a phenomenon that should be accounted for, just like the other sound features. The fact that most orthographies do not represent intonation patterns consistently, and tend to concentrate on the smaller sound chunks of language like syllables or consonants and vowels, may *explain* the theoretical neglect of intonation, but it surely doesn't *justify* it. Secondly (*pace* Matthew 1981: 33–34), it *is* possible to show that intonation patterns express systematisable meanings, just like other forms of structure, and that these patterns work together with the other patterns more readily recognised as syntactic (Halliday 1967–68: Part 2), such as those we have already examined in the previous chapters.

As we listen to a spoken text like this one, we can recognise particular points that are more prominent than others. In Chinese, a so-called 'tonal language' where intonation contours are also used to distinguish different words from each other, such prominence tends to take the form of a particular syllable being longer and louder than surrounding syllables. If we represent this intonational prominence by bold font, the opening of our extract looks like this:

(1)A **Zhēn**.de   hē-zuì   .le,
      really   drink drunk   ASP:perf
      '(If someone) is really drunk'

(2)   nǐ   **kàn**-de-chūlái.
      you   look POT out
      'you can tell'

(3)B O, **zhēn**   hē-zuì   .le,
      oh really   drink drunk   ASP:perf
      'Oh (if someone) is really drunk'

(4)   nǐ   **qiáo**-de-chūlái.
      you   look POT out
      'you can tell'

Thus we can see that as well as being emphasised by repetition, the main pieces
of information *zhēn* 'really' and *kàn* or *qiáo* 'look'(in the idiom *kàn/qiáo -chulai*
'see out – tell (by looking)')[1] are also emphasised intonationally.
     The following part of the extract shows a similar pattern, with in some cases
only one piece of information being emphasised out of a succession of clauses,
or in other cases, merely the affirmative noises being emphasised:

(5a)A **Zhēn**   hē-zuì   .de rén…
       really   drink drunk   SUB person
       'A person who's **really** drunk…'

(6)B   **Ng**
       INT
       '**Mm**.'

(5b)A …tā **pà**   (7)   rén shuō   (8)   tā   zuì   .le
       s/he fear   people say   s/he drunk ASP:perf
       'he's **afraid** people will say he's drunk.'

(9)B   O,   tā   dào   **pà**   zhè.yang.
       Oh   s/he however   fear   this-way
       'Oh, he's **afraid** of that.'

(10)A **Ng**
       INT
       '**Mm**.'

(11)B Shì   a.
  be   MOD:excl
  'Yeah.'

Because intonational prominence may single out any part of a clause, or succession of clauses, it allows elements to be emphasised that would not normally be so. In the following two clauses, we might expect the emphasis to be on *he* 'drink' in 12 and *zui* (*le*) 'drunk' in 13:

(12)A Liǎ rén   zài yíkuài'r   **hē** jiǔ,   a?
  two-MEAS person   at together   drink alcohol   INT
  'Two people are **drinking** together, eh?'

(13) Liǎ rén   dōu **zuì**   .le.
  two-MEAS   person   all   drunk   ASP:perf
  'Both of them are **drunk**'

This expected pattern turns out to be only a third right. The actual pattern is as follows:

(12)A Liǎ rén   zài yíkuài'r   **hē** jiǔ,   **a**?
  two-MEAS person   at together   drink alcohol   INT
  'Two people are **drinking** together, **eh**?'

(13) Liǎ   rén   **dōu** zuì   .le.
  two-MEAS person   all   drunk   ASP:perf
  '**Both** of them are drunk'

The main speaker first stresses the fact that the two characters – whom he goes on to mimic – are drinking, and he makes sure that this point will get across by following this up with a separate 'checking' word *a* 'eh'. He then goes on to emphasise that *both* of the characters are drunk, and in fact this theme of 'bothness' is continued in the following clauses, where the intonational prominence is on such words as *duì* 'mutual', and the paired expression *shéi*… (*shéi*), literally 'who…who' but used here with a negative to express the notion of 'neither one':

(14)B Zěn.meyàng?
  how
  '(So) **what** (happens)?'

(15)A Nǐ **kàn** .ne,
    you look MOD:op
    'You **look**'

(16) liǎ rén **duì**chuī
    two-MEAS person mutual-boast
    'the two of them boast **to each other**'

(17)B O, liǎ rén **chuī**+niú.
    Oh two-MEAS person boast cow[2]
    'Oh, the two of them **boast**'

(18)A **Shéi** yě bù chēngrèn (19) shéi zuì .le
    who even NEG admit who drunk ASP:perf
    '**Neither** of them will admit they're drunk.'

(20)B **Shì** .a?
    be MOD:excl
    '**Is** (that so)?'

As we can see in these examples, patterns of intonation prominence ignore clause boundaries: in principle, any piece of information may be singled out for emphasis. In many cases, there will be one intonation prominence per clause, as in clauses 1–4 or 12–14. However, there is always the option to emphasise two or more pieces of information *within* a clause, as in 22 below, said very slowly and carefully by the one drunk to the other:

(21)A 'Wǒ kàn **nǐ**,
    I look you
    ' 'I think (consider) **you**,'

(22) nǐ.de **jiǔ** wa, **bù** xíng'.
    you SUB alcohol TEXT NEG okay
    'Your **drinking**, is **no** good' '

(Note that the second intonation group in 22 has an 'unusual' prominence on the negative *bù* 'not').

The opposite phenomenon, i.e. one intonation prominence over more than one clause, is of course also possible, as we saw above:

(5b)A   ... tā **pà**   **(7)** rén shuō   **(8)** tā zuì .le
    s/he fear   people say   s/he drunk ASP:perf
'he's **afraid** people will say he's drunk.'

However patterns such as those identified above are not the whole story. Just the fact that all languages have intonation, does not mean to say that they all identify important or salient information specifically or exclusively by intonational prominence (see Chapter 12 for another possible use of intonation in language). In the following Scottish Gaelic text, which we examined for different purposes in Chapter 2, we can identify intonational prominence in each clause as follows:

(1)R   De **nì**   sinn a-nochd ma tha?
    what will-do we   tonight   then
'What'll we **do** tonight then?'

(2)D   Nach teid   sinn gu **disco** neo gu **dannsa**?
    not-Q will-go we   to disco   or   to dance
'Why don't we go to a **disco** or to a **dance**?'

(3)M   Cha teid   mise   co-**dhiù**.
    not-S will-go I-EMPH   anyway
'I'm not going **anyway**.'

(4)   Tha mi ro **sgìth**.
    be   I   too tired
'I'm too **tired**.'

(5)   Bha mi air mo chasan **fad** an latha.
    was I   on my feet   long the day
'I was on my feet **all** day.'

(6)   B'fhèarr   leam   fuireach **a-staigh** a-nochd.
    were better with-me staying   at-home   tonight.
'I'd rather stay **home** tonight.'

Though for the most part the intonation prominence falls in the places where we would expect it to, clause 3 has an extra feature, the use of the emphatic particle *–se* to indicate what we may call informational saliency. In this case, as we can see, the intonational prominence actually falls elsewhere, on the attitudinal word *co-dhiù* 'anyway'. The emphatic particle here seems to be indicating a meaning of contrast.

If we examine the immediately following part of the text, we find, in clause 11, an example of another way of indicating informational saliency:

(7)S   Nach **fhuirich** sinn   a-staigh
        not-Q will-stay   we   at-home
        'Why don't we **stay** at home'

(8)   's nach   **coimhead**   sinn   air film   air bhidio?
       and not-Q   will-watch   we   on film   on video?
       'and **watch** a film or a video?'

(9)R   Am bu **toil**   leibh   idir   a'dhol a-mach   a dh' àite air choireigin?
        Q-were pleasure with-yous   at-all   to go out   to place of some-kind
        'Wouldn't you **like** to go out somewhere or other?'

(10)D   Bu toil   leamsa   **sin**   co-dhiù.
        were pleasure   with-me-EMPH   that   anyway
        '*I'd* like **that** anyway.'

(11)   Chan ann **tric**   a gheibh sinn   an cothrom   a dhol   a-mach   còmhla.
        notS-is in-it often   REL will-get we   the chance   to go   out   together
        'It isn't **often** that we get the chance to go out together.'

In clause 10, we have another example of the emphatic particle, in this case in another of its variant forms *–sa*, again indicating a meaning of contrast. Then in clause 11, we have a structure which emphasises a particular piece of information **structurally**, *chan ann tric* 'it's not often...', a feature of Gaelic that corresponds very closely to a similar usage in English. This special emphasis marker involves a form of the verb *is* 'is', abbreviated as *'s*, plus another word, *ann* literally 'in it' which in this case marks this particular piece of information as an adjunct, with the rest of the clause structurally an embedded or relative clause introduced by the relative marker *a / an / am*. Below is a simple example of this using a modified version of clause 5:

(5') 'S   ann **air mo chasan** a   bha   mi fad an latha.
      is   in-it on my feet   REL was   I   long the day
      'It was **on my feet** I was all day.'

Such a strategy may also be used with complements, in this case using the verb (*i*)*s* 'is' plus *e* 'it', which marks the information as a complement (in the broadest sense, i.e. including both subjects and complements proper − if the complement is a pronoun, it is normal to add the emphatic particle -*se* / -*sa* / -*san* to it):

(5″) Is **mise** a bha air mo chasan fad an latha.
     is I EMPH REL was on my feet   long the day
     'It's **me** that was on my feet all day.'

This then explains our original example in clause 11 above. The principle of this structure is to 'dress up' the clause as a copular clause in two parts around the predicator, with *gu tric* 'often' in the stressed form *ann tric*, as subject, and the rest of the clause as a sort of complement following it, i.e. 'it is not (P) often (S) that we get the opportunity to see each other (C)', with subject linked to complement by the relative clause joiner *a*. The original clause is repeated below with two sets of clause functions, the original, and the 'dressed-up' version:

```
                    A          P          S     C
      P       S           C
(11) Chan ann tric     a gheibh sinn    an cothrom a dhol  a-mach    còmhla.
      notS-is in-it often   REL will-get we    the chance  to go     out       together
      'It isn't often that we get the chance to go out together.'
```

We saw a similar use of the verb be to identify informational salience in the Chinese text we looked at in Chapter 8, where the normally non-salient adjunct is singled out for emphasis: e.g.

```
      S                                    P     C
                                                 A      P
(6)  Mèng.li nà.me duō rén     dōu     .shi  nǎ'r   lái .de?
      dream in  so many person      all      be    where  come SUB
      'So many people in dreams, where do they all come from?'
```

Here the subordinating particle *de* is used to mark the clause following *shi* as embedded, with a very similar effect to that of the relative clause in Gaelic.

In Gaelic, such 'focusing' is very common, and in parts of the syntax of the language has almost completely taken over from the 'unfocused' form. For example, in clauses that identify someone as a particular role or profession, the older simpler PSC form would be as follows:

```
P       S           C
Is      oileanach   mi.
is      student     I
```
'I am a student'

However, in contemporary Gaelic, it is much more common to use the emphatic *'s e* 'it's' followed by a relative *a tha* 'that be' with what would be the subject in the unfocused version expressed as a prepositional pronoun at the end of the clause:

```
P       S           Cr      P       A
's  e   oileanach   a       th'     annam.
is  it  student     REL     be      in-me
```
'I am a student' – literally 'it's (the role of) a student that is in me.'

The use of this prepositional pronoun also makes possible the expression of fine representational distinctions, as for example between a role, which is 'in one' in Gaelic as in the above example, versus a label, which is 'on one': e.g.

```
's  e   Seumas   an t-ainm   a     th'   orm.
is  it  Seumas   the name     REL   be    on-me
```
'It's Seumas the name that's on me, my name is Seumas.'

Such examples which 'rearrange' the order of the clause in different ways, raise the question of the significance of word order. If we think back to the discussion of word order in Chapter 8, we saw that each language has a most common or ordinary order of elements, a **default** word order: in other words, the order that will be chosen unless there's a good reason for doing otherwise. For Gaelic, we saw that the default order was PSCA, i.e. Predicator – Subject – Complement – Adjunct. If we reorganise the 'focussed' clause 11 above to follow this default order, we'd get something like the following:

```
       P              S       C                                        A
(11')Chan fhaigh   sinn    an cothrom   a dhol  a-mach   còmhla   gu tric.
       notS will-get   we      the chance    to go    out      together  often
```
'We don't often get the chance to go out together.'

The principle behind the notion of default word order is in fact an order of *clause functions*, i.e. subject, predicator, complement and adjunct, and these clause functions are one of the main ways in which a particular language represents experience (the other being the relationships between clauses that we looked at in the previous chapter). As we saw in Chapters 7 and 8, word order is not the only means of identifying clause functions, since we must also take collocational restrictions, and in some languages inflectional markers, into account. Conversely, word order may also play other roles aside from identifying clause functions, and even in languages like Gaelic which make great use of it in expressing clause functions, there is still the option to use word order for informational purposes, not all of which fall under the 'focussing' rubric used above.

Let's take a look back at the beginning of the 'Eagle' text we analysed in Chapter 8, and see what sorts of patterns we can find.

```
       A          P          S
(1)  Uair    dha    robh        an saoghal
     time    to-it  be+PAST+DEP  the+MASC world
     'Once upon a time,'
```

```
       P            S       A
(2)  bha         iolaire  anns na beanntan        a-muigh  taobh Loch Trèig.
     be+PAST+IND  eagle    in the+PLUR mountain+PLUR  away    side   Loch Treig
     'there was an eagle in the mountains beside Loch Treig.'
```

```
       P-          S      -P         A        A
(3)  Bha         i      a' fuireach ann an  coire an sin
     be+PAST+IND  she    at live+NOM  in       corry  there
     'She was living in a corry there'
```

```
       A       P      S    C
(4)  ris   an  can       iad    An Coire Meadhain.
     to-it  REL say+FUT+DEP  they   the corry middle+GEN
     'which they call the Middle Corry.'
```

```
       A               P            S
(5)  A' bhliadhna seo  thainig      geamhradh fuar   agus mòran sneachda,
     the+FEM year this  come+PAST+IND winter cold+MASC  and much snow+GEN
```

```
       A
     le    cur   is  cathadh,
     with  fall  and drift
     'One year (there) came a cold winter with much snow, in fall and drift,'
```

    A   P-   S

(6) oidhche   dhe na h-oidhcheannan,   bha   an iolaire

    night   of the+PLUR night+PLUR   be+PAST+IND   the+FEM eagle

    -P   C

    a' faireachdainn   an fhuachd.

    at feel+NOM   the+GEN cold+GEN

    'one night, the eagle was feeling the cold.'

Here we find the 'default' order P-S-(C)-A only in clauses 2 and 3, while clauses 1, 5, and 6 all take the option of putting the A(djunct), not in its default position at the end of the clause but rather at the very beginning, as does clause 4, using the special 'relative' structure. What is the significance of these options? The case of clause 4 is perhaps easiest to explain. As we saw in Chapter 11, these kinds of clauses tend to 'follow on' or 'pick up' from a particular piece of information in the preceding clause, in this case *coire* 'a corry' in clause 3. So it seems reasonable that the relative element *ris an* 'to which' should follow directly on from the previous clause and thus appear at the beginning of its clause. But what about the adjuncts at the beginning of clauses 1, 5, and 6?

Clause 1 is obviously a standard formula, like *once upon a time* in English, so we can probably leave it out of consideration here. But in 5 and 6, we can note that both adjuncts refer to time – *a' bhliadhna seo* 'this year' and *oidhche dhe na h-oidhcheannan* '(on) a night of the nights – one night' – and that they appear to be 'setting the scene' for the story, which goes on to detail the eagle's search for another animal who has experienced a colder night that this one. Structurally speaking, the predicator is always at or near the beginning of the clause and cannot really be moved around. Thus for the purposes of this discussion we can ignore it and see the contrast as one between subject at the 'beginning', as in clauses 2 and 3, as opposed to adjunct at the beginning, as in clauses 5 and 6.

Let's now see how the patterns of intonational prominence interact with those of word order (for ease of exposition, the intonational prominence, marked in bold font, it taken to apply to the whole group / phrase in which it appears):

    A   P   S

(1) Uair dha   robh   **an saoghal**

    time   to-it   be+PAST+DEP   the+MASC world

    'Once upon a time,'

      P   S   A

(2) bha   iolaire   anns na beanntan   **a-muigh taobh Loch Trèig.**

be+PAST+IND   eagle   in the+PLUR mountain+PLUR away   side   Loch Treig

'there was an eagle in the mountains **beside Loch Treig.**'

      P-   S   -P   A   A

(3) Bha   i   **a' fuireach**   ann an coire an sin

be+PAST+IND she at live+NOM   in   corry   there

'She was **living** in a corry [depression in the mountain side] there'

      A   P   S   C

(4) ris   an   can   iad   **An Coire Meadhain.**

to-it   REL say+FUT+DEP   they   the corry middle+GEN

'which they call the Middle Corry.'

      A   P

(5) **A' bhliadhna seo** thainig

the+FEM year this   come+PAST+IND

      S   A

geamhradh fuar agus **mòran** sneachda **le cur** is cathadh,

winter cold+MASC   and much snow+GEN   with fall and drift

'One year (there) came a cold winter with much snow, in fall and drift,'

      A   P-   S

(6) **oidhche dhe na h-oidhcheannan,** bha   an iolaire

night   of the+PLUR night+PLUR   be+PAST+IND the+FEM eagle

      -P   C

a' faireachdainn an fhuachd.

at feel+NOM   the+GEN cold+GEN

'one night, the eagle was feeling the cold.'

This analysis shows that there *are* instances where the first element in the clause is given intonational prominence, as in clauses 5 and 6, but there are also cases where the intonational prominence tends to come at the end, rather than the beginning of the clause, as in clauses 1, 2 and 4; as well as cases where it appears somewhere in between, as in clause 3, and (a number of times) in clause 5. So this suggests that there are two separate things going on here. Intonational prominence, or its structural equivalents, identifies the **focus** of the clause, in the sense of the main item of information that the speaker / writer is trying to get across. First position in the clause, in contrast, seems to be indicating the **topic** of the clause: that is, what is being taken as its starting point, what the clause is going to be about.

An analysis of the pieces of information singled out as **focus** in the above text might be paraphrased something like this (using the clauses in English translation as a convenient summary):

1. 'at one time **the world** was like this'
2. 'there was an eagle **over there by Loch Treig**'
3. it was **living** there in a corry'
4. 'which is called **the Middle Corry**'
5. 'one year, there was a cold **winter**, and **lots of** snow, in **fall** and drift'
6. '**one night**, the eagle was feeling the cold'

What we see here is a fairly obvious pattern of emphases, with (apart from the formulaic clause 1), focus falling mainly on where the eagle was (clause 2); what it was doing there (clause 3); what its home was called (clause 4); multiple focuses on the severity of the weather (clause 5), and finally the particular time when the eagle was moved to do something (clause 6).

An analysis of the pieces of information singled out as **topic** by being put in first or almost first position, gives a slightly different picture (the remainder of the clause apart from the topic is given in brackets):

1. 'once upon a time'
2. '(there was) an eagle'
3. 'it (was living in a corry)'
4. 'which (is called the Middle Corry)'
5. 'one year (there was a cold winter)'
6. 'one night (the eagle was feeling the cold)'

What this pattern does is provide a series of 'hooks' to follow as the text unfolds, giving us the main characters, times and places of the narrative.

If we now go back to Chinese, we see that initial position in the clause has a special significance as opposed to final position, in that a noun or nominal group in this position takes on the status of 'known information':

Rén   lái   le.
person   come   ASP:compl.
'The person (you were expecting) has arrived.'

Lái   rén   le.
come   person   ASP:compl.
'Someone has arrived (there's someone here to see you).'

In this case, with only two functions in the clause – subject and predicator – the distinction is basically between subject first – a known entity is arriving; and subject last – an unknown entity is arriving. In a clause where there are other functions, for example, complements and / or adjuncts, some further options are possible, in the example from the Tommy text below, with relation to the position of the adjunct:

```
     A          S
(14) Měi tiān, wǒ    dōu   dài   Bàobǐ   qù   gōngyuán   sànbù,
     each day  I     all   take  Bobby   go   park       stroll
```
'Every day I take Bobby to the park **for a walk**,'

```
      S     A
(14') Wǒ    měi tiān   dōu   dài   Bàobǐ   qù   gōngyuán   sànbù,
      I     each day   all   take  Bobby   go   park       stroll
```
'I take Bobby to the park **for a walk** every day,'

If we tried to paraphrase the difference here, clause 14 is about 'what happens every day', clause 14' about 'what I do everyday'. In Chinese most adjuncts precede the predicator, so the choice is between first and second position; whereas in English adjuncts most normally follow the predicator, so the realisation is different in each case, but the meaning distinction seems pretty similar. In Chinese, as in English, it is also possible to have a complement in initial position. Compare the two clauses below, adapted from the Ghosts text analysed in Chapter 8. Here in both cases *tā.men.de míng.zi* 'their names' is focus, but in the second version, it gains double prominence by being also used as topic:

```
Nǐ     zhǐ    tīngshuō.guo          tā.men.de míng.zi
you    only   hear-say   ASP:exp    s/he+PL SUB  name
```
'You've only heard their names.'

```
Tā.men.de      míng.zi   nǐ   méi       tīngshuō.guo
s/he+PL SUB     name      I    NEG:perf  hear-say   ASP:exp
```
'Their names you haven't heard.'

This double emphasis, commonly seen with elements like complement that would not normally be at the beginning of the clause and thus a candidate for topic, can also be reinforced with a special structure of paired conjunctions *lián* 'even' and *yě* 'also, even':

Lián	**tā.men.de**	**míng.zi**	nǐ	yě	méi	tīngshuō.guo
even	s/he SUB	name	you	also	NEG:perf	hear-say ASP:exp

'Even their names you haven't heard.'

Such analyses cannot be easily justified in brief explanations such as given above, since they require the analysis of significant portions of text in order to demonstrate their validity. However, they do go to show that a particular **realisational device**, such as word order, can be used to express a range of different **syntactic meanings**. The range of expression in any one language tends to depend on how 'fixed' the word order of the clause is: i.e. how much of its ordering potential is taken up in expressing clause functions. Of the languages we have examined here, Chinese probably shows the greatest potential for using word order for marking information status, and Gaelic the least, with English falling somewhere in between.

The expression of these types of informational meaning has tended to be sidelined or ignored in many studies of syntax. There are several reasons for this. Firstly, there is the marginal position given to intonation, which tends to be regarded as a 'peripheral' means of expression – 'peripheral', one suspects, largely because only in special circumstances is it noted by the writing systems of most languages. Secondly, intonational distinctions tend not to affect the representational meaning of the clause and thus can be relegated to the rag-bag category of 'stylistic variants'. And thirdly, the sorts of distinctions identified here really only make sense in the context of a whole text, so if the analyst is working with single sentence examples, often invented, these sorts of structures are either unlikely to come up or else to be explained in terms of clause internal functions. In the following chapter, we will go on to look at another class of structures that have also tended to be sidelined, and see how here too it is both 'peripheral' expression and 'peripheral' meaning that has led to such patterns being overlooked.

Notes

1   The use of *kàn* in this idiom is standard Chinese, while *qiáo* represents the colloquial Pekingese equivalent.

2   This idiom, literally 'blow cow' (sic), means 'to boast'.

12 Full words and empty words

When looking at clauses in the context of a whole text, we will almost inevitably find elements that seem to be functioning in ways not explained by any of the principles we have examined so far. From the viewpoint of traditional Chinese linguistics, the words in a text can be divided into two main kinds: what were called *shizi* (modern *shici*) or 'full words', and *xuzi* (modern *xuci*) or 'empty words'. In Old Chinese, as we saw in Chapter 4, each written **character**, which was not distinguished from the syntactic concept of **word** (the term *zi* being used for both), normally corresponded to a single syntactic word that could function more or less independently in the clause. However, it was clear to Chinese scholars that, semantically at least, while some words had an independent identifiable meaning, others had meaning only in relation to other words. It was the first kind that they named **full** – translated variously as 'substantial words' or 'content words'; while the second were **empty** – 'function words', or 'grammatical words'. Since in European languages the kinds of meanings expressed by 'empty words' in Chinese were mostly indicated, not by separate words but by inflections on the 'full words', European linguistics never felt the need to make such a distinction.

In these terms, the majority of the elements we have been analysing so far would be 'full' rather than 'empty'. Of course we have considered empty words in certain cases where their analysis was relevant to the understanding of the full words – for example, the function of the subordinating particle *de* in marking embedded clauses within a nominal group in Chinese, or that of conjunctions in linking clauses together – but our main focus was on relationships between full words. Such relationships have been described using a number of concepts – valency, transitivity, taxis, information – but they all have in common the fact that they ultimately relate to Tesnière's notion of each clause as a little drama with its action, actors and setting. Tesnière's own notion of **valency**, as well as the more traditional notion of **transitivity**, are directly concerned with modelling that 'drama'; while the notion of **taxis** deals with how separate 'scenes' of the drama relate to each other; and the notion of **information**, first brought to prominence by linguists of the Prague School under the label of 'functional sentence perspective' (cf Mathesius 1929, Daneš (ed.). 1974), concerns how that drama can be packaged or presented in different ways.

Another aspect of human experience that also finds expression in language, if often less obviously, is 'drama' in another sense: that is, **interaction** (Halliday 1985/1994: Section 4.1). Human beings not only perform actions on and are acted on by other human beings and objects in their surroundings, they also interact with each other. The following text, a continuation of the story of the drunks we looked at in the previous chapter, contains at least two layers of interaction: that between the two drunks in the story boasting to each other; and that between the main speaker and the feed. It therefore contains numbers of elements that signal the nature of those interactions, and which as such do not fall within any of the frameworks introduced in previous chapters.

We take up the story, with a bit of overlap, from where we left off in the previous chapter (A refers to main speaker, B to feed).

(21)A 'Wǒ   kàn   nǐ,
     I   look   you
    ' 'I think you,'

(22) nǐ.de   jiǔ   wa,   bù   xíng.'
    you SUB   alcohol TEXT NEG   okay
    'Your drinking, is no good' '

(23)B O, rénjiā   bù   xíng!
    Oh other-person   NEG   okay
    'Oh, the other one's no good!'

Here the main speaker is imitating the two drunks trying to outdo each other, and representing one of them casting aspersions on the drinking capacity of the other. At this point the feed interjects with a comment underlining this point. He introduces his interjection with the vocable *o*, which both sounds and means something very similar to English *oh*. The fact that such elements, often called **exclamations** (Chinese *gantanci*) do seem to occur in very similar forms across a range of languages, has led to them being considered as peripheral to the main system of the language itself. And it is true that in a number of ways such elements don't 'conform' to the main pattern of the language: Yuen Ren Chao in his *Grammar of Spoken Chinese* (1968: 815–819) lists numbers of them containing sounds that do not otherwise occur in the language.

The function of a sound like *o* can largely be explained, unlike the distinctive sounds or phonemes of the language, in purely physiological terms: it is the sound produced when the jaw and tongue drop and the lips become rounded, as in a reaction of surprise. Halliday has explained such elements as a leftover from what he calls the **protolanguage** stage (Halliday 1994: 95) which precedes the development of adult language. But the exceptional status of such elements in relation to the language as a whole does not mean that they are in any way irrelevant in actual language use. Just as we saw in the case of intonation, exclamations are normally theoretically separated from the study of syntax proper: traditionally in terms of some concept such as **style**, and more recently under the rubric of **pragmatics**, i.e. the study of language in use. However, if we follow the basic principle put forward in this book, that the study of syntax concerns all the meaningful elements of language, then it is hard to find a good reason to exclude such interactional elements.

The next section of the text introduces yet another new kind of element not so far accounted for:

(24)A 'Zài   hē   liǎng   bēi,
     further drink two   cup
     ' 'Drink another two glasses,'

(25) nǐ   jiù   zuì   .le.'
      you   then   drunk   ASP:compl
      'and you'll be drunk.' '

(26)B Shì   .a?
       be   MOD:moll
       'Yeh?'

(27) Nèi.ge   .ne?
      that MEAS   MOD:op
      'What about that one?'

The main speaker continues his imitation of the first drunk, this time issuing a direct challenge to the other drunk that he won't be able to hold his drink, and again the feed responds. But this time he does so in two distinct stages: first in clause 26 he **confirms** what has just been said; then in clause 27 he **questions** how the other drunk responds. And in doing this, he 'tacks on' two little words to the end of his clause: *a* in clause 26, and *ne* in clause 27. What exactly are these elements?

In traditional Chinese linguistics they are known as *zhuzi* 'auxiliary words', and in more modern studies as *yuqi zhuci* 'mood particles'. The concept of **mood,** as referred to in Chapter 2 in the context of discussing the parsing of different kinds of negatives in Gaelic, is a very old one in European linguistics.

In its non-technical sense, also reflected in its Chinese equivalent *yuqi*, 'mood' refers to an emotional state; but technically it refers to the interactional function of the clause as a whole as a statement, a question etc. If we think about it, a statement is not simply a specification of information: it is rather an **offer** of information to another interactant. Likewise a question is a **demand** for information from an interactant (Halliday 1985/1994: Section 4.1). Unlike the sorts of functions we have seen above in the representational or informational aspects of syntax, such interactional meanings tend to apply not to 'chunks' of the clause, but rather to clauses as a whole. From this point of view, it therefore seems to make sense for them to be realised by a particle that comes at the very end of the clause, as we have seen in the Chinese examples above.

From a sound point of view, however, there is yet another feature that distinguishes a statement like clause 25 above, from a question like clause 27: their **intonation contour**. The basic distinction in Chinese, as in English, is between a **rising** contour and a **falling** contour: in what seems like a fairly iconic way, a rising contour is used for questions (demanding information) and a falling contour for statements (offering information). How this works out in practice in Chinese is complicated by the use of lexical tone, i.e. intonation used to distinguish one word from another. It is, however, possible to distinguish a statement from a question in Chinese simply by intonation, even when the lexical tone is in both cases the same: e.g.

Nǐ qù.   ↘   Nǐ qù?   ↗
you go   you go
'You're going.'   'You're going?'

In the first case, the falling tone falls to the bottom of the range, thus giving an overall **falling contour** to the clause; whereas in the second case, the falling tone on *qù* 'go' doesn't fall as low as normal, thus making the intonation contour of the clause as a whole higher than normal, and thus giving an overall **rising contour** to the clause. However, a more normal practice in Chinese would be to add a final modal particle, which being like most particles **atonic**, i.e. without lexical tone, can take its intonation from the contour of the whole clause: e.g.

Nǐ qù ma.   ↘   Nǐ qù ma?   ↗
you go MOD:evid   you go MOD:interrog
'You're going (of course).'   'Are you going?'

In this case, the 'same' particle, if analysed simply in terms of its consonant + vowel structure, has two completely different effects: an affirmation of obvious knowledge in the first case, a request for confirmation in the second.

In fact the concept of mood was originally used by Latin grammarians in order to explain three large sets of verbal inflections in Latin. The first set, known as **indicative**, from *indicāre* 'to point out', was used to present situations as real (technically, **realis**) i.e. that had happened, or were currently happening, or would happen in future: e.g. in Caesar's famously terse report of his victory in battle:

> Veni,   vidi   vici.
> come+PERF+INDIC+1SG   see+PERF+INDIC+1SG   conquer+PERF+INDIC+1SG
> 'I came, I saw, I conquered.'

The second set, traditionally known as **subjunctive**, from *subjungere* 'to subjoin', since they commonly appeared in a hypotactic clause attached to another clause, were used to present situations as unreal (technically, **irrealis**), i.e. as hypotheses about what might happen or should happen. Thus we can compare the original line from the Aeneid, when Aeneas responds to Dido's request to speak about the fall of Troy, where the key verb *renovāre* 'renew' is in the infinitive, or tenseless and moodless form:

> Infandum,   Regina,   iubes   **renovāre**
> unspeakable+ACC+SG   queen   order+PRES+INDIC+2SG   renew+INFIN
>
> dolorem
> sorrow+ACC+SG
> 'An unspeakable sorrow, oh Queen, you order me **to rehearse**.'

with a description of the occasion in the indicative, on the one hand:

> Aeneas   coram Reginā   dolorem
> Aeneas   in-presence-of queen+ABL+SG   sorrow+ACC+SG
>
> **renovāvit.**
> renew+PERF+IND+3SG
> 'Aeneas **rehearsed** (his) sorrow in the presence of the Queen'

and, on the other hand, a representation of a counsellor's advice to the Queen before the event in the subjunctive:

Regina,	ut	Aeneas	dolorem	**renovet.**
queen	that	Aeneas	sorrow+ACC+SG	renew+PRES+SUBJ+3SG

'Oh Queen, let Aeneas **rehearse** (his) sorrow'

The third set, known as **imperative**, from *imperāre* 'to order', were used to issue commands, as in the famous advice from Horace which has become proverbial in English:

Carpe	diem	quam	minimum	**credula**	postero
pluck+IMP+2SG	day+ACC+ SG	as-much	least	believe+IMP+2s	afterwards

'**Seize** the day (i.e. take advantage of the present moment), **believe** as little as possible in tomorrow.'

These three types were also formally distinguished in a language like Old English: for example in the sparrow text we examined in Chapter 9, where the bulk of the verbs are in the subjunctive mood, since the whole story is a parable of how we might conceivably regard this present life. Although these are the most consistent and obvious mood distinctions made in Latin, there were a number of other grammatical categories, variously realised, that could be brought under the same heading. Firstly, the **interrogative**, from *interrogāre* 'to question', which was used to ask questions. In Latin this did not take the form of a verbal inflection, but was instead expressed by interrogative particles very similar to those we saw in Chapter 2 for Gaelic, but which could be attached to different parts of the clause depending on emphasis: e.g.

Veniet	-ne	Aulus?
come+FUT+INDIC+3SG	INTER	Aulus+NOM+SG

'Will Aulus *come*?'

Aulus	-ne	veniet?
Aulus+NOM+SG	INTER	come+FUT+INDIC+3SG

'Will *Aulus* come?'

Finally there was a special form of the verb usually dealt with under a separate head, since it also had the effect of turning a verb into a type of adjective known as the **gerundive**, which in conjunction with forms of the verb *esse* 'be' was used to express obligation or necessity, as in the famous rallying-cry of Cato:

Delenda	est	Carthago.
destroy+GER+FEM+SG+NOM	be+PRES+INDIC +3SG	Carthage+FEM+SG+NOM

'Carthage must be destroyed.'

To come back to our Chinese text, in Chinese most such meanings of mood are expressed through *yuqi zhuci* 'mood particles', similar to those found in the Latin interrogative, but restricted to the position at the very end of the clause. In traditional Chinese linguistic scholarship, such particles, along with other kinds of empty words, were simply listed in lexicons with illustrative quotations. In more modern studies, under the influence of European linguistics, the different particles are normally listed under the different basic mood types, those usually recognised for Chinese being declarative (*chenshu*), interrogative (*yiwen*), and imperative (*qishi*), although many particular forms tend to appear with more than one mood type.

Of these particles in modern Chinese (Mandarin), the particle *ne* used in clause 27 is perhaps the easiest to explain:

(27)B Nèi.ge   **.ne**?
       that MEAS MOD:op
       'What about that one?'

The particle *ne* may be glossed 'open-ended', and is often used in clauses in interrogative mood to express questions where, as here, a single piece of information is being singled out for further specification. So *nei.ge ne?* could be translated 'And that one?' 'What about that one?' The same particle also appears in indicative or imperative clauses where it adds an emphasis hard to convey in English translation, but which has the effect of 'attracting' the attention of the addressee, as in part of the same text looked at in the previous chapter:

(15)A Nǐ   kàn   **.ne**,
      you   look   MOD:op
      'You look'

(16) liǎ   rén   duìchuī
     two-MEAS person   mutual-boast
     'the two of them boast to each other'

The widely-used particle *a*, as seen in clause 26, varies in both form and meaning:

(26)B Shì   .a?
     be   MOD:moll
     'Is that so?'

This particle can show up simply as *a*, as in clause 26 above; or as *ya* in clauses 34, 36 and 43 below; or may even 'blend' with another particle such as the aspect marker *le*, to give forms like *la* in clauses 41 and 42 below. Its general effect is to vary the force of the statement, question or command: with statements it could be glossed as 'heightening' or 'exclamative', that is, can turn a plain statement into an exclamation: e.g.

(34)A Nèi.ge   yě   shuō   dà huà   .ya.
      that MEAS also   talk   big speech   MOD:excl
      'That one's bragging too.'

Such a clause has an exclamative or heightened effect as opposed to the form without (*y*)*a*. With questions or commands, however, it has the opposite effect, which could be glossed as 'softening' or 'molliative' (which, however, can only be represented indirectly in English translation): e.g.

(26)B Shì   .a?
      be   MOD:moll
      'Yeah? Is that (really) the case?'

If we compare such a clause with a variant using the 'biased' interrogative particle *ma*, which marks the question as expecting a yes answer, there is a clear difference in degree of certainty:

(26′)B Shì   ma?
       be   MOD:inter
       'Yeah? That's so, is it?'

Moving on to the immediately following segment of the text, we have the first drunk continuing his boasting, his claim immediately repeated by the feed, along with the special contrastive emphasis on the pronouns:

(28)A 'Nǐ   kàn,
      you   look
      ' 'You look,'

(29) **wǒ**   méi   guān.xi.'
     I   NEG+exist   connection
     'there's nothing wrong with *me*.' '

(30)B **Tā**   méi   guān.xi?
      s/he   NEG +exist connection
      'There's nothing wrong with *him*?'

The drunk's statement, without any mood particles, come across as very direct and unmodulated, as is the feed's reaction. But when the drunk proceeds to be more specific in his boasting in clauses 31 and 32, the feed is moved to comment in clause 33:

(31)A ' Wǒ zài   hē   bàn jīn
       I   further drink half catty
      ' 'If I drink another half catty,'

(32) méi   guān.xi.'
     NEG+exist connection
     'it won't make any difference.' '

(33)B Chúncuì shuō dà huà.
      sheer   talk big speech
      'Sheer bragging.'

In the feed's reaction, clause 33, we see another device for expressing interactive meaning: the use of what is often called an **attitudinal adjunct**. The word *chúncuì* literally means 'pure, unadulterated'; but here it is not being used referentially to indicate some objective characteristic or quality of the speaking, it is instead expressing the speaker's attitude towards the behaviour of boasting. The main speaker then reacts to the feed's comment, this time using the particle (*y*)*a* in what we characterised above as its 'heightening' effect:

(34)A Nèi.ge   yě   shuō dà huà   .ya.
      that MEAS also talk big speech MOD:excl
      'That one's bragging too.'

The feed continues this focus on the other drunk, and the main speaker goes on to imitate *him*:

(35)B Nèi.ge   rén   zěn.meyàng?
      that MEAS person like-what
      'What's that one doing?'

(36)A ' Nǐ méi   zuì   .ya?'
      you NEG:perf drunk MOD:excl
      ' 'You're not drunk?' '

(37)B Hng.
     EXCL
     'Hm.'

Here the feed's reaction in clause 37 is an example of what has been called 'channel checking', in other words a way of showing that he is still paying attention. Such elements can also be classified under the general heading of exclamations, and again they tend to utilise sounds that are not used elsewhere in the language: here the sound represented *hng* is simply a brief vocalisation or grunt through the nose. Then the main speaker continues to imitate the second drunk, again eliciting a reaction from the feed:

(38)A 'Zán   liǎ   yíduì   yìpíng'r.de   hē.'
     you-me   two+ MEAS   one pair   one bottle MAN   drink
   ' 'Let's match each other bottle for bottle.' '

(39)B Huo, yòu   chuī-shang   .le!
     EXCL   further   boast on   ASP
     'Ha, (he's) boasting even more.'

Clause 39, as well the clearly exclamative element *huo* 'ha, wow' with which it starts, also contains another interactive element which, unlike those we've looked at before, is not wholly interactive in meaning. The adverb *yòu* literally refers to the completed repetition of an action – in contrast to *zài* 'again' which indicates the potential repetition of action or another action following on from a first – but unlike *zài*, *yòu* also has a attitudinally heightening effect, as can be seen in the following conversational example:

     Wa, nǐ   yòu   lái   .le!
     EXCL   you   further   come ASP:compl
     'Oh, here you are again – not you again!'

In this context, the use of the 'completed aspect' particle *le*, often used in conjunction with *yòu*, could also be seen as having a heightening role, with the effect of 'that's it, that's over and done with'. In the following segment of the text, this particle again appears twice with this interactional colouring, in this case in conjunction with the 'heightening' *a* (*le* + *a* = *la*):

(40)A 'Nǐ,nǐ   shuō   huà   shí,
     you you   talk   speech   time
   ' 'You, (when) you speak,'

(41)   shé.tou dōu   duǎn   .la.'
   tongue   already   short   ASP:compl+MOD:excl
   '(your) tongue's got shorter.' '

(42)B Tā   nèi   shé.tou   yě   bú   lìsuǒ   .la.
   s/he   that   tongue   also   not   nimble   ASP:compl+MOD:excl
   'His tongue's not nimble either.'

The final segment of the text examined here again has the drunk repeating his claim, with an exclamative response from the feed, here a conventionalised representation of laughter:

(43)A 'Méi   hē‑zuì   .ya.'
   NEG:perf   drink drunk   MOD:excl
   ' '(I'm) not drunk.' '

(44)B He,   he.
   EXCL   EXCL
   'Ha, ha!'

Most of these interactional features of language tend to be treated only piece-meal under the heading of syntax, or are shifted off to 'pragmatics'. Again, in line with the principle we have adopted throughout this book, any meaningful elements of language are by definition syntax. But it is clear that, not only are these interactional meanings a far cry from the representational meanings that tend to be treated as the central aspect of linguistic meaning, their structural realisations are also very different from the complex layered structures of traditional syntax.

As we have stressed throughout Part 2, the biases of traditional syntax can be explained in terms of the features of language brought to prominence by the writing system, by the realisational characteristics of different languages, and by certain philosophical ideas about what constitutes meaning. So at this point, having gained an overall view of what syntactic description consists in, we need to get away from language description proper and examine some of the theoretical principles and descriptive traditions that have underpinned the creation of frameworks for analysing syntax.

Part 3

Theorising syntax

Earlier, I described the field of syntactic studies as a 'tangled forest' of different theories. It is as well to remember that this state of affairs in a relatively recent phenomenon. In his review of Tesnière's *Éléments de syntaxe structurale* (Tesnière 1959), British linguist R.H. Robins finished up with the following eloquent appeal (Robins 1961 / 1966: 395):

> There is altogether too little material on syntax in general linguistic
> publications for anyone to neglect any serious work on the subject
> because he does not agree with the author's assumptions about language
> and linguistic analysis. Serious students in any branch of linguistics will
> study Tesnière's *Éléments* with profit, and if his approach annoys them the
> proper response is a book of equal length, detail, and insight, written in a
> technical language and within a theory of linguistic description of which
> they approve.

From the perspective of the early 21st century, it seems incredible that there could ever have been 'too little material on syntax' available, let alone 'written in a technical language'. While it was certainly not the case that no work on syntax was done before the mid 20th century, as the title of Graffi's recent book *200 Years of Syntax* (Graffi 2001) amply demonstrates, it would be true to say, as we shall see in Chapter 13, that syntax occupied a somewhat marginal position in the discipline as a whole. That marginal status has now changed to one of absolute centrality, and 'serious students' are faced with an absolute *embarras de richesse* in relation to the range and detail of different theoretical proposals. What does not seem to be of much interest to most linguists, however, is providing some way of navigating *between* different theories (see discussion in Martin 1986 and a rare counter-example in Butler 2003). In Part 2 of this book, we chose one solution to this problem – the usual one – which is to select one particular framework and work within it, though the aim in doing so was not the usual one – to demonstrate the superiority of that framework over all others – but so that we could get an idea of what the nitty gritty of syntactic analysis actually involves.

In Part 3 we take a different tack, attempting the much less often undertaken task of attempting to *compare* different theories. The diversity of syntactic theorising tends to be dealt with in books of this kind by identifying various 'schools', usually starting from a broad division between 'formalist' and 'functionalist'. There are a number of problems with such an approach. Firstly it misrepresents the complexity of intellectual influences, which tend to run across such simplistic divisions. For example, the theory known as Functional Grammar (see Chapter 16) associated with the work of the late Simon Dik and his colleagues in Holland and Belgium is, despite the name, in many ways a continuation of – albeit mostly in the form of a reaction against – themes first put forward in the work of the 'Father of Formalism', Noam Chomsky, while also acknowledging significant influences from European functional traditions like that of the Prague School. Moreover, such divisions also have the tendency to be treated politically, with particular 'schools' tracing their influences, and therefore their legitimacy, back to some influential founder figure, or as part of some respected lineage, and thus tend to be used to draw 'battle lines' between different schools.

What I plan to do here instead is to trace certain influential theoretical 'themes' through some of the syntactic theories of the past half century. In Chapter 13, I set the scene with an account of two of the most influential syntactic theorists to emerge in the 1950s: Lucien Tesnière and Noam Chomsky. These two theorists in effect represent different reactions to the impact of structural linguistics on traditional grammar. Both of them clearly recognised the then marginal status of syntax, and both argued strongly for its 'autonomy', though for very different reasons. Although their specific claims turn out to contain some surprising similarities, their overall frameworks point in very different directions, and show that it was in no way inevitable that syntax should have taken the Chomskyan path, so often now regarded as the default one.

Once syntax is established as an independent field of study, there are two major theoretical decisions to be made: firstly, how to theorise syntactic **relations**, including the relationship between syntactic categories and semantic ones; and secondly, how to model syntactic **patterning**. In Chapters 14 and 15 we explore the first of these themes, tracing the theorisation of syntactic relations in terms of two concepts from traditional grammar which both date back to Greek and Roman antiquity: **case** and **transitivity**. Both concepts are in origin morphological ones, used to explain aspects of the inflectional patterning of Greek and Latin, but in the last half-century have been reinterpreted syntactically, and in some cases semantically, to characterise clause structure in terms of an array of noun functions (Chapter 14) or of clause types (Chapter 15). The history of these concepts, which show up in some form or other in most current syntactic theories, shows how in syntax, as in most fields, old ways of thinking have remarkable staying power if they can be reinterpreted to meet current needs.

In Chapters 16 and 17, we move on to the second of these themes, how to model syntactic patterning. Here we pick up on one of Saussure's key distinctions, that between the 'horizontal' syntagmatic aspect and the 'vertical' paradigmatic aspect of language (see Chapter 3), and show how it can be used to characterise the emphases and biases of different theories. While it is sometimes assumed that 'syntax' is necessarily 'syntagmatic' (both deriving from the same Greek root meaning 'joint arrangement') – something that is certainly true of mainstream approaches to the subject – there are significant minority traditions which instead take the paradigmatic as their starting point. Here again, as in the case of 'formalist' and 'functionalist', there is no necessarily clean break between the two, with most paradigmatic approaches dealing also with the syntagmatic, and many basically syntagmatic approaches also incorporating aspects of the paradigmatic.

Finally in Chapter 18, I take Firth's advice on the necessity of what he called 'renewal of connection' (Firth 1957 / 1968: 175–6) between theory and data, to complete the circle that has taken us from data through description to theorising, by presenting a specific case study of one attempt to apply a particular theory – systemic functional linguistics – to the description of a particular language – Mandarin Chinese. As I noted in the Briefing, syntactic analysis is not just about theories, it is about languages, and an exploration of the difficulties and contingencies of a concrete attempt to account for syntactic patterning in one language, an attempt that also involves mediating between two very different linguistic traditions, should drive home the essential relationship between theories and languages. I finish up with a 'Debriefing' which sets out the main conclusions that can be drawn from the exploration undertaken in this book.

13 Delimiting syntax

One way of looking at the development of the study of language in the Western tradition would be to see it as a gradual progression from smaller to larger units of analysis. The Greek term for the study of language was *tekhnē grammatikē*, literally 'the art of letters', from which our term 'grammar' derives, and grammars of Greek normally started off with a discusssion of the letters of the alphabet in terms of their shapes and sounds. Such grammars then moved on to setting out the *analogiai* or 'regularities' of the language, by which they meant the inflectional patterning of its words (Robins 1993: 47–49). As we have noted before, Greek and Latin were highly inflected languages, so in classical Greek and Roman linguistics, as well as in the 19th century comparative study of the family of Indo-European languages to which they belonged, the study of syntax was to a large extent swallowed up in morphology. Because so much of the 'syntactic' work, in the broader sense of that term as used in this book, was done word-internally in these languages, the word-external patterns didn't seem to warrant so much attention.

Despite the great flowering of linguistic study on phonology, with the identification of the phoneme in the 1920s to 1930s, as well as the work on morphology from the 1930s to the 1940s, descriptions were still very much based on the smallest units of 'letter' – albeit 'renamed' **phoneme** – and **word**. In line with this tradition, what we are here calling the syntactic level of language continued to be divided into two sub-fields with the word as the boundary marker: morphology, covering relationships *within* words; and syntax proper, covering relationships *between* words. Even in 20th century American descriptive linguistics which overturned many of the preconceptions of the European tradition, since American Indian languages were also morphologically highly complex, the attitude was pretty much that after you'd covered the phonology and morphology, you'd effectively 'done' the language.

So when from the 1950s syntax came to be given attention in its own right, it was first of all necessary to argue that it covered a separate domain from morphology. Tesnière, most of whose work on syntax was published only after his premature death in 1954, but who had been developing his ideas on 'structural syntax' since the 1930s (Tesnière 1934), makes this point very clearly. First of all he harks back to the distinction between linear sequence and structural order that we discussed in Chapter 3 (Tesnière 1959: 34, numbering and emphasis omitted):

> Once arranged in the linear sequence of the spoken chain, the structural scheme of the sentence is ready to receive the phonetic dress which will give it its external form.

> But this external form, a perceptible element destined to be heard, should not be confused either with the structural scheme nor with the linear scheme from which it proceeds, [which are] abstract elements from which it differs profoundly by its essentially concrete nature.

In other words, both the structural scheme, Hockett's 'structure-in-depth', and the linear sequence are *abstractions* from the perceptible form of an utterance, abstractions which account for, in Hockett's formulation quoted in Chapter 1, 'the collusion between the structure of utterances and the strategy of listeners by virtue of which correct interpretation and understanding are possible'.

Tesnière goes on to draw a distinction between what he calls the **internal form** and the **external form** of a sentence, and to thereby delimit the study of syntax from that of morphology (1959: 34):

> The structural scheme and the semantic scheme, then, constitute in opposition to the external form of the sentence a veritable internal form...

> The study of the external form of the sentence is the object of morphology. The study of the internal form is the object of syntax.

Note what it is that Tesnière does here. Firstly, he reverses the order of priority of morphology and syntax implicit in earlier accounts, by making the study of morphology analytically dependent on that of syntax. Secondly, he groups syntax together with semantics as constituting the internal form of the sentence, a stance which has both theoretical and descriptive implications, and which we will explore further below. Tesnière then drives home the priority of syntax in this new conception even more forcefully (1959: 34):

> Syntax is therefore quite distinct from morphology. It is independent of it. It has its own laws: it is autonomous.

A conception of syntax as 'autonomous' in quite a distinct sense from that put forward by Tesnière is given in the very different model of syntactic analysis presented by the American linguist Noam Chomsky in his 1957 work *Syntactic Structures*. Chomsky's view of language shows the very clear influence of the letter- and word-based tradition refracted through the mathematical concept of 'set' (Chomsky 1957: 13, original emphasis):

> ...I will consider a *language* to be a set (finite or infinite) of sentences finite in length and constructed out of a finite set of elements. All natural languages in their spoken or written forms are languages in this sense, since each natural language has a finite number of phonemes (or letters in its alphabet) and each sentence is representable as a finite sequence of these phonemes (or letters), though there are infinitely many sentences.

The striking similarity of this 'additive' view of language to that of Priscian quoted in Chapter 1 should not need pointing out. In putting forward this model of language, Chomsky was also greatly influenced by his first teacher of linguistics, Zellig Harris, whose *Methods in Structural Linguistics* (1951) was largely concerned, as the title suggests, with reducing linguistic analysis to a set of methodological procedures, to be applied consistently at all levels from phonetics and phonology right up to discourse. A key feature of Harris's analysis, and a major trend among some American linguists in the 1940s and 1950s – ironically characterised by Hockett who was one of them himself as 'temporarily dizzy investigators' (Hockett 1968: 25, footnote 14) – was the attempt to carry out *all* types of linguistic analysis, even of meaningful elements, i.e. at the levels of morphology and syntax, *without* reference to meaning.

If meaning was not to be appealed to in analysis, as had been the implicit practice of linguists since antiquity, there needed to be another concept to take its place, otherwise there would be no way of telling whether a particular description of a language was accurate or not. To this end, Chomsky identi-fied as central a new notion of **grammaticality** (Chomsky 1957: 13, original emphasis):

> The fundamental aim in the linguistic analysis of a language L is to separate the *grammatical* sequences which are the sentences of L from the *ungrammatical* sequences which are not sentences of L and to study the structure of the grammatical sentences. The grammar of L will thus be a device that generates all of the grammatical sequences of L and none of the ungrammatical ones.

This programmatic statement deserves further elucidation. Firstly, we can see that Chomsky, like Tesnière, gives syntax the theoretical priority in the study of language by making the central unit of language, not the word, but rather the **sentence** (in effect, what we have been calling a clause). The language itself, as we saw in the previous quotation, is identified as a set of sentences, specifically those sentences defined as grammatical by the **grammar**, that is, by the linguist's description of the language. Secondly, we can note the emphasis on **formalisation**, with the grammar described as a 'device' that will automatically 'generate' all and only the grammatical sentences of the language. The term 'generate' is taken over from mathematics, and as Chomsky clarifies in his second book *Aspects of the Theory of Syntax*, in syntax it refers to the process of 'in some explicit and well-defined way assign[ing] structural descriptions to sentences' (Chomsky 1965: 8). This mechanistic, formalistic bias was no doubt influenced by current work on machine translation which at the time was holding out great hopes – soon to be proved false – of being able to translate from one language to another without a human intermediary; it is interesting to note, however, that Chomsky makes no attempt to explicitly *argue* for the advantages of formalisation – it is seen as an obvious benefit in its own right.

Chomsky then considers three concepts which might be thought to at least partly overlap with the notion of grammatical in defining a language. One is the **corpus**: that is, the data of naturally occurring language forms. Chomsky immediately dismisses this possibility: 'the set of grammatical sentences cannot be identified with any particular corpus of utterances obtained by the linguist in his fieldwork' (Chomsky 1957: 15), on the grounds that any corpus will be 'finite and somewhat accidental' in relation to the 'presumably infinite' set of grammatical utterances in a language (Chomsky 1957: 15). On one hand, this is simply the perennial problem of scientific investigation, that the number or types of actual observed data can never exhaust the potentially possible phenomena. In Chomsky's view of language, this also ties in with the theorised 'behaviour of the speaker', who on the basis of a strictly limited data of sentences actually heard, can 'produce or understand an indefinite number of new sentences' (Chomsky 1957: 15). Such a view, however, also displays a downgrading of the importance of the observable data which would become quite characteristic of Chomskyan-style linguistics

The second concept, presumably suggested by another then new and promising field of study, information science (e.g. Shannon and Weaver 1949), is that of **probability**: in other words, that the set of grammatical sentences of English could be 'identified…with the notion 'high order of statistical approximation to English'…' (Chomsky 1957: 16). Chomsky again dismisses this possibility, and on very similar grounds: 'one's ability to produce and recognize grammatical utterances is not based on notions of statistical approximation or the like' (Chomsky 1957: 16). This on the face of it seems a little surprising: one might have thought that the notion of probability could supply a fairly efficient way of reaching a first approximation of the notion of grammatical, given sufficient computing power, but it again shows Chomsky's determination to distance the basic idealisation of his theory from patterns directly observable in the data.

Alongside these two concepts, Chomsky raises, only to immediately dismiss, the possibility of a useful criterion being **meaning**. It is interesting to see how he sets up his argument against meaning (Chomsky 1957: 15):

> ...the notion 'grammatical cannot be identified with 'meaningful' or 'significant' in any semantic sense. Sentence (1) and (2) are equally nonsensical, but any speaker of English will recognise that only the former is grammatical.
>
> Colorless green ideas sleep furiously
> Furiously sleep ideas green colorless.

Interestingly, Tesnière also argues for the theoretical independence of syntax from semantics by inventing two very similar examples (Tesnière 1959: 41–42):

> ...a sentence may be semantically absurd while structurally being perfectly correct. Take for example the sentence *Le signal vert indique la voie libre* 'The green signal indicates [that] the way [is] free', which has a reasonable meaning; if I replaced all the meaning-bearing words by words of the same kind which immediately follow them in alphabetical order in the dictionary, I arrive at the sentence *Le silence vertebral indispose la voile licite* 'The vertebrate silence indisposes the allowable sail'.

What is significant here is that both scholars unthinkingly give priority to what Firth called **colligational** relations (links between grammatical categories) over **collocational** relations (links between lexical items), with only the former seen as clearly syntactic. On the one hand, as we saw in the analysis of *Jabberwocky* in Chapter 3, the two types of relation actually work together with each other in 'making sense' of a text. On the other hand, it is perhaps harder than either scholar admits to render something completely 'meaningless': there have been explanations of Chomsky's sentence (1) which make perfect sense, and it is not too hard to think of perhaps some surgical context in which Tesnière's second sentence would be interpretable; while in a poetic style of English, Chomsky's sentence (2) would be by no means out of place.

However by contrast with Chomsky, Tesnière uses this type of example to argue that what he calls the structural plane, i.e. the syntactic level of language, while independent of the semantic plane, is by no means unrelated to it (1959: 42):

> …the structural plane and the semantic plane are independent of each other. But this independence is only a theoretical point of view. In practice, the two planes are in fact parallel, because the structural plane has no other object than to make possible the expression of thought, that is to say of the semantic plane. There is not identity between the two, but there is parallelism…This parallelism can be formulated in other terms by saying that the structural expresses the semantic.

For Tesnière, both the independence of syntax from semantics and the relatedness of the two levels are equally stressed (Tesnière 1959: 40):

> If syntax is distinct from morphology, it is no less so from semantics. The *structure* of a sentence is one thing, the *idea* which it expresses and which constitutes its meaning is another thing…The *structural plane* is that on which the linguistic expression of thought is elaborated. It belongs to grammar and is *intrinsic* to it. The *semantic plane*, on the contrary, is the proper domain of thought, an abstraction made from every linguistic expression. It does not belong to grammar, to which it is *extrinsic*, but only to psychology and logic.

There are problems with Tesnière's unquestioning identification of 'meaning' with 'idea', particularly since he does not explain how he thinks the 'semantic plane' is organised. But it is interesting to note that, even when Chomsky later came to put forward a very similar mentalistic view of semantics to that put forward here by Tesnière (Chomsky 1965), he still refused to admit meaning as a criterion in syntactic analysis.

Following on from the examples quoted above, Chomsky cites two more pairs of examples for which he claims 'there is no semantic reason to prefer' the grammatical (3) and (4) to the ungrammatical (5) and (6) (Chomsky 1957: 15):

> have you a book on modern music?
> the book seems interesting
> read you a book on modern music?
> the child seems sleeping

He concludes from this that 'any search for a semantically based definition of 'grammaticalness' will be futile' (Chomsky 1957: 15). This very short discussion comes in the middle of his dismissal of corpus data and probabilistic models as candidates for determining grammaticalness, and seems to assume the highly dubious proposition that a clear semantic parallel can be found for every 'rule of grammar', a closeness of linkage between the two levels which, as we have seen, Tesnière clearly rules out. Despite this, Chomsky goes on to make an even more strongly-phrased statement (Chomsky 1957: 17): 'I think we are forced to conclude that grammar is autonomous and independent of meaning…'.

It is nonetheless clear that Chomsky realises he is on rather shaky ground here, since in a later chapter of the book he returns to the attack on the opposing point of view – i.e. that syntax is *not* independent of semantics – by ingeniously reversing the burden of proof (Chomsky 1957: 93):

> A great deal of effort has been expended in attempting to answer the question: 'How can you construct a grammar with no appeal to meaning?' The question itself, however, is wrongly put, since the implication that obviously one can construct a grammar *with* appeal to meaning is totally unsupported. One might with equal justification ask: 'How can you construct a grammar with no knowledge of the hair color of the speakers?' The question that should be raised is: 'How can you construct a grammar?' I am not acquainted with any detailed attempt to develop the theory of grammatical structure in partially semantic terms…

The absurd reference to hair color shows that Chomsky is not at all concerned to take this opposing view seriously. On the face of it would seem a fairly obvious hypothesis that semantics *would* be related to syntax, since no-one, not even Chomsky, denies that the basic data of syntactic study *are* meaningful, and so even the separation of 'meaning' (semantics) from 'form' (syntax) as two distinct levels of language is a theoretical hypostatisation for which we have no direct evidence: in Tesnière's formulation quoted above – 'only a theoretical point of view'. Since it is clear that, in contrast to the distinctive units of phonology, syntax *is* directly concerned with describing the patterns formed by significant, i.e. meaningful, units, it would seem that the burden of proof would be rather on someone who wanted to claim that there was *no* connection between semantics and syntax.

It is evident that the whole argument hinges on the prior setting up of the notion of **grammaticality** as the fundamental idealisation of syntactic description. Since Chomsky does not at any point explicitly define what he means by 'grammatical', apart from citing examples of 'grammatical' vs 'ungrammatical' sentences, it is difficult to pin down exactly what he means by this. However, numbers of references to the inability of other concepts to account for the creative ability of the speaker to produce new sentences show that what he has in mind must be some sort of mental capacity, presumably the sort of faculty he later went on to name 'competence' (Chomsky 1965: 4). But even this faculty, or 'intuition', is not allowed to have any relationship to meaning (Chomsky 1957: 94):

> It is undeniable that 'intuition about linguistic form' is very useful to the investigator of linguistic form (i.e., grammar). It is also quite clear that the major goal of grammatical theory is to replace this obscure reliance on intuition by some rigorous and objective approach. There is, however, little evidence that 'intuition about meaning' is at all useful in the actual investigation of linguistic form.

An appeal to something like intuition is also made by Tesnière, but again for quite different reasons. In the process of arguing for the priority of syntax over morphology, he acknowledges that in many cases there is no direct morphological marking of syntactic connections. This means that any attempt to base a syntax wholly on morphological evidence is doomed to failure, unless the analyst is able 'to supplement the morphological material by the direct knowledge of purely syntactic material': in other words, where 'external' means of information are lacking, to rely on 'internal' means (Tesnière 1959: 37). Tesnière therefore concludes (Tesnière 1959: 37):

> The very conditions under which the facts of syntax are presented to us thus impose at least the partial use of the introspective method. In fact, the activity of the speaking subject on the structural plane can only be analysed by an introspective tour into itself.

Tesnière's appeal to introspection is thus for him a supplementary means of analysis, required by the fact that syntax deals with part of the abstract internal form of language facts, not its concrete external form. This appeal is in the context of prejudices inherited from 19th century linguists towards a too narrow conception of the data of linguistics – basically simply its phonology and morphology – prejudices which led, for example, to the myth that isolating languages like Chinese 'had no grammar' because they had very limited if any morphological variation. But it can also be understood as relating to Tesnière's own distinction between 'linear sequence' and 'structural order' – cf Hockett's notion of 'structure in depth': i.e. an acknowledgment that the elements of language are bound together in ways more complex than appears from their basic linearity, an insight that would lead Chomsky to later make his famous distinction between 'surface structure' and 'deep structure' (see next chapter).

Tesnière's understanding of 'the structural [as] express[ing] the semantic' is carried over quite consistently into his treatment of syntactic relations, or what he calls the **connections** of the sentence (1959: 39):

> We will term the function of words the role which is assigned to them in the mechanism of the expression of thought…The controller [in a dependency relationship EMcD] has the function of joining in a single bundle the different connections by which several dependents are joined to it. We will give this function the name of nodal function…the superior term of such a group has only one and the same function, the nodal function…[while] the different dependents take on different functions with regard to the controller.

In other words, the representation of syntactic structure in terms of dependency relations aims to capture the nature of connections between elements as 'the mechanism of the expression of thought', and to do so in terms of syntactic functions – the **process**, **participants**, and **circumstances** – which are not the same as but are nevertheless the expression of the semantic categories of **action**, **actors** and **setting**. As Tesnière pithily characterises such a view of syntax, and the model he has developed on the basis of this view (1959: 39):

> …there can only be structure insofar as there is function. It follows from the preceding that structural syntax is at the same time functional syntax, and that as such it is essentially the study of the different functions necessary to the life of the sentence.

In contrast, Chomsky's very different view of the relationship between syntax and semantics leads him to put forward a model of syntactic analysis in which the basic concepts are not 'grammatical functions' like 'Subject' and 'Object', but rather 'grammatical categories' like 'noun phrase' and 'verb phrase'. Again such a model needs to be understood in the light of Chomsky's preoccupation, inherited from Harris, with what are known as **distributionalist** approaches to linguistic analysis (see Chapter 16). This methodological concept, most comprehensively applied in Harris's *Methods in Structural Linguistics* (1951), but already foreshadowed in Bloomfield's *Language* (1933), holds that the most useful way of capturing the structural regularities of linguistic units is in terms of their patterns of mutual distribution: in other words, the possible combinations of elements with each other. Syntactic classes, or what Chomsky calls syntactic categories, may be very efficiently and accurately identified by distributionalist methods. Such a methodology also allows analysts to ignore meaning in the *definition* of linguistic units, although they may of course appeal to questions of meaning as a *support* for their analyses. Chomsky starts off with what he calls a **phrase structure** analysis, i.e. the type of immediate constituent 'tree' with the 'nodes' labelled for class, or in Chomsky's terms 'category', that was introduced in Chapter 5, and then derives the functions from this representation. Thus rather than structure being *identifiable* with (a configuration of) functions, as in Tesnière, functions are made *derivable* from structure (see Chapter 14).

Chomksy thus took over from Harris a bias against appealing to meaning in linguistic analysis, but went beyond his teacher in making it a matter of theoretical principle that syntax could, or rather should, be treated separately from semantics (Chomsky 1957: 100):

> …only a purely formal (i.e. non-meaning-based EMcD) basis can provide
> a firm and productive foundation for the construction of grammatical
> theory.

He likewise stressed the priority of syntax, not over morphology which is effectively subsumed within syntax in his model, but over semantics (1957: 102):

> …relations between semantics and syntax can only be studied after the
> syntactic structure has been determined on independent grounds.

This comparison of Chomsky and Tesnière is very enlightening for the state of syntactic studies just on the verge of the great 'explosion' in the field. Their numerous similar concerns, especially significant since it is highly unlikely that either would have known of the other at the time, show that the task of defining syntax as a separate area of study was very much 'in the air' at the time. However, their almost opposite answers to these similar problems seem to demand some further explanation. Although there is no place here to go into this subject in the detail which it deserves, it seems to me that Tesnière's work, while innovative and full of original insights, is a clear continuation of the tradition of linguistics from which he comes, and that the innovations he introduces are designed either to extend that tradition in the direction of a more detailed treatment of the data, or to fill in gaps and correct biases.

Chomsky's work, on the other hand, shows a strange mixture of the highly traditional and the boldly reformist. His attitude towards the basic categories of linguistic tradition is mostly to take them over without argument – a trend which is continued in his next book *Aspects of the Theory of Syntax* (Chomsky

1965). Thus, unlike Tesnière who carries out a wholesale reanalysis of the traditional 'parts of speech' (Tesnière 1959, Part V) and rejects the traditional split between 'subject' and 'predicate' as inapplicable to language, Chomsky makes these traditional categories the very basis of his analysis. His notion of 'grammaticality', never clearly defined, seems to be calqued on the traditional notion of a 'grammatical rule', and thus in many ways seems to stem from the 18th century notion of 'correct language' that was one of the key underpinnings of traditional school grammar. But Chomsky's innovation is to rephrase these traditional notions in logical, mathematical terms (for example, defining language as a 'set of sentences'), and to weld his whole descriptive enterprise, not like Tesnière to the traditional goal of language teaching, but to the new goal of formalisation – again a goal assumed as worthwhile rather than argued for – that was being made available by advances in computational technology. Chomsky's theory thus combined the maximum ideological power of the comfortingly familiar with the excitingly up-to-date.

In the decades that followed, syntax became the cutting edge of linguistics, and many new theories sprang up, each reacting in its own way to the sorts of problems raised by Tesnière and Chomsky. In the chapters that follow, we take a look at some of these, not in terms of a full-blown history of syntactic theories, but by identifying some of the influential 'themes' which were drawn on by various theorists in their attempts to account for the patterning of the significant elements of language.

14 Theorising syntactic relations (i): case

In this chapter, we will explore the origins and development of one of the oldest syntactic concepts in the Western tradition, that of **case**. As explained in Robins (1993), case, along with tense, was one of the earliest concepts devised by Greek grammarians to explain the morphological patterning of words in the Greek language. It was Aristotle who coined the term *ptōsis* 'fall', of which the Latin *casus* is a direct translation, as a general term 'for virtually any morphological difference in a word form, from an assumed prior basic form, which had a distinctive syntactic or semantic function' (Robins 1993: 215). The Stoics took over this term, but restricted it to noun inflections, as has subsequently been its meaning. In this model the 'assumed prior basic form' of the noun was the nominative, dubbed *euthêia* or *orthē* 'upright', and the remaining cases were collectively *plágiai* 'slanted', from whence later come the Latin *casus rectus* 'upright case' versus the *casūs obliquī* 'oblique cases'. Each case was given a name based on 'a prominent or characteristic function'. The usual Greek terms and their Latin equivalents are given below (adapted from Robins 1993: 215):

Greek term	meaning	Latin translation	normal function
nomastikē	naming	*nominativus*	subject
klētikē	calling	*vocativus*	address form
genikē, ktētikē	familial, possessive	*genitivus*	possessed
dotikē	giving	*dativus*	recipient (indirect object)
aitiatikē	caused, affected	*accusativus*	acted upon (complement, direct object)

From the Latin translations of the original Greek terms come the familiar 'nominative', 'genitive', 'dative', etc. of traditional grammar. The only term that needs some explanation here is the 'accusative', which should really be something like 'causative'; but the first Latin translator, the Roman grammarian Varro, was misled by the double meaning of the Greek noun *aitía* – 'cause' but also 'accusation' – thus 'accusative'. This mistranslation, like the similar one from Latin to English of *partes orationis*, as 'parts of speech', rather than the more accurate 'parts of the sentence', has stuck and is now standard.

As Robins notes, these terms were chosen on the basis of 'a prominent or characteristic function' of each case, but apart from perhaps the vocative, none of the cases had a single function, instead playing numbers of different roles in the clause. In later scholarship during Hellenistic and on into Byzantine times, parallels were drawn between the three main oblique cases – genitive, dative, accusative (omitting the vocative which played no role in clause structure) – and a systematic series of locative adverbs. Thus the notion came into being that the 'basic meaning' of these three cases was in fact a **locative** or 'localist' one. As Robins (1993: 225) summarises the history of this concept:

> It is possible to trace a sequential conception of a localist case theory among Greek grammarians. The *Téchnē* [by Dionysius Thrax 2nd century BC EMcD] lists the three denominal locative adverbs *oíkoi* 'at home', *oíkade* 'homeward', and *oíkothen* 'from home', paraphrased by *en tópōi* 'in a place', *eis tópon* 'to a place', and *ek tópou* 'from a place', but without reference to the three cases involved.… The commentators on the *Téchnē* in general say no more than this, but one such, Heliodoros (? 7th century) brings the cases into a more direct relationship with the three locative relations… 'the locative states are three in number, out of a place, in a place, and into a place; 'out of' is specific to the genitive, 'in' is specific to the dative, and 'into' is specific to the accusative'… Planudes [mid 13th to early 14th century EMcD] treats case as the principal marker of location and movement, with or without an accompanying preposition, making the three local relations the basic distinction between the three Greek oblique case forms.

Following on from the introduction of a structural view of language in the early 20th century, similar attempts to generalise a concept of case that would explain the variety of meanings attached to case forms in languages were made by a number of scholars, the most prominent being the Danish scholar Hjelmslev's 1935–7 study *La catégorie des cas* [The category of cases]. However, the direct application of the concept of case to syntax, as opposed to morphology, was in direct response to one of the key distinctions put forward in Chomsky's second major work, *Aspects of the Theory of Syntax* (Chomsky 1965), between, to simplify somewhat, an underlying form of its sentence, which he dubbed its **deep structure**, and its perceptible form or **surface structure**. This distinction depends on a conceiving of the grammar of a language as made up of a number of 'components', where the 'syntactic component' is at the centre and determines the other 'components' of the grammar, the 'phonetic' on the one hand, and the 'semantic' on the other. As Chomsky puts it (1965: 16, original emphasis):

> The syntactic component specifies an infinite set of abstract formal objects, each of which incorporates all information relevant to a single interpretation of a particular sentence.... Both the phonological and semantic components are therefore purely interpretative. Each utilizes information provided by the syntactic component concerning formatives [i.e. words and morphemes EMcD], their inherent properties, and their interrelations in a given sentence. Consequently, the syntactic component of a grammar must specify, for each sentence, a *deep structure* that determines its semantic interpretation and a *surface structure* that determines its phonetic interpretation.

In this conception of language, the link between deep structure and surface structure is made by a series of modifications or **transformations** of the deep structure, thus the name given to the theory at this time, 'transformational generative grammar'. The deep structure was further specified as the **base** of the syntactic component, in other words, the basic structure from which everything else was generated (Chomsky 1965: 17, original emphasis):

> The *base* of the syntactic component is a system of rules that generate a... set of *basic strings*, each with an associated structural description called as *base Phrase-marker*. The base Phrase-markers are the elementary units out of which deep structures are constituted.... Underlying each sentence of the language there is a sequence of base Phrase-markers, each generated by the base of the syntactic component. I shall refer to this sequence as the *basis* of the sentence... In addition to its base, the syntactic component of a generative grammar contains a *transformational* sub-component. This is concerned with generating a sentence, with its surface structure, from its basis...

In this analysis of English, Chomsky assumes a description of the sentence essentially identical to that given by traditional grammar, which he sees as 'substantially correct and essential to any account of how the language is used or acquired' (Chomsky 1965: 64 – as noted in the previous chapter, this constituted a major break with previous linguistics which had rejected many of the assumptions of what came to be known as 'traditional grammar'). What he set out to do was **formalise** this account in a way that was generative, i.e. by which a structure could be derived from its 'underlying' representation through an explicit series of steps. The initial stage of the derivation starts from the 'categorial component' of the base, so-called because it contains the fundamental (non-derived) **categories** of the theory, corresponding to traditional parts of speech, or word and phrase classes. The role of the categorial component is to 'define implicitly the basic grammatical relations that function in the deep structures of the language' (Chomsky 1965: 120). It does this by providing, for each surface structure sentence, a deep structure constituent tree with categorial (i.e. class) labels, from which the different grammatical functions may be derived. The basic grammatical functions are thus theoretically **relational**, that is, they are derived from the relations between certain labelled constituents: technically, they are defined in terms of the 'domination' of certain categories by others, i.e. by part-whole relationships between immediate constituents. In this model the four main grammatical relations are the following:

1. Subject-of, defined as   [NP, S] i.e. NP immediately dominated by S
2. Predicate-of, defined as   [VP, S] etc
3. Direct-Object-of, defined as [NP, VP]
4. Main-Verb-of, defined as   [V, VP]

Chomsky points out that the rules of the categorial component 'carry out two quite separate functions: they define the system of grammatical relations, and they determine the ordering of elements in deep structure' (1965: 123). He notes that the second function could be eliminated, i.e. that the elements in deep structure could be unordered; but immediately, though without justification, dismisses this alternative as unviable. In fact, though Chomsky does not acknowledge this, his reliance on constituent ordering and categorial labels obliges him to posit an ordered deep structure, because unordered sequences of categorial elements would leave the model with no way of defining grammatical relations. His description of a possible alternative model as 'a set of syntactically related structures with a single network of grammatical relations [in which] each member is directly related to the underlying abstract representation, and there is no internal organization... within the set of structures' (1965: 125) could be applied almost wholesale to the conception of grammatical relations developed by Charles Fillmore, as an explicit reaction to Chomsky's 1965 model, under the title of 'case'.

In *The Case for Case* (1968), Fillmore sets out to modify Chomsky's *Aspects* model, in the context of theorising about language universals, by first taking up the problem of the ordering of elements in the base component of the syntax. On this point he adopts the opposite line to Chomsky's (Fillmore

1968: 1, original emphasis): 'A common assumption is that the universal base specifies the needed syntactic *relations*, but the assignment of sequential order to the constituents of base structure is language specific.' Fillmore's solution is to put forward a model very close to that rejected by Chomsky above, where each element of deep structure is 'directly related to the underlying abstract representation', and directly labelled for its syntactic relation, i.e. function (Fillmore 1968: 21):

> The substantive modification to the theory of transformational grammar which I wish to propose amounts to a reintroduction of the 'conceptual framework' interpretation of case systems, but this time with a clear understanding of the difference between deep and surface structure. The sentence in its basic structure consists of a verb and one or more noun phrases, each associated with the verb in a particular case relationship...

In this model, Fillmore relegates the ordered relations, in other words, 'subject', 'object' etc., to surface structure phenomena which correspond to an array of deep structure **cases**, covering such notions as agent, instrument, location, beneficiary, and so on. This extension of the morphological phenomenon of case to the syntactic level is used to capture generalisations about the predication relations of nouns in a sentence to the main verb (Fillmore 1968: 23):

> In the basic structure of sentences...we find what might be called the 'proposition', a tenseless set of relationships involving verbs and nouns (and embedded sentences, if there are any), separated from what be called the 'modality' constituent. This latter will include such modalities on the sentence-as-a-whole as negation, tense, mood, and aspect.

Although Fillmore thus sees his conception of case as still fitting within the syntactico-centric model of language put forward by Chomsky, he defines the actual cases themselves in clearly semantic terms (Fillmore 1968: 24–25):

> The case notions comprise a set of universal, presumably innate, concepts which identify certain types of judgments human beings are capable of making about the events that are going on around them, judgments about such matters as who did it, who it happened to, and what got changed. The cases that appear to be needed include:
>
> > *Agentive* (A), the case of the typically animate perceived instigator of the action identified by the verb.
> >
> > *Instrumental* (I), the case of the inanimate force or object causally involved

in the action or state identified by the verb.

Dative (D), the case of the animate being affected by the state or action indentified by the verb.

Factitive (F), the case of the object or being resulting from the action or state identified by the verb, or understood as part of the meaning of the verb.

Locative (L), the case which identifies the location or spatial orientation of the state or action identified by the verb

Objective (O), the semantically most neutral case, the case of anything representable by a noun whose role in the action or state identified by the verb is identified by the semantic interpretation of the verb itself; conceivably the concept should be limited to things which are affected by the action or state identified by the verb. The term is not to be confused with the notion of direct object, nor with the name of the surface case synonymous with accusative.

Exactly twenty years after Fillmore's seminal paper, though based on work since the early 1970s, the American linguist Stan Starosta published his new version of case theory known as 'lexicase' (Starosta 1988). Starosta's theory also takes its place in the tradition both stemming from and reacting against Chomsky's work, incorporating some of the revisions to that theory during the intervening two decades, as well as work in related frameworks (Anderson 1971; Hudson 1976, 1984). Starosta criticises the notion of 'case' in the Fillmorean tradition, as well as similar work stemming from Gruber 1965 (in which predication relations are termed 'thematic relations'), as being based on extralinguistic intuitions about the numbers and types of cases necessary for a particular verb, in other words a 'situation-oriented procedure' (Starosta 1988: 117) for identifying case relations. Starosta criticises the use of paraphrase in this procedure, which he defines as follows (p.117): 'two sentences are paraphrases if they have the same truth values, which is a more precise way of saying that they characterize the same external situations'. He concludes that '[s]ince such determinations are typically made on the basis of prelinguistic intuitions, there is no way to bring linguistic evidence to bear in deciding the issue' (1988: 118). He thus argues for the recognition of what he calls, borrowing a term from later work of Fillmore's (Fillmore 1977), different 'sentence-specific PERSPECTIVES of...situations', so that 'if two different sentences refer to the same situation but portray it from different viewpoints, they may contain quite different arrays of case relations' (1988: 119).

The 'lexi-' part of lexicase theory refers to the fact that Starosta does away with the distinction between deep and surface structure, and indeed in principle with the notion of a syntactic rule, reducing the representation of syntactic relations to that of the interaction of lexical items in a sentence. Applying an idea from Chomsky 1970, he basically allows **features** marked on each lexical item to capture all syntactic generalisations. All syntactic features, including case, are thus marked on individual lexical items, and syntactic rules are seen as extrapolations from sets of lexical items bearing specific syntactic features.

Starosta argues that the concept of 'case' can be extended from its traditional usage to capture the 'semantic-syntactic relationship[s]' of the clause (Starosta 1988: 114):

> In traditional grammar, the term 'case' refers to an inflectional category, for example 'Nominative', 'Accusative', which is marked on nouns to indicate particular semantic-syntactic relations which they bear to other words in the sentence, especially to regent [i.e. 'governing' EMcD] verbs or prepositions. In generative grammar, 'case' in the context of Fillmorean 'case grammar' refers to the syntactic-semantic relationship itself, for example 'Agent', 'Patient', etc.... In lexicase grammar, the term 'case' is a cover term for all these phenomena and more. A lexicase grammar distinguishes among 'case relations' (similar to Fillmorean cases...), 'case forms' (similar to case in traditional grammar...), 'case markers' (incorporating the case inflections of traditional grammar and other classes of overt grammatical markers), and the 'macroroles' actor and undergoer.... By allocating case-like phenomena among these various subsystems, the grammar is able to eliminate redundancy, limit the case role inventory to a small fixed universal set, and capture important generalizations....

Alongside this theoretical proliferation of the concept of case, Lexicase theory also reflects earlier traditions in the concept of case by drawing a distinction between a basic case, like the 'upright case' of Greek grammars, the Patient, which appears 'in the case frame of every verb' (Starosta 1988: 128); and by characterising most of the remaining cases in localistic terms. By further allowing these localistic cases to have both an 'inner' and 'outer' form, where 'inner case relations' relate directly to a particular 'regent' (in effect, a 'participant' in Tesnière's terms), while 'outer case relations occur freely with all predicates' (Starosta 1988: 128), the theory is able to work with 'only five 'deep'case relations' (Starosta 1988: 126):

> Patient (PAT): the perceived central participant in a state or event (formerly also Object or Theme)
>
> Agent (AGT): the perceived external instigator, initiator, controller, or

experiencer of the action, event, or state (formerly also Dative, Experiencer, Force, Instrument)

LOCUS (LOC):

inner: the perceived concrete or abstract source, goal, or location of the Patient (formerly also Source, Goal, or Path)

outer: the perceived concrete or abstract source, goal, or location of the action, event, or state (formerly also Place)

CORRESPONDENT (COR):

inner: the entity perceived as being in correspondence with the Patient (formerly Dative, Experiencer, Range, Increment)

outer: the perceived external frame or point of reference for the action, event, or state as a whole (formerly Benefactive, Reference)

MEANS (MNS):

inner: the perceived immediate affector or effector of the Patient (formerly Instrument, Material, Vehicle)

outer: the means by which the action, state or event as a whole is perceived as being realized (formerly Instrument, Manner)

Although this very brief account cannot do justice to the ways in which the concept of case has been used, and continues to be used, in many syntactic theories, nevertheless from even as a sketchy a treatment as this we can still extract some useful generalisations about the modern use of this ancient term.

- In most modern theories, case is envisaged as belonging to what Tesnière called the 'internal form' of language: that is, it is not essentially a morphological phenomenon, although particular cases may of course be realised morphologically, but is rather an abstract notion set up to account for a range of syntactic phenomena.

- Unlike traditional notions of case, which were clearly language-specific (despite the frequent use of the same case labels across different languages), modern theories of case all make claims of universality: in other words, case notions are taken to apply to all languages. This can cause problems for theorising case, most clearly demonstrated in the frequent modifications to and finally abandonment of Fillmore's theory of case (Fillmore, 1968, 1977), since it is not immediately obvious what sorts of generalisations can be made across languages in this area, or exactly what is the status of the case concept – syntactic, semantic, semantico-syntactic, and so on. In Halliday's terms (see Chapter 18), case might be regarded as a descriptive category that has been pressed into service as a theoretical category, with all the problems that entails.

- In most modern syntactic theories that employ a notion like case, case categories are linked to another set of categories which tend to represent 'surface' rather than 'deep' phenomena, e.g. 'subject' and 'object' in Fillmore's framework; or are generalised across the whole set of cases, usually in terms of highly general categories with which all cases can be cross-classified, e.g. 'actor' and 'undergoer' in Foley and Van Valin 1984, or as adapted in Starosta's framework. Here again there is often ambiguity in the way such notions are applied: as 'purely' structural notions, as in Fillmore's 'subject' and 'object'; as representing the speaker's 'perspective' on the presentation of the situation, as in Dik 1979, 1989, where 'subject' and 'object' are in effect similar to 'pragmatic' or 'informational' notions such as 'topic' and 'focus'; or as what Foley and Van Valin 1984 and Starosta following them call 'macro-roles', i.e. generalised cases.

The original metaphor of *ptōsis* / *casus* as 'fall' seems not to have been a very fruitful one, in that its semantic implications, rather vague and limited from the first, seem to have been quickly forgotten, requiring further metaphors, such as location or role, to 'syntacticise' it. By contrast, in the following chapter we go on to look at another ancient morphological motion adapted to syntactic use, that of transitivity, which unlike case has proved since ancient times to be a highly useable and adaptable metaphor in explaining syntactic patterns.

15 Theorising syntactic relations (ii): transitivity

The concept of **transitivity**, like case, was orginally devised by Greek grammarians to explain various aspects of the inflectional marking of Greek. As Robins explains (Robins 1993: 30):

> It seems that Apollonius [Dyscolus, 2nd century A.D. EMcD] introduced the specifically syntactic concept of transitivity (and its counterpart intransitivity). Transitivity involved a construction having two non-referential persons or things, represented overtly by a noun or a pronoun, or 'understood' in the personal inflection of the verb... The words used for transitivity were *diábasis* 'passing across' and *metábasis* 'transference'....But we see that this syntactic relation is not referred to a syntactic element like subject or object...but to case forms... 'It is clear that the activity proceeds from the nominative to the accusative'...The descriptive priority of morphology over syntax is plain to see...

However, in contrast to Aristotle's concept of *ptōsis* 'fall' or case, it seems that the metaphor involved in the notion of *diábasis* 'passing across' lent itself more easily to being extended to syntax. Robins sees a connection between it and 'the later Byzantine term *ekpompē* 'sending out' for the transitive construction in general, involving a process or activity proceeding out of the agent (nominative) to something or somebody outside' (Robins 1993: 37). This notion was suggested by certain morphological phenomena of Greek, such as those involved in verbs of perception, that were readily interpretable within the notion of 'passing across' (Robins 1993: 37):

> A regular feature of Greek case syntax is that verbs of sensation other than sight regularly construct with the genitive, such as *háptomai* 'touch', *osphraínomai* 'smell', *akoúō* 'hear', *geúomai* 'taste', but that verbs like *horō* and *blépō* 'see, look at' take the accusative case only...Byzantine grammarians explain [this distinction EMcD]...in terms of *ekpompē*

'sending out' in verbs of seeing, which construct with the accusative only, and *eispompē* 'introduction from outside' in other verbs of perception, which may take the genitive as well as the accusative.

Modern adaptations of the concept of transitivity take up this metaphor of 'passing across' or 'extension', as well as different kinds or degrees of 'passing across' which may be used to categorise clauses or verbs into different classes. For M.A.K. Halliday, whose earliest published work on transitivity was in a series of articles in the *Journal of Linguistics* in 1967–8 (here we will draw mainly on a 1970 paper which presents the framework in briefer and more accessible form), the notion of transitivity plays much the same role as that of valency in Tesnière's framework, with indeed many similarities of substance and terminology between the two (Halliday 1970: 146–147):

> Let us consider the expression of processes: of actions, events, states and relations, and the persons, objects and abstractions that are associated with them. For this purpose we will focus our attention on one unit of linguistic structure, namely the clause. In any language, a vast number of different processes can be distinguished; but these are reducible to a small number of process types, and the grammar of every language comprises sets of options representing broad categories of this kind. The most familiar, and simplest, model is that which groups all processes into the two categories of 'transitive' and 'intransitive'.

> Associated with each type of process are a small number of functions, or 'roles', each representing the parts that the various persons, objects or other classes of phenomena may play in the process concerned...
> The roles which appear in the expression of processes are of different kinds. First there is the process itself, usually represented by a verb...
> Then there are the participant functions, the specific roles that are taken on by persons and objects...; and finally there are what we may call the circumstantial functions, the associated conditions and constraints such as those of time, place and manner....

Halliday recognises three main types of 'process' for English, which 'possibly' may be generalisable to other languages (Halliday 1970: 155–156):

> As far as the ideational component of grammar is concerned, the English clause shows the three principal types – action, mental process and relation – and associates with each a set of different inherent roles, or structural functions. The system of clause types is a general framework

for the representation of processes in the grammar; possibly all languages distinguish three such categories.

However, unlike most case theories, Halliday does not claim universality for either the particular process types or indeed the notion of transitivity itself, with another model, ergativity, also put forward as an alternative or copresent one (Halliday 1970: 157–158):

> These two ways of representing processes, the transitive and the ergative, are very widely distributed; possibly all languages display one or the other, or (perhaps always) both in different mixtures. In English, the two occur side by side. The transitive system asks 'does the action extend beyond the active participant or not?'; the ergative, 'is the action caused by the affected participant or not?'…the ergative pattern, whereby a process is accompanied by a obligatory 'affected' participant and an optional 'causer', is more readily generalizable than that of actor and goal. It extends beyond action clauses to those of mental process, and perhaps even to clauses of relation as well.

This brief sketch of Halliday's transitivity theory shows the use he has made of this concept: semanticising it in a very similar way to Tesnière, in both cases by using the metaphor of 'process'; and recognising a number of different types of process, analogous to Tesnière's classification of types of valency, with each process having its associated participant roles, and less closely linked circumstance roles.

A quite different adaptation of the concept of transitivity is undertaken by Paul Hopper and Sandra Thompson, as a way of accounting for certain types of both 'morphosyntactic marking' and 'semantic interpretations' of clauses and clause elements, but whose ultimate explanatory value lies in the realm of discourse context. Hopper and Thompson characterise their understanding of transitivity as follows (Hopper & Thompson 1980: 251, original emphasis):

> Transitivity is traditionally understood as a global property of an entire clause, such that an activity is 'carried-over' or 'transferred' from an agent to a patient. Transitivity in the traditional view thus necessarily involves at least two participants (a view which we will later qualify), and an action which is typically EFFECTIVE in some way. This intuitive understanding is one which we shall attempt to characterize explicitly and in universal terms.

The idea that such a detailed concept of transitivity could be in any ordinary sense 'intuitive' is rather a strange one (see discussion in Chapter 18), particularly since the notion of 'effective' seems to be borrowed directly from Halliday 1967. But this rhetorical strategy of justifying their argument as a development of 'traditional' or 'pre-theoretical' notions (see again Chapter 18 for a critique of this latter term) seems quite characteristic of their approach (Hopper & Thompson 1980: 253, original emphasis):

> Transitivity…viewed in the most conventional and traditional way possible – as a matter of carrying-over or transferring an action from one participant to another – can be broken down into its component parts, each focusing on a different facet of this carrying over in a different part of the clause. Taken together, they allow clauses to be characterized as MORE or LESS Transitive…. Again, this notion is in general consonant with our pre-theoretical understanding of Transitivity.

Hopper and Thompson identify a number of features which define a continuum of 'transitiveness', in other words, of degrees of Transitivity from 'high' to 'low' (Hopper & Thompson 1980: 252):

		HIGH	LOW
A.	PARTICIPANTS	2 or more participants, A and O.	1 participant
B.	KINESIS	action	non-action
C.	ASPECT	telic	atelic
D.	PUNCTUALITY	punctual	non-punctual
E.	VOLITIONALITY	volitional	non-volitional
F.	AFFIRMATION	affirmative	negative
G.	MODE	realis	irrealis
H.	AGENCY	A high in potency	A low in potency
I.	AFFECTEDNESS OF O	O totally affected	O not affected
J.	INDIVIDUATION OF O	O highly individuated	O non-individuated

This 'graded' conception of transitivity certainly seems consonant with the original metaphor of 'passing over', reinterpreted as not simply an absolute binary distinction – either passing over (transitive) or not (intransitive) – but as a scale of degrees, more or less transitive. However, in contrast to the many explanations of case in terms of 'location' or 'role', Hopper and Thompson do not attempt to put forward an overarching semantic notion to explain this phenomenon (Hopper & Thompson 1980: 279–80):

> It is tempting to try to find a superordinate semantic notion which will include all the Transitivity components. If there is one, it has not so far been discovered; terms such as 'activity', 'intensity', and others which we have considered all fail to capture the essence of the relationship among these components. Yet it is crucial to posit some unifying principle, since otherwise there is a danger of circularity in our argument. This circularity would not necessarily be vicious, but the hypothesis is more convincing and stronger if the Transitivity components can be shown to follow from a unitary underlying principle.

This on the face of it seems rather strange, particularly since the notion of 'transitivity' is itself a semantic one, certainly as applied by Hopper and Thompson. However, as they make clear in the conclusion to their argument, they regard *any* syntactic account which remains within the confines of the sentence as avoiding the question of the ultimate motivation for such patterns (Hopper & Thompson 1980: 295, original emphasis):

> In general,…we suggest that phrasocentric ('sentence-level' or sentence-internal) accounts of morphosyntax can have only a provisional and incomplete validity, and that a fully coherent theory of language must begin at (and not merely include) the level of discourse MOTIVATION for individual sentences.

Their solution in the case of transitivity is to identify the syntactic distinction between high and low transitivity with a discourse distinction between **foregrounding** and **backgrounding** of information (Hopper & Thompson 1980: 295, original emphasis):

> Users of a language are constantly required to design their utterances in accord with their own communicative goals and with their perception of their listeners' needs. Yet, in any speaking situation, some parts of what is said are more relevant than others. That part of the discourse which does not immediately and crucially contribute to the speaker's goal, but which merely assists, amplifies, or comments on it, is referred to as BACKGROUND. By contrast, the material which supplies the main points of the discourse is known as FOREGROUND. Linguistic features associated

with the distinction between foreground and background are referred to as GROUNDING....

Hopper and Thompson make a link between transitivity and grounding which they theorise as explaining some universal features of syntax (Hopper & Thompson 1980: 294):

> ...Transitivity is a global property of clauses...it is a continuum along which various points cluster and tend strongly to co-occur, and...the foci of high Transitivity and low Transitivity correlate with the independent discourse notions of foregrounding and backgrounding respectively. The fact that semantic characteristics of high Transitivity such as perfective Aspect, individuated O, and agentive subject tend strongly to be grammaticized in the morphosyntax of natural languages points to the importance of the foregrounding/backgrounding distinction, and suggests that this distinction is valuable in explaining certain universals or near-universals of morphosyntax.

To sum up, the notion of 'transitivity', although not as widely utilised as 'case', has nevertheless proven itself a very useful one, although again in contrast to case, the original metaphor of 'passing across' has been retained relatively unchanged in modern accounts. On the basis of the two frameworks briefly described here, we can make the following generalisations:

- the notion of transtivity can be interpreted in two main ways: as (defining) a **typology**, as in Halliday's work (roughly comparable to Tesnière's classification of valency types); or as a **scale**, as in Hopper and Thompson's framework, where the 'canonical' notion of transitivity is interpreted as the highest degree of 'passing across'.

- both interpretations seem equally consistent with the original notion as put forward in grammars of Classical Greek and Latin, as well as quite consonant with each other; indeed, in a more recent account of transitivity in English (Halliday 1985 / 1994), the different process types are envisaged as 'shading into' each other, with the three main types – material, mental and verbal – connected by the transitional types of behavioural (coming between material and mental, and sharing features of both), verbal (mental and relational) and existential (relational and material).

Modern syntactic theories are not simply, of course, updated versions of traditional ideas about syntax. In the following two chapters, we go on to see how different theories can be characterised in terms of the two major perspectives of syntagmatic and paradigmatic originating in the work of Saussure whose ideas were foundational for modern linguistics. These two principles, while not necessarily explicitly acknowledged in the construction of theories, are nevertheless fundamental in modelling syntactic patterning.

16 Modelling syntactic patterning (i): syntagmatic approaches

As has been mentioned several times before, the first great flowering of modern structural linguistics was in the field of phonology, and in many linguistic circles, particularly in the United States, it was seen as an obvious next step to apply the techniques so successfully worked out for phonology to the 'higher' levels of morphology and ultimately syntax. The epitome of this approach is represented by Zellig Harris's 1951 work *Methods in Structural Linguistics* which, as the title suggests, attempts to define a set of procedures which linguists can successively apply to the raw data of language. These procedures are based squarely on the notion of **distribution** (Harris 1951: 5):

> Descriptive linguistics, as the term has come to be used, is a particular field of inquiry which deals not with the whole of speech activities, but with the regularities in certain features of speech. These regularities are in the distributional relations among the features of speech in question, i.e. the occurrence of the features relatively to each other within utterances. It is of course possible to study various relations among parts or features of speech, e.g. similarities (or other relations) in sound or in meaning, or genetic relations in the history of the language. The main research of descriptive linguistics, and the only relation which will be accepted as relevant in the present survey, is the distribution or arrangement within the flow of speech of some parts or features relatively to others. The present survey is thus explicitly limited to questions of distribution, ie. of the freedom of occurrence of portions of an utterance relatively to each other.

The concept of distribution in Saussure's terms is concerned primarily with the **syntagmatic** aspects of language. There are several historical reasons for this emphasis on the syntagmatic in American linguistics at the time. The linguistic tradition to which Harris belonged took the work of Leonard Bloomfield, particularly his 1933 text *Language* as foundational, and is thus often known as

neo-Bloomfieldian linguistics. Its other common label, **descriptive** linguistics, used by Harris in the quotation above largely as a synonym for structural linguistics, suggests that linguistics was largely directed towards practical descriptive concerns. This school placed great stress on the formal aspects of language analysis, an approach to dealing with language that emphasised linguistic **form** over meaning in characterising the patterns of language, and made use of an array of explicit procedures in doing so, including segmentation, substitution and later transformation.

Such methods had proven their worth in the study of the sound aspects of language, and the crucial distinction later expressed by Martinet as one between such **distinctive** elements and the **significant** units of morphemes, words etc., was insufficiently understood at the time that it seemed quite plausible for both types of element to be treated in broadly the same way. As Harris explicitly states (Harris 1951: 6–7):

> The whole schedule of procedures…, which is designed to begin
> with the raw data of speech and end with a statement of grammatical
> structure, is essentially a twice-made application of two major steps:
> the setting up of elements, and the statement of the distribution of these
> elements relative to each other. First the distinct phonologic elements
> are determined…and the relations among them investigated…. Then
> the distinct morphologic elements are determined…and the relations
> among them investigated….There are various differences between
> the application of these steps in phonology and the application of the
> same steps in morphology. These derive from the differences in the
> material…and from the fact that when the operations are repeated for
> the morphology they are being carried out on material which has already
> been reduced to elements. Nevertheless, the two parallel schedules are
> essentially similar in the type and sequence of operations.

The methodology known as **immediate constituent** or IC analysis developed by American linguists in the immediately preceding period to analyse syntactic patterning was firmly based on distributionist principles. It was seen by its proponents as a more explicit and more rigorous alternative to the traditional dependency type of analysis derived from the analysis of the classical languages (see Chapter 6). IC analysis, under the label of **phrase structure** analysis, formed the starting point for Chomsky's analysis of syntax, as providing the basic structure for the subsequent permutations of morphemes that he dubbed transformations.

We have already in previous chapters gained some idea of the conception of syntactic structure in transformational generative grammar, and we will come back to a more recent version of this model later in this chapter. Firstly, however, we can take a look at another approach to syntactic description which *ideologically* arose in direct opposition to Chomsky, but which *analytically* preserved the basically syntagmatic orientation of this tradition: the theory known as **Functional Grammar** or FG, and associated with the work of the late Simon Dik and his colleagues in Holland and Belgium. For ease of presentation, the following description draws mainly on Anna Siewierska's (1991) introductory account.

From the organisation of the overall model, it is clear that Functional Grammar unproblematically regards **structure** as the fundamental relevant abstraction (Siewierska 1991: 10):

In FG each clause is characterized in terms of an abstract clause structure which is mapped onto actual linguistic expressions by a set of expression rules specifying form, order and intonation. This is shown schematically in (9).

> (9) underlying structure
>
> ↓
>
> expression rules
> ↓
> linguistic expressions

This notion of 'underlying structure' recalls Chomsky's concept of 'deep structure', with the difference that the 'underlying clause structures posited in FG are...essentially semantic' (Siewierska 1991: 10, summarising Dik 1989: 7). Furthermore, rather than being seen as characterising a basic set of relationships between syntactic elements which are then modified by various transformational processes, this structure in the Functional Grammar model is envisaged as multi-layered, with each layer representing a different kind of meaning (Siewierska 1991: 10–11):

Under the current version of FG (Dik 1989), the underlying structure of the clause is seen to consist of several nested *layers*, *levels* or *domains* (the three terms are used more or less interchangeably) of organization which correspond to the different communicative functions that a clause fulfils.... The major layers in question are:

> (10) clause   - 'speech act'
>   proposition   - 'possible fact'
>   predication   - 'state of affairs'

> predicate   - 'property/relation'
> term   - 'entity/entities'

Accordingly, the structure of the clause is built up as follows: a predicate is applied to an appropriate number of terms (referential expressions) which results in a predication designating a given state of affairs...; the predication is built into a proposition designating a 'propositional content', and finally the proposition is built into an illocutionary frame defining a given speech act....

In terms of formalisation, the theory abandons structure trees in favour of a notation drawn from logic (Siewierska 1991: 11):

> The underlying structure of the clause is depicted by means of a schema, inspired by predicate logic, which takes the form of a predicate frame flanked by a series of brackets and parentheses depicting various levels of structure. A simplified example is shown as (12)

(12) clause $(E_i:[X_i:\text{etc.}(X_i)\,)]\,(E_i))$
      proposition $(X_i:[(e_i:\text{etc.}(e_i))]\,(X_i))$
      predication $(e_i:[\text{pred.}_B(x_i)^n]\,(e_i))$
      term $(x_i:\text{pred.}_N(x_i))$

The main metaphors employed here to characterise structure are those of **nesting**, with different levels of structure seen as contained within or embedded inside each other, and **expansion**, whereby a basic structure is progressively specified in more and more detail (Siewierska 1991: 11–12):

> The derivation of fully fledged sentences is achieved by the gradual building up of structures rather than the mapping of one structure onto the other. Thus a predicate frame which is seen to contain only the predicate and its arguments...is successively expanded by specifications of, for example, aspect, tense, manner, time, place, reason, possibility, probability, evidentiality and illocutionary force into, first, an (extended) predication, then a proposition and finally a clause. All the information required for the surface realization of the clause is incorporated in its underlying structure.

A quite different set of metaphors for structure is evident in the latest version of generative grammar, known following Chomsky 1995 as the **Minimalist**

Program, and presented here in the version given in Radford's most recent introductory account (Radford 2004: 9, original emphasis):

> One component of a grammar is a **Lexicon**…and in forming a given sentence out of a set of words, we first have to take the relevant words out of the Lexicon. Our chosen words are then combined together by a series of syntactic computations in the **syntax** (i.e. the **syntactic/computational component** of the grammar), thereby forming a syntactic structure.

What we have here is clearly a **processual** model which identifies different levels of language linked by various processes of **combining** (later more technically termed **merging**), **mapping**, **interfacing**, and so on. This processual orientation can also be seen in the conception of syntactic structure, which is worth quoting at length (Radford 2004: 66–67, original emphasis):

> …the simplest way of forming a phrase is by merging two words together: for example, by **merging** the word *help* with the word *you*…, we form the phrase *help you*. The resulting phrase seems to have verb-like rather than noun-like properties…. So, it seems clear that the grammatical properties of a phrase like help you are determined by the verb *help*, and not by the pronoun *you*.
>
> Using the appropriate technical terminology, we can say that the verb help is the **head** of the phrase *help you*, and hence that *help you* is a **verb phrase**…. If we use the traditional labelled bracketing technique to represent the category of the overall verb phrase…and of its constituent words…, we can represent the structure of the resulting phrase as in (4) below:
>
> $[_{VP}[_V \text{ help}] [_{PRN} \text{ you}]]$
>
> An alternative (equivalent) way of representing the structure of phrases like *help you* is via a **labelled tree diagram** such as (5) below…:

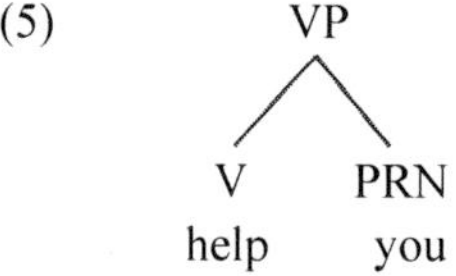

What the tree diagram in (5) tells us is that the overall phrase *help you* is a verb phrase (VP), and that its two **constituents** are the verb (V) *help* and the pronoun (PRN) *you*. The verb help is the **head** of the overall phrase…; we can say that conversely, the VP *help you* is the **projection** of the verb *help* – i.e. it is a larger expression formed by merging the verb *help* with another constituent of an appropriate kind.

Despite the familiar constituency model represented by the notational conventions of bracketing, tree diagrams, and category (class) labels, some of the terminology, e.g. 'head', draws by contrast on dependency notions, and these two models seem to operate side by side in the framework. What could be seen as a conflict between constituency and dependency modelling does, however, emerge when Radford, following Chomsky, critiques such representations of structure, applied below to the analysis of the clause *I will survive*, for not being sufficiently 'minimal' (Radford 2004: 94–95):

(66)

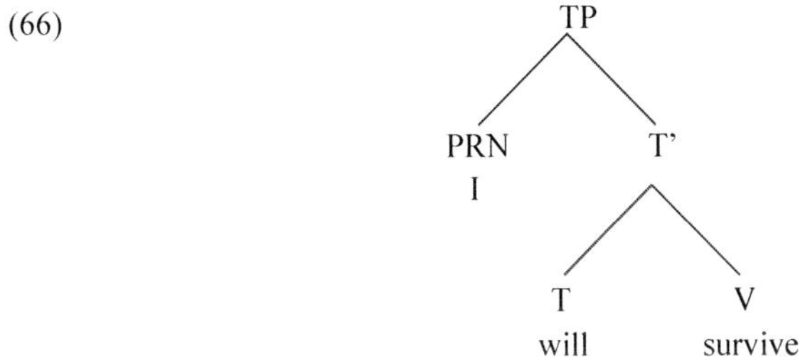

The bar notation used in (66) posits that there are three different levels of projection (i.e. types of expression): (i) heads (also called minimal projections) like the T/tense auxiliary *will*; (ii) intermediate projections like the T-bar *will survive*; and maximal projections like the TP *I will survive*. However…[w]hen the word *will* is taken out of the lexicon, its lexical entry specifies that it has a set of properties represented by the category label T in (66). But the tree in (66) tells us that when *will* is merged with its complement *survive*, the resulting string *will survive* belongs to the category T-bar – in other words, it is an intermediate projection of *will*. Likewise the tree in (66) also tells us that the larger string *I will survive* is a TP – in other words, it is the maximal projection of *will*. But this information about intermediate and maximal projections is not part of the lexical entry for *will*, and hence must be added in the course of the syntactic computation.

In effect, though this is not how the issue is represented here, this problem demonstrates a conflict between a clause-based constituency model and a word-based dependency model that goes right back to the so-called Lexical Hypothesis (Chomsky 1970), where rather than lexical items being 'fitted into' syntactic structures, syntactic structures are rather derived from the combination of syntactic features specified on individual lexical items. The constituency model defines the structure of the clause in terms of multiple constituent **relations** between elements labelled for category (class), such as we see in the tree diagrams above. In contrast, the dependency model, also taken up by Starosta in his Lexicase framework (Starosta 1988 – see Chapter 14), works by specifying **features** attached to individual lexical items which then determine their syntactic relations to other lexical items. As Radford concludes (Radford 2004: 95–96, original emphasis):

> Given the possibility…that categorial information…can be represented
> in terms of grammatical features (and hence subsumed within the set
> of features which characterise the idiosyncratic properties of individual
> words), a further possibility is that category labels like those in (68) can
> be entirely replaced by sets of features, so opening up the possibility of
> developing a theory of **bare phrase structure** – i.e. a theory in which
> there are no category labels in syntactic trees.…

(69)

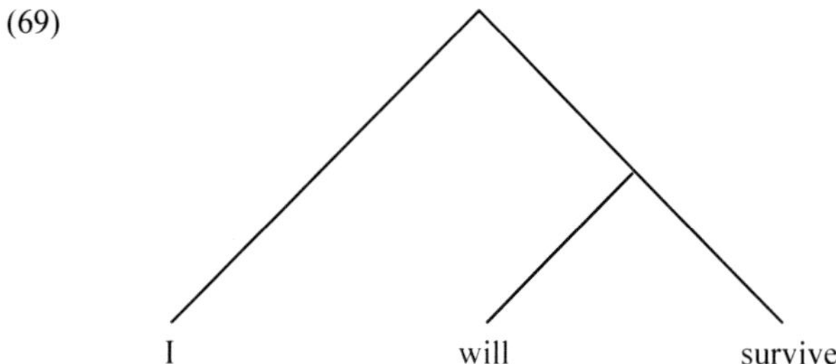

> An unlabelled tree diagram like (69) tells us that the constituents of (69)
> are *I*, *will*, *survive*, *will survive*, and *I will survive*. The lexical entries
> for the items *I*, *will*, and *survive* comprise sets of features which include
> information about their grammatical and selectional properties.… As
> before, the relative position of the relevant constituents within the overall
> structure tells us that *will* is a minimal projection (of itself), *will survive*
> is the intermediate projection of *will*, and *I will survive* is the maximal
> projection of *will*.…

This brief account of two syntagmatically oriented theories – out of a wide range of candidates – which are of course far more detailed than has been possible to show here, allow us to make the following generalisations:

- syntagmatic (structural) relations are unproblematically taken as the basic patterns to be accounted for

- paradigmatic (systemic) relations are normally not seen as relevant or essential

- both models depend heavily on constituency, represented either in terms of bracketing (Chomsky) or nesting (Dik)

- the main technique for elaborating the description is by adding further layers of structure

- both models use some type of process metaphor, with particular structures, or levels of structure leading to or derived from other structures or levels

As I noted above, 'syntax' tends to be taken as 'syntagmatic' by default, so this way of modelling syntactic patterning is usually not seen as requiring explicit justification. The case is very different with the other main type of modelling, the paradigmatic, where the modelling is normally justified both in terms of the internal nature of language, and in terms of its external contexts, as we will see in the following chapter.

17 Modelling syntactic patterning (ii): paradigmatic approaches

At the beginning of his *Methods in Structural Linguistics*, Harris sums up his approach to linguistic analysis, an approach which can be seen as, in effect, a formalisation of a long tradition dating back to Aristotle of 'building up' language from its minimal units. Such an approach, of course, assumes the existence of basic **elements** or 'atoms' of analysis, which can be distinguished from each other by similar analytical procedures going from small to large (Harris 1951: 1):

> This volume presents methods of research used in descriptive, or, more exactly, structural linguistics. It is thus a discussion of the operations which the linguist may carry out in the course of his investigations, rather than a theory of the structural analyses which result from these investigations. The research methods are arranged here in the form of the successive procedures of analyses imposed by the working linguist upon his data...

> Starting with the utterances which occur in a single language community at a single time, these procedures determine what may be regarded as identical in various parts of various utterances, and provide a method for identifying all the utterances as relatively few stated arrangements of relatively few stated elements....

Saussure, however, put forward a quite different conception of language, one which can be summed up in his dictum (Saussure 1916 / 1983: 107, my emphasis): 'language is characterized as a system based entirely on the *opposition* of its concrete units'. One of the consequences of this radical rethinking of language, one whose implications are still largely ignored in the practice of many linguistic theories, is the replacement of the notion of element with that of **relation** as the fundamental way of modelling language. The Danish linguist Louis Hjelmslev was one of the main scholars to take up the challenge of interpreting and extending Saussure's conception of language in his major theoretical work *Prolegomena to a Theory of Language* (Hjelmslev 1953 / 1961: 22):

…the important thing is not the division of an object into parts, but the conduct of the analysis so that it conforms to the mutual dependences between those parts, and permits us to give an adequate account of them.…both the object under examination and its parts have existence only by virtue of these dependences; the whole of the object under examination can be defined only by their sum total; and each of its parts can be defined only by the dependences joining it to other coordinated parts, to the whole, and to its parts of the next degree, and by the sum of the dependences that these parts of the next degree contract with each other. After we have recognized this, the 'objects' of naïve realism are, from our point of view, nothing but intersections of bundles of such dependences. That is to say, objects can be described only with their help and can be defined and grasped scientifically only in this way. The dependences, which naïve realism regards as secondary, presupposing the objects, become from this point of view primary, presupposed by their intersections.

Such a **relational** approach calls for quite a different approach to linguistic analysis from that assumed by the **elemental**, building-block approach adopted by linguists such as Harris. Hjelmslev contrasts the two in the following terms (Hjelmslev 1953 / 1961: 12–13):

In its typical form [previous] linguistics ascends, in its formation of concepts, from the individual sounds to the phonemes (classes of sounds), from the individual phonemes to the categories of phonemes, from the various individual meanings to the general or basic meanings, and from these to the categories of meanings. In linguistics, we usually call this method procedure inductive. It may be defined briefly as a progression from component to class, not from class to component. It is a synthetic, not an analytic, movement, a generalizing, not a specifying, method.…

If we start from the supposed empirical data, these very data will impose the opposite procedure. If the linguistic investigator is given anything… it is the as yet unanalyzed *text* in its undivided and absolute integrity. Our only possible procedure, if we wish to order a system to the process of that text, will be an analysis, in which the text is regarded as a class analyzed into components, and so on until the analysis is exhausted. This procedure may therefore be defined briefly as a progression from class to component, not from component to class, as an analytic and specifying, not a synthetic and generalizing, movement, as the opposite of induction in the sense established in linguistics.

Going from **component** to class, as in Harris's approach, implies a **syntagmatic** orientation, where elements are classified on the basis of their combinational relations to each other. Conversely, going from **class** to component, as in Hjelmslev's approach, implies a **paradigmatic** orientation, where the data is classified in terms of ever smaller sets of contrasts. The theoretical implications of a paradigmatic approach are clearly laid out in Hjelmslev's work, but given that it is self-characterised as 'prolegomena' i.e. 'introductory remarks', it concentrates more on general theory-building than language description. One of the earliest scholars to apply Hjelmslev's relational approach to actual language description was the American linguist Sydney Lamb, whose approach shows the clear influence of Hjelmslev (Lamb 1966: 3):

> A language may be regarded as a system of relationships. As such, it is
> not directly observable. The linguist can only observe the manifestations
> of linguistic structure, i.e. samples of speech and /or writing, and the
> situations in which they occur. From analyzing such data he must
> try to construct a representation of the system of relationships which
> underlies it. Such a representation may be taken as a description of
> (part of) a language. Thus the goal of a linguistic description should be
> a characterization, as precise as possible, of the structural relationships
> which underlie the linguistic data.

Lamb combines the relational conception of language with another notion adapted from Hjelmslev, i.e. that language analysis needs to distinguish different planes or **strata**, thus the name given to his theory, **stratificational** (Lamb 1966: 8, original emphasis)

> I consider a language to be a system of relationships. It may be analyzed
> into a series of subsystems, called STRATAL SYSTEMS, each of which has a
> syntax of tactics and certain other characteristic patterns of relationships.
> The elementary relationships of which these patterns are composed are of
> a very small number of types.

The types of relationship recognised *within* each stratum, known as **tactic**, are clearly distinguished from those obtaining *between* strata, which are known as **realizational** (Lamb 1966: 4–5, original emphasis):

> It is convenient to distinguish two general types of linguistic analysis,
> concerned with two kinds of linguistic patterning. They may be called
> TACTIC ANALYSIS and REALIZATIONAL ANALYSIS…this process of isolating

recurrent partial similarities is the basis of tactic analysis…. [and] leads the analyst to distribution classes and constructions which describe arrangements in the simplest possible terms….Analysis concerned with the parts of a stratal system other than its tactics may be called REALIZATIONAL ANALYSIS.

Lamb formalises his model in terms of a **network** of relations whose basic links are nodes specifying relations of basically two kinds, paradigmatic 'or' relations, and syntagmatic 'and' relations, combined with two other pairs of dichotomies, expressing 'upward' versus realising 'downward' relations, and 'ordered' versus 'unordered' choice relations (Lamb 1966: 8–10, original emphasis):

> Three fundamental dichotomies provide eight types of nodes, of which at least seven play a very important role in characterizing linguistic structures. These dichotomies are AND:OR, UPWARD:DOWNWARD, ORDERED:UNORDERED….
>
> The directions UPWARD and DOWNWARD are in keeping with the diagramming convention according to which meaning is at the 'top' and speech at the 'bottom' of linguistic structure. Thus UPWARD means 'towards meaning' while DOWNWARD means 'towards expression'….
>
> The OR is an exclusive OR; and the ordering with respect to the AND relationship is temporal ordering, while ordering with respect to an OR is an ordering of priority; i.e., that which comes first takes priority over the second if both are possible.

Lamb early on saw such a formalisation as providing an analogue for the cognitive processing of language, a three-decade-long line of research which culminated in his recent book *Networks of the Brain* (Lamb 1999), (Lamb 1966: 10 original emphasis):

> These relationships are perhaps most easily understood in terms of the dynamic interpretation which can be given to linguistic diagrams, which enables them to serve as models of the processes involved in producing and decoding speech. For the dynamic interpretation, IMPULSES are allowed to move along the lines, in either direction. Impulses move downward during the production process and upward during the decoding process.

A similar approach to the modelling of language, though seen more in terms of the social rather than cognitive context of language, was taken in the London tradition of linguistics, particularly in the work of its founder, J.R. Firth. Firth, like Hjelmslev, was unimpressed by what he saw as the over-simplified view of language exemplified by the phonological theory of many scholars in the United States (where this distributional approach to the description of sound was known as 'phonemics'), which as he saw it, was incapable of handling statements of meaning, always for Firth the main goal of linguistics (Firth 1957 / 1968: 192):

> Some linguists seem to regard phonemics as a kind of pure mathematics handling ultimate linguistic units....Such analysis does not go beyond the basic principle of linear and successive segmentation, and therefore proves inadequate for statements of meaning of such complexes as a sentence or paragraph, or any suitably abstracted longer piece of discourse. From the present point of view such meaningful complexes are described as a relational network of structures and systems at clearly distinguished but congruent levels....

For Firth both the paradigmatic aspect of language, which he dubbed **system**, and its syntagmatic aspect, **structure**, played an equally important role in linguistic description (Firth 1957 / 1968: 186, original emphasis):

> The first principle of phonological and grammatical analysis is to distinguish between *structure* and *system*.... The terms *structure* and *elements of structure* are not used to refer to a whole language or even to what may be called part of a language, but exclusively to categories abstracted from common word form or textual form. And quite similarly, *system*, *systems*, *terms* and *units* are restricted to a set or sets of paradigmatic relations between commutable units or terms which provide value for the elements of structure. Though structures are, so to speak, 'horizontal' while systems are 'vertical', neither are to be regarded as segments in any sense. Elements of structure, especially in grammatical relations, share a mutual expectancy in an *order* which is not merely a *sequence*.

Firth worked out his system-structure theory, as it has been called, mainly on phonology, in developing the theory known as prosodic phonology (Palmer 1970). It was one of Firth's students, M.A.K. Halliday who took up the challenge of applying it to syntax, first of all to Chinese (Halliday 1956), and then just over ten years later in the form of a detailed description of clause structure in English (Halliday 1967–68). By this stage, Halliday had gone beyond system-structure theory, where the paradigmatic and the syntagmatic were on an equal level, to give theoretical priority to the paradigmatic, just as Hjelmslev had done. This is how he explains the model in terms of a network of systems (Halliday 1967: 37):

> The formulation is in terms of a 'systemic' description…in which the grammar takes the form of a series of 'system networks', each such network representing the choices associated with a given constituent type: clause system network, nominal group (noun phrase) system network and so on. A system is a set of features one, and only one, of which must be selected if the entry condition to that system is satisfied; any selection of features formed from a given system network constitutes the 'systemic description' of a class of items. Such a 'selection expression' is then realized as a structure, the structural representation being fully derived from the systemic; each element of the structure is a point of entry into a further system network, so that constituency is based on the concept of 'rank', with minimal bracketing.

Unlike Lamb, who included both the paradigmatic ORS and the syntagmatic ANDS in the same network, Halliday separates his paradigmatic systems and his syntagmatic structures into two stages of description, with a particular set of options from a system, a **selection expression**, being realised by a combination of **structural functions**. For example, the main options in the clause system of Transitivity, which we looked at from a different point of view in Chapter 14, can be captured in the following network (Halliday 1967: 43):

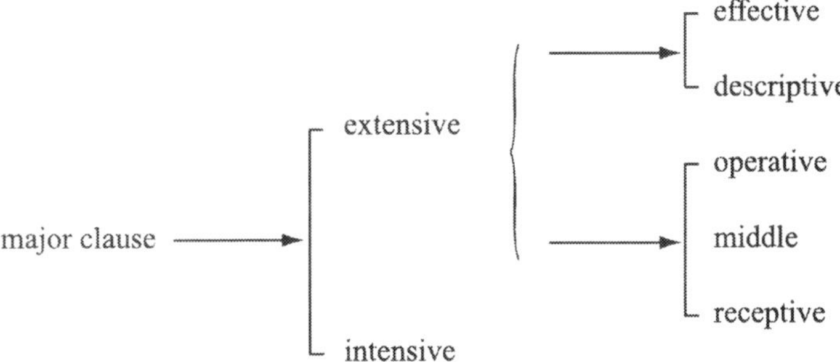

Without going into detail of the structural realisations of these options, the 'extensive' part of the paradigm can be briefly exemplified as follows (Halliday 1967: 43, 'S' represents 'Subject'):

	operative	middle	receptive
effective (directed action)	S actor *she washed the clothes*	S actor and goal *she washed*	S goal *the clothes were washed*
descriptive (non-directed action)	S initiator *he marched the prisoners*	S initiator and actor *the prisoners marched*	S actor *the prisoners were marched*

From this very sketchy account of these two paradigmatic approaches, the following conclusions can be drawn:

- unlike the 'default' syntagmatic modelling, paradigmatic modelling is 'novel' and therefore requires explicit justification

- although many – most? – syntagmatic approaches ignore the paradigmatic, all paradigmatic approaches feel obliged to incorporate the syntagmatic, presumably since linear structure must be accounted for somewhere in the model

- the two basic options are to treat paradigmatic and syntagmatic as equal, as in stratificational linguistics (Lamb) or system-structure theory (Firth); or to prioritise the paradigmatic, as in systemic functional theory (Halliday)

- although syntagmatic models tend to be purely language internal in terms of their justification of the modelling, paradigmatic models tend to find analogues outside language for their modelling, either in terms of cognitive processing (Lamb), or access to social resources of meaning making (Halliday).

18 'Doing syntax': aims and methodologies

After this brief survey of some of the 'consumer's choices' in the field, we should have a better idea of where to place the particular kind of 'syntax' that has been 'done' in the first two parts of this book. From the point of view put forward here, the notion of 'doing syntax' is actually rather a strange one, despite the fact that it reflects a common discourse in the field, with claims like 'I do syntax and a bit of semantics' or 'I do syntax and morphology' being not unusual self-descriptions for many linguists. However, it should be clear from the view of the nature and aims of syntactic analysis as sketched in the foreword and early chapters of Part 1, and demonstrated in actual analysis in the remainder of Part 1 and Part 2, that such remarks display a clear reversal of what I would argue should be the real priorities.

First of all, professionally speaking, I am far from convinced that the specialisation as currently constituted is in a sufficiently developed state to warrant any real confidence about what 'doing syntax' really should consist in. The sorts of questions dealt with in this book would no doubt be regarded by many syntacticians as falling not just within the purview of syntax 'proper', but as moving over, or perhaps even trespassing on, the concerns of semantics, morphology and occasionally phonology. And as I have already pointed out, the whole of Part 1 of this book deals with issues normally completely ignored by accounts of syntax, despite the clear relevance of the concerns of glossing and parsing for the recognition of syntactic categories and functions.

Secondly, the idea that one can or should 'do syntax', as some sort of abstract process removed from the context and demands of a particular description, seem to me to be blatantly putting the theoretical cart before the descriptive horse. This reversal of priorities has unfortunately been only too characteristic of much linguistics, particularly formal syntax, over the last fifty years. As I have argued theoretically, and demonstrated in practice throughout this book, the basis data of linguistic and therefore syntactic analysis is **text** or **texts**, in that handy grammatical ambiguity of English that allows us to conceptualise either the ongoing unfolding of discourse (*text*), or a more or less complete stretch of language (*a text*). From either point of view, text is the living stuff of human interaction, and any process of removing it from the immediate context of that interaction, in order to render it amenable to analysis, must be recognised as a static simplexification of a phenomenon whose dynamic richness ultimately eludes *all* analysis.

There is a certain humility in the face of linguistic, as of any phenomenal reality, a necessary respect for the irreducible complexity of linguistic data, which has been largely conspicuous by its absence from much syntactic theorising and model-building over the last half century. When Chomsky dismissed the work of his immediate predecessors in the United States as 'taxonomic' (Chomsky 1965: 54) i.e. concerned merely with the assemblage and cataloguing of facts, and 'data-driven' (Chomsky 1965: 15), i.e. ignoring the presumably more significant challenge of theory construction, he was contemptuously turning his back on the very empirical basis of the discipline. The greatest challenge in syntactic description, as in any descriptive project in the semiotic sciences, lies not in constructing the 'perfect theory', as though there *could* be any perfection in theory without reference to application, but in the messy struggle to apply theoretical tools, always at the same time too sharp and too blunt, to the fluid 'mush' of linguistic facts, facts which are, as Saussure pointed out, in a very real sense created by the theory.

In this final chapter, I would like to show how this struggle between theoretical consistency and descriptive adequacy has been played out through a particular case study: my own attempt to develop a text-based description of the grammar of Mandarin. With all necessary apologies for navel-gazing, it seems to me that only by having access to the actual process of decision-making – as well as I can recreate it – something which linguists and indeed most scientists would not normally consider worthy of mention, can we gain a real sense of what is involved in developing a description of a language.

I referred above to a 'handy grammatical ambiguity' in the use of the word *text* in English to refer either to an ongoing process or a delimited object, both necessary concepts for linguistic analysis. A far better-known ambiguity routinely called upon in linguistics is that between 'grammar' as the inherent patterning of a language (in this usage often including phonology and morphology + syntax), and 'grammar' as the description put forward to account for that phenomenon. Such an ambiguity is widespread in English, where the same word, for example 'psychology' is used to cover both the **phenomenon** under examination, which might more accurately be characterised as the 'human psyche', and the theoretical **account** of that phenomenon. What is referred to by Chomsky as a 'systematic ambiguity' between these two senses of the word 'grammar' (Chomsky 1965: 152) is utilised by Chomsky and other linguists following him in a quite deliberate way.

But the fact than such an ambiguity is widespread does not mean it should be left untheorised or uncritiqued. Chomsky draws attention to this problem largely, it seems, so that he can dismiss it as being of any real significance; but in so doing he and a whole generation of generative grammarians signally fail to grapple with the crucial issue of what exactly *is* the relationship between the objective phenomenon and its theoretical modelling. In fact, by ignoring the necessary gap between the two, generative grammarians may feel themselves licenced to concentrate on theory-building without being required to rigorously measure up their theories against the data they are ultimately supposed to be accounting for.

So in the following account of one particular struggle to reconcile linguistic theory and language facts, I will try to show that the relationship between theory and description is much more of a two-way street, a process of mutual influence, that most workers in the field are generally willing to admit. Since talk of 'reconciling' facts and theory seems to assume the independence of these two concepts, we must recall again Saussure's dictum that in linguistics the object of study, the 'facts', are *not* given in advance, but rather created, in the sense of demarcated, distinguished and classified, by the theory. Of course I am not denying the objective existence of the phenomenon Saussure referred to as *langage*, which we might translate into English in a dynamic, processual way as **languaging**, but rather pointing out that in order to have access to that phenomenon, we must 'reduce' it to a network of interconnected facts. And as Goethe had already pointed out a century before Saussure: *alles Faktische schon Theorie ist* – 'everything factual is already (part of) a theory' (significantly used by Firth as an epigraph to his summary account of his own theoretical framework (1957 / 1968)).

The case of Chinese syntax provides an interesting challenge for description, both in terms of accounting for the facts and in developing theories to explain them, since the bulk of the 'facts' and the 'theories' were only 'created' just over a hundred years ago. For reasons to do with the isolating nature of Chinese grammar, and the concentration of traditional linguistic scholarship on interpreting the features of the written graphs or characters, the area of study known as *xiaoxue*, often translated 'philology', contained no concept analogous to 'grammar' or 'syntax'. There was a recognition of the different kinds of significant elements in the language, again focusing on the classification of characters, which were divided into two large sets: either 'full', representing lexical or content words, and 'empty', representing grammatical or functional words. Within full words, a further distinction was also drawn between 'living' words, roughly 'verbs', and 'dead' words, 'nouns'. Since classical Chinese syntax made no use of inflection, with structures that were for the most part very simple and words able to change their syntactic function according to context, a word-based account of syntactic patterns which could be understood as a concatenation of lexical items, 'helped' out by the occasional grammatical item, worked very well for the needs of literacy and textual exegesis.

When syntactic analysis was introduced to China in the late 19th century, for what were in fact political reasons, as part of a reform of the country's education system in order to resist the incursions of the Western powers (see McDonald 2002), it was as a component of a foreign concept of 'grammar' – originally rendered phonetically as *gelangma*, and then calqued as *wenfa* 'rules of writing' or later *yufa* 'rules of language' – which was closely based on the model of Latin grammar. Since, then the Chinese scholarly tradition of *yufaxue* 'grammatical studies' – which following Halliday (1996: 2) and in order to avoid any ambiguity, systematic or not, we may call **grammatics** – has gone through successive phases of borrowing terms and concepts from the European tradition, and modifying or even rejecting those same terms as not suited to the 'facts' of Chinese. This pull between adoption and adaptation continues to characterise the field today, and has certainly been a live issue in my own work on Chinese.

My own work on Chinese grammar has also been characterised by a kind of cross-cultural movement, starting with my BA (Hons) thesis at the University of Sydney, undertaken very much within European traditions of the description of Chinese; continuing in my MA thesis at Peking University, where I was for the first time introduced on a large scale to the traditions of Chinese linguistics, discovered how different those traditions were to those of European language scholarship, particularly in the area I was working on, and attempted to combine insights from both traditions; and then in my PhD thesis at Macquarie University where I extended the study of Chinese grammar into its discourse contexts in order to come up with what I dubbed a 'text-sensitive' description. By good luck, and a certain amount of good management, most of that work has been published, at least in part, which means that the results of the process I will be describing are already on public record, as it were, and can be consulted to flesh out the necessarily abbreviated account I will be giving here.

My research into Chinese grammar was initiated in the final year of my undergraduate studies at the University of Sydney, where my supervisor Prof. Michael Halliday suggested I take on the challenge of describing within a systemic-functional framework one of the 'hard nuts' of Chinese grammar: a structure, made up of two verb-like elements, which is commonly known in English as a 'resultative verb compound'. The rider 'in English' is particularly necessary in this case, since in the Chinese language literature such structures tend to be not only named but conceptualised quite differently. One of the earliest Chinese accounts of these combinations, Wang 1944, gives examples which include the following (glossing and translation added by myself: verb combinations in bold):

(1) Zhè yòu .shi shéi .de zhǐjiǎ **guā- pò** .le?
this again be who SUB fingernail scratch damaged ASP:compl.
'Whose fingernail was it that **scratched** this again?'

(2) Kěqiao nà rì .shi wǒ **ná- qù** .de.
lucky that day be I hold go SUB
'Luckily that day it was I who **took** (it) **away**.'

These clauses exemplify the two most commonly recognised subtypes of this class of verb combinations: the **resultative**, as in (1), where we have an action *gua* 'scratch' and its resulting state *po* 'damaged, broken'; and the **directional**, as in (2) where we have a potential motion, here *na* 'hold (in hands), and a direction *qu* 'go – away from speaker'. In order to appreciate the meaning of such combinations, it needs to be understood that in Chinese the use of a verb indicates an attempt – *gua* thus means 'apply force with a sharp object' – without assuming the success of that attempt: it is therefore necessary to add an extra element in order to explicitly indicate the result (see Halliday & McDonald 2004). While the outlines of this class and its two main sub-classes are fairly clear, most accounts are not able to say much about the main descriptive challenge in accounting for this class: viz., to be able to predict which first elements, which we can call simply **verbs**, can combine with which second elements, **postverbs**. Such a descriptive challenge requires a mixture of syntactic and lexical analysis, a characteristic which has no doubt contributed to their resistance to comprehensive description.

The three stages in my exploration of this phenomenon could be summarised in point form as follows:

1   BA Honours thesis: *Completive verb compounds in modern Chinese* (revised version published as McDonald 1994)

Challenge: how to predict the combination of verbs and postverbs.

Literature: European language tradition – Halliday 1956, Cartier 1972, Thompson 1973.

Problems:

- structural (colligational) analysis only goes a short way;

- what is needed to capture patterning is an ordered list of collocations;

- SFL theory predicts that collocational categories should be more delicate instances of colligational categories (cf Hasan 1987 'grammarian's dream'), i.e. fit into process types established structurally;

- however, sets given by collocational analysis cut across process types;

- postverb not part of transitivity structure as such, rarely has an effect on it.

Solution: recognise two relevant systems: transitivity, realised by clause structure, and phase; realised by verbal group structure.

Conclusion: need to modify original descriptive categories in course of more detailed description.

2   MA thesis: *The 'complement' in Chinese grammar: a functional reinterpretation* (published in part as McDonald 1996)

Challenge: how to reconcile differing descriptions (and delimitations) of this class – 'verb-complement construction' (Chinese) vs 'resultative verb compound' (English).

Literature: European language tradition – as in (1); Chinese language tradition – Wang 1944, Zhou 1957, Lu 1964, Liu et al. 1983.

Problem: how to make sense of the differing range of forms subsumed under the 'complement' label.

Solutions:

- make a distinction between an experiential type (completive), expressed through a verbal group compound, and a textual type, which tends to take final position in the clause (carrier of New information);

- multifunctional approach helps to reconcile English-language and Chinese-language tradition by providing a principled basis for their differing conclusions;

- description of one part of the grammar inevitably involves other parts as well.

Conclusion: taking different descriptive traditions seriously, looking for areas of disagreement between them as pointers to significant insights.

3   PhD thesis: *Clause and verbal group systems in Chinese: a text-based, functional approach* (published in part as McDonald 2004)

Challenge: account for all verbal elements in the clause.

Literature: Halliday 1956, Simons 1958, Li 1990.

Solutions:

- sort out the domain of clause structures – delimitation of clause boundaries – as well as verbal group boundaries;

- multifunctional approach leads to recognition of number of different structures;

- all verbs can be seen as forming a logical structure, like a serial verb construction, which can then be interpreted in different ways according to other functions;

- verbal group as expansion of clause only relevant experientially, in terms of various compound and embedded structures;

- interpersonally, modal verbs better understood as part of mood structure of the clause;

- textually, some relational verbs used to give special information status to particular elements of clause.

Conclusions: benefit of 'playing around' with descriptive categories, examining same phenomenon from numbers of points of view, in order to reach a deeper more nuanced understanding.

These three stages in my research into verb systems and structures in Chinese also show an increasing awareness of meta-theoretical complexity. In the first project, the main focus was on working within systemic functional theory, and drawing on all the resources of that theory to model the phenomenon under examination, though always remaining aware of areas in which there seemed to be a mismatch between theory and data. The second project was explicitly meta-theoretical, as signalled by the quotation marks round 'complement' in the title, and sought to reconcile the data with two different traditions of description, the European language one (English & French) and the Chinese language one. Here the main focus was on using this cross-theoretical comparison to provide an integrated way of accounting for patterns in the data. Finally, the third project, which was part of a broader attempt to develop a 'text-sensitive' grammar of Chinese, deliberately used systemic functional theory as a heuristic, trying out number of different ways of accounting for the data, and revealing the benefit of drawing on different perspectives.

This, again very sketchy, account of a particular ongoing project of syntactic description should hopefully give some idea of the complexity of the process.

As argued in the Briefing, not only do syntacticians need to be multilingual in different languages, they need to be multi-*meta*lingual in different syntactic theories, in order to have a genuinely contextualised understanding of the fundamentally contingent nature of both descriptions and theories.

Having thus 'completed the circle' between theory and description, we can now reflect on what we have learned. In Part 1 of this book we took a close look at the basic data of syntactic analysis, texts, and what needed to be done to them before they could be analysed syntactically. In Part 2, we went on to examine a number of different texts in terms of particular syntactic phenomena and the sorts of descriptive categories often used to account for them. In Part 3, we moved away from both data and description in order to examine some of the different theoretical themes that show up in different syntactic frameworks, and in terms of which analyses like those given in Parts 1 and 2 make sense.

The respective focuses of each part of this book – data, description, theory – represent distinctions that are vital to make, but are at the same time inextricably interrelated. As I have continually pointed out, every descriptive decision, from the earliest choices of transcription and glossing, is made in terms of a particular theoretical framework. For example, the process of romanising Chinese, i.e. representing it in terms of the orthographic conventions of the Roman alphabet, assumes – and forces – a recognition of word boundaries which Chinese character orthography allows one to leave undecided. At the other end of the spectrum, no theory develops in isolation from the data on which it is worked out: for example, the distinction between syntax and morphology that looms so large in the Western tradition because of the nature of the Greek and Latin languages would never even have arisen in a language like Chinese; while conversely that between 'full' (lexical) and 'empty' (grammatical) words in the Chinese tradition, would never have arisen in Greek linguistics, since the equivalent of the 'empty words' of Chinese were mostly expressed in Greek through inflectional affixes which were not recognised as separate elements.

So at this point, it would be useful to take a look at the relationship of theory, so often the inordinate focus of discussions on syntax, with data on the one hand, and with description on the other.

Theory and data

As was noted in the Foreword, the explosion of syntactic theorising from the 1960s was in some quarters accompanied by a move away from a data-oriented approach towards a theory-oriented one. This supposed dichotomy between data and theory, like most such dichotomies which are more usefully viewed as complementarities, is an unnecessary and misleading one. From one point of view, as Saussure pointed out, the data presents itself to the analyst as a bewilderingly multifarious phenomenon and it is only our particular point of view, our theory, however implicit, which transforms that data into facts that can be delimited and categorised.

For instance, all of the text data in this book could in fact have been approached, not in terms of their significant patterning as **wordings** but rather in terms of their distinctive patterning as **sounds**. If we had been concerned solely with the sound patterning of these texts, the types of processing or parsing would have been quite different (hinted at briefly in the examination of the Chinese text in Chapter 4); as would have been the sorts of analysis, in terms of phonological structures, intonation prosodies and the like. There is nothing in the data itself that forces us to analyse it *either* as sound *or* as wording: rather, the data is open to any number of different kinds of processing and analysis, including viewing the texts in terms of their overall structure as texts, or as evidence of cognitive processing, or as artefacts of their social context, or as a reflection of the genetic potential of the human brain, or for a host of other purposes.

So in adopting any particular viewpoint, we need to be very clear about what we are including and what we are leaving out. I have argued throughout this book that the study of syntax, as currently constituted, in fact leaves out too much that can insightfully be brought under the general heading of significant patterning in language. Historically this stems from a tradition which started off treating the significant elements of language in the same way as its distinctive elements – in the work of Zellig Harris as a heuristic strategy, but by his student Noam Chomsky as a matter of principle: that is, without reference to meaning.

In one sense, then, it is true to say that the theory, the point of view, takes priority, since it is the theory which creates the object of study. But in another sense, if we think of any theory as a kind of model of the phenomenon which it seeks to account for, the theory is only a faint adumbration of the data in all its richness and complexity. As Pike points out (see below), a model, in order to be of any use, must be a simplification of the original. In order to grasp the complexity of reality, we need to reduce it to an outline, an outline which takes its cues from the particular point of view adopted. Thus it is absolutely crucial not to blur the distinction between the original phenomenon, the **language**, and the derived **metalanguage**. In this connection, Firth's call for a continual 'renewal of connection' between theory and data is a very salutary one.

Theory and description

A theory of language has a special status, as has often been pointed out (for example, Firth's definition of linguistics as 'language turned back on itself'), in that it is cast in the same 'stuff' which it is describing: that is, language. In our discussion of glossing in Chapter 2, we already talked of the simplification and distortion that inevitably takes place when we go from one language to another. But there is an equally inevitable simplification and distortion involved in going from the language being described to the metalanguage being used to describe it. In a sense, the only way to fully 'capture' a language analytically would be to *use* it, taking advantage of all the lexical and grammatical relations of its own internally created network in its external contexts of use. So when we freeze the dynamic functioning of a language in context in order to focus on a particular aspect of it, we are making use of only a small part of that network.

But we cannot *not* model the phenomenon we are examining, we cannot do without a metalanguage, however distorting: otherwise, we are unable to identify recurring patterns in the data, and derive useful generalisations from these patterns which will aid us in whatever context of application our description is designed for. So we need to strongly reject the common misconception, even among some linguists, that description can be done *without* theory. A term such as 'pre-theoretical', despite belonging to a common discourse in the field, is on the face of it totally meaningless. What people tend to mean by this is 'not aligned to any particular theory in particular', ignoring that their own 'intuitive' understanding of language (another common but highly misleading notion in this context) has already been shaped by a whole range of theoretical conceptions, whether explicit or not, about what sort of thing language is; and ignoring the fact that there are huge discrepancies among different linguistic schools and traditions on just this very 'intuitive' notion. (For example, the suggested rendering above of Saussure's *langage* as 'languaging' may hint that what we should be talking about here should perhaps not be thought of as a *thing* at all, but rather a *process*.)

Two well-known linguists, highly experienced 'describers' if nothing else, who have also lived through and themselves contributed significantly to the huge proliferation of syntactic theorising over the last fifty years, provide their own insights into this relationship between theory and description.

Pike addresses the question of why we need theories in an extended discussion worth quoting at length (Pike 1982: 5–7, original emphasis):

A theory is like a window.

The intellect, in order to get outside itself and to interpret the sense data impinging on the body, needs in advance some kind of idea of the way in which the data may turn out to be organised.

A theory in this sense is *directional*...[different theories] lead to partial insight into one's surroundings, but in different directions...If we look at the same data through different theories, we may see different aspects of a pattern.

A theory must be *simpler* than reality if it is to be helpful. It attempts to strip away from attention those items which are not important to the observer *at the moment*....

Any theory may have a weakness at the point of its greatest strength. Since a theory looks in a particular direction...it may tell us nothing about data or characteristics of reality which must be seen from some other vantage point. A scientific theory is good only if it *leaves out wisely* those materials which are relevant to other questions but not to those immediately being answered....

A good window is like a smooth, clean window. A bad theory...[is like a] dirty window [which] allows us to see something, even though what one sees may be blurred. To have a poor theory is better than having no theory at all.

Halliday takes up the question of the relationship between the categories of a general theory and the categories of a particular description (Halliday 1993: 4–5):

Theoretical categories are general to all languages: they have evolved in the construction of a general linguistic theory. They are constantly being refined and developed as we come to understand more about language; but they are not subject to direct verification. In contrast, descriptive categories are language-specific: they have evolved in the description of particular languages and can be defined in such a way as to make them subject to verification. What is usually called a 'universal category' is not a theoretical category as such but rather a descriptive category that is said to be present in every language.

Much of the theorising about Universal Grammar or the like falls into this trap of over-generalising descriptive categories from particular languages or language families to human language in general. Such categories as 'subject', whose utility for the description of Chinese at least I cast some doubts on in Chapter 7, are commonly given some sort of spurious existence as 'ideal forms' whose realisation in specific languages is only partial or distorted (see discussion in Hasan & Fries 1995). The current approach recommends what Firth characterised as an *ad hoc* approach to both theoretical and descriptive categories (1957 / 1968: 190), recognising that all analytical categories are 'created' in order to capture some regularity in linguistic patterning, and it is the patterning itself, rather than the category, to which any sort of 'reality' should be attributed.

Debriefing

So at the end of the voyage of 'exploration' promised at the beginning of this book, what have we learned about 'doing syntax', and what useful lessons can we draw for future explorations? At this point, I am obliged to drop the 'inclusive' *we* employed throughout this book to represent author and readers jointly exploring questions of mutual interest, and revert to the bald *I* of personal, but I hope informed, opinion. My conclusions here are obviously tentative, but are based on three decades of exposure to 'syntax' in the form of learning foreign languages, two decades of study and thinking in the areas of linguistic theory and language description, and over a decade of attempting to communicate my understanding of the topic to students.

My three main conclusions, which I briefly discuss below, relate to our three main focuses of data, description, and theory respectively, and can be expressed in slogan form as follows:

data:	Respect the text
description:	Take meaning as central
theory:	Only contextualise

'Respect the text'

The basic data of syntactic analysis, text, is one of the most complex phenomena in the universe, involving as it does the sound-producing and sound-perceiving physiology of the human body, the meaning-creating and meaning-recognising faculties of human cognition, and the interactional abilities of humans as social beings. Syntax in some sense sits at the very core of these human abilities, since it is the meanings created by syntactic patterns that motivate the communicative exchange of energy (cf Halliday 2005), meanings which both depend on and contribute to human cognitive and social functions.

The complexity of most contemporary syntactic theories, however, is a complexity of theoretical constructs, one which tends to ignore or sideline the far greater inherent complexity of the data. As shown in Chapter 2 in relation to glossing, and in Chapters 4 and 5 in relation to transcription and delimitation of syntactic units, the work of describing this complexity begins right from the processing of the text, and all sorts of theoretical choices – albeit often implicit ones – are made at this stage, with major implications for subsequent analysis. Contrary to most syntactic practice, such analytical constructs as units (word, group / phrase, clause, etc.), class and function categories, constituent bracketing, etc., are *not* given in advance, but need to be worked out anew for each language, with a clear understanding of the purposes for which such constructs are posited, and of their nature *as* constructs, in Firth's terms, *ad hoc* concepts designed for specific purposes, without any claims for universality.

Given the nature of modelling – by which I include both theoretical frameworks and descriptions developed within those frameworks – as a process of **simplification** of the original data, we as analysts always need to remain aware of what I referred to earlier as the 'irreducible complexity' of the data, and acknowledge that our efforts to represent the patterns in the data are *representations* that will always fall short of the richness of the original *presentation* that is language use in context. Respecting the text, to again repeat an earlier formulation, thus implies a 'modesty' in the face of language, an awareness of the primacy of linguistic data, and of the importance of Firth's notion of 'renewal of connection' between theory and data.

'Take meaning as central'

Every syntactic theory, of whatever stripe, acknowledges that the study of syntax in ultimately concerned with the meaningful elements of language – of its significant as opposed to distinctive units, in Martinet's terms. But with the rise of the tradition epitomised by the work of Zellig Harris in the 1940s, and continued by his student Noam Chomsky from the 1950s, meaning became increasingly placed outside the purview of syntactic theory and description, firstly as a heuristic *reductio ad absurdum* – something that to a certain extent proved very fruitful – but then as a principled exclusion which, in my opinion, has led to a pathological narrowing of theoretical concerns.

With the advent of Chomskyan 'formal syntax', and its subsequent move to the mainstream of the discipline, at least in the sense of setting the baseline for syntactic study which one must either agree with or react against, other syntactic traditions which retained meaning as one of the key phenomena to be accounted for in syntactic description found themselves grouped, whether or not in direct reaction to Chomsky's work, under the label of 'functional syntax', or more commonly in this context, 'functional grammar'. This formal-functional split is another complementarity in the study of language that tends to be misconstrued as a dichotomy.

All syntactic study is by definition *formal*, since in order for it to treat syntax at all it is obliged to deal with linguistic *form*. However, linguistic form is not, in a common architectural metaphor, simply the structural beams and joists that hold up the semantic roof of language, not even in the stronger version of that metaphor where particular formal structures are specially adapted to their own particular function in 'supporting' meanings. Syntactic form, like all linguistic form, exists ultimately only for the expression of meaning, and without meaning is simply a jumble of uninterpretable sounds.

In a fairly restricted sense, all syntactic study is likewise *functional*, in that every theory is concerned with modelling the ways syntactic units pattern that allow them to function in the expression of meanings. But many formal theories deny a necessary role to meaning in determining the form of this patterning, as if someone were to construct a building simply on physical and engineering principles of what would stand up, without any thought of the purposes for which the building might be used. Even some functional theories in effect deny the meaningfulness of syntactic patterning, looking for meaning elsewhere in the cognitive correlates or discourse contexts of syntactic forms, like a building that accidentally turns out to be useful for particular purposes, even though it was not designed with them in mind.

What I am arguing here, to put my claim in the strongest possible form, is that any theory of syntax which does not put meaning at the very centre of syntactic theorising and description, as a *sine qua non* of 'doing syntax', is in fact both theoretically incoherent and descriptively barren. The idea that 'syntax' can be 'done' *without* reference to meaning, though it still seems to me somewhat paradoxical, is possible to understand from the perspective of the historical development in the 1940s and 1950s of the 'no-meaning' strategy in linguistic analysis, given its success in the study of sound patterning, and what was seen at the time as the intractable nature of the study of meaning. But with our currently much more sophisticated theories of meaning (see Halliday 1986 and Lamb 1999 for two complementary perspectives on dealing with meaning in a syntactic context), there is no need to keep on carrying the historical baggage of that tradition, baggage which is seriously impeding our understanding of syntactic patterning.

The epitome of this 'purely' formal approach to syntax, what is now generically referred to as 'generative grammar', has gone through many developments since Chomsky's first work in the 1950s, and many of the once basic tenets of the theory put forward in *Syntactic Structures* have been discarded, or modified almost out of recognition. But one theoretical step that has never been reconsidered is that by which meaning was excluded from the study of syntax proper, and it is that misstep, barely and badly justified from the beginning as shown in Chapter 13, which continues to vitiate the study of syntax within this paradigm. Together with the associated bias *towards* theory construction and *against* accountability to the data, the exclusion of meaning has ensured that the only genuine progress possible in generative grammar is one of increasing theoretical sophistication. But this very sophistication, and the impressive battery of results built up within the theory, mask the bare fact that, at its very best, all the theory can hope to account for is **pattern recognition**, as long as it continues to avoid the challenge of developing a theoretically informed understanding of the ultimate purpose of those patterns, to express meanings.

One of the key rhetorical strategies of generative grammar since its inception has been its claim to be 'scientific', and the associated dismissal of most other theories of language, apart from some carefully selected and reinterpreted 'predecessors', as failing to meet that demanding standard. But in terms of the 'scientific results' we should be able to expect, both in terms of a detailed understanding of the range of linguistic phenomena in descriptions of individual languages, and more general insights into nature of language, generative linguistics still provides only a promissory note. When Chomsky describes the most recently outmoded version of generative grammar, the Principles and Parameters approach, as 'a radical break from the rich tradition of thousands of years of linguistic inquiry' which 'maintains that the basic ideas of [that] tradition, incorporated without great change in early generative grammar, are misguided in principle' (Chomsky 1995: 5); and then goes on in almost the next breath to argue for 'a picture of language that differs considerably from even its immediate precedecessors' (Chomsky 1995: 10), what he has dubbed the Minimalist Program, a sceptical outsider could be forgiven for wondering whether the whole purpose of the theory has not now become simply a need to constantly renew itself.

In his evaluation of the philosophical underpinnings of generative grammar, Hockett remarked that most of the theory's problems seemed to have been created by the theory itself (Hockett 1987: 84); and four decades later, it seems to me that most of its 'progress' is also theory-created. We may now have more elegant and economical solutions to questions raised in the course of theory-building within the generative tradition, but as long as the study of meaning in syntax continues to be marginalised, as long as individual languages are seen more as convenient – and expendable – cannon fodder for defending theoretical positions, generative grammar, in my opinion, will continue to fail the basic test of any syntactic theory: to provide insights into the complex ways in which linguistic forms express meanings.

'Only contextualise'

In *Syntactic Structures*, Chomsky raised the possibility of providing an 'evaluation procedure' (1957: 51) for 'grammars' – in the sense of 'theories of language' – which would enable the analyst to judge the relative success of different theoretical proposals for what he defined as the central goal of any theory of language: providing an explicit and rigorous account of syntactic patterning. Almost half a century on, we seem no closer to that elusive goal, and have no clearer idea of how to apply the vague criteria of simplicity, economy, and so on, that Chomsky put forward then and continues to call on.

I hope that the brief trawl through some of the prominent 'themes' in syntactic theorising given in Part 3 of this book has shown that such a goal is not only elusive but illusory. Given the fundamental and far-reaching differences among different theories of language revealed in even this brief sketch, there is no way we could ever come up with any such set of criteria that could be independently justified. This is not simply the result of the empirical challenge of evaluating the complexity of substantive issues involved, but stems from the very contingent nature of theory itself.

It is this 'contingency' that I have summed up in my final slogan – with apologies to E.M. Forster – 'only contextualise'. Like the phenomenon of language which it models, no linguistic theory can be understood in isolation from its **contexts**: in the case of linguistic theories, their differing historical backgrounds and applicational goals. All the theories described in this book, as well as the many I have not been able to cover, are defined, in the sense of both 'characterised' and 'limited', by where they came from and what they are aimed at. In Halliday's instrumental conception of theory (Halliday 1985 / 1994: xxix), a theory is a 'means of action', a tool designed for a specific range of purposes, and as such there are likely to be just as many things it *cannot* do as it *can*.

So how does the 'student' of syntax, in the old-fashioned sense of that term, deal with the bewildering variety of syntactic theories on offer? The usual strategy, among the minority of linguists who seem at all interested in looking across different theories, is to rhetorically manoeuvre the 'opposing' party onto your own theoretical turf, where not surprisingly, you manage to successfully dispose of the 'wrong' theory as failing to measure up to the criteria you have chosen to judge it by, criteria which may bear very little relation to the stated aims of the theory itself (e.g. Newmeyer 1998). It may indeed seem to some readers, that this is a good description of what I myself did in the previous section, in arguing that the generative tradition is 'theoretically incoherent' in excluding meaning from the core of its model of syntax. In fact, I would claim that it is precisely this kind of criticism, in contrast to the Newmeyerian polemical kind, which holds the key to how the student of syntax should make the decision about what sort of theory he or she will find useful to work with.

There are two ways in which one may evaluate any theory, not limiting ourselves here to syntactic theories in particular: by how well it fulfils its own claims about what it sets out to do; and by how well it measures up to the challenge of accounting for the phenomenon it is modelling. Both types of evaluation are crucial: on the one hand, because every different theory makes different claims about the nature of the phenomenon, and thus different predictions about what should be found by an analysis of that phenomenon; and on the other, because although no *account* of a phenomenon can be 'pretheoretical', or rather non-theoretical, the *phenomenon* itself does exist outside any theoretical claim about it. To put the matter in a nutshell, although different linguists do *not* agree on the exact nature of 'language', they all agree that there *is* something we could call 'languaging' that does go on, and which all their theories are attempting to account for.

Thus my advice to the student of syntax – only contextualise: decide which tradition seems to suit your own ideas about what language and syntax is, and which framework will be useful for the sort of purposes for which you intend to engage with syntax. To modify my earlier image somewhat, any theory provides a certain path through the 'trackless forest' of syntactic phenomena, and whatever path you choose to take is bound to provide opportunities for observing and learning much along the way. And as workers on and with syntax, we can certainly distinguish between the theoretical claims of a particular framework – which we may disagree with – and the descriptive results achieved within that framework – which we may nevertheless be able to use. I myself have certainly benefited from work on Chinese syntax carried out within the generative tradition (e.g. Li 1990) for my own functional description of that language, and expect to continue to do so in future.

But alongside the tolerance of diversity of opinion, which I would see as one of the key academic virtues, since it is ultimately a recognition of the contingent nature of one's own views, I believe there is also a need for intellectual honesty about those views, and other views with which one disagrees. So while I accept the legitimacy of claims made within the tradition of generative grammar for what it is attempting to achieve, I would nevertheless maintain that *by the terms of those very goals*, as well as in relation to the nature of syntactic patterning, there is a fundamental inconsistency in attempting to account for the meaningful elements of language without reference to meaning. This critique will certainly come as no surprise to any reader of this book; but the fact that the very formulation of its title, 'meaningful arrangement', as referring to syntax, will no doubt strike many syntacticians as odd, seems to me a paradox that called for explanation.

I started this book by casting doubt on claims for syntax as a well-founded and developed field of study whose results could be dependably used both within and beyond the discipline. It is just this exclusion of meaning from many syntactic theories that causes my doubt about the validity of many of the theoretical and empirical claims made by those theories. In the words of the Latin poet, as processed by myself earlier in this book:

Natūram	expellas	furcā	tamen
nature+ACC+SG	drive-out+SUBJ+2SG	fork+ABL+SG	however

usque	recurret.
back	return+FUT+3SG

'You may drive Nature out with a pitchfork, but (she) will come back'

It is **meaning** that is the 'nature' of syntax, in the sense both of its wider environment and its basic characteristic, and it seems to me that the syntacticians' meaning-removing pitchfork will ultimately prove, if it has not already, not only ineffectual, but debilitating to the discipline. I hope that this book has at least been successful in putting forward some ideas about how to bring meaning back into the fold.

References

Anderson, John M. 1971. *The Grammar of Case: Towards a Localistic Theory.* London: Cambridge University Press.

Becker, A.L. 1993. The elusive figures of Burmese grammar: An essay. In Foley, W. (ed.). 61–85.

Bloomfield, Leonard. 1933. *Language.* New York: Holt & Reinhart.

Boyd, Robertson & Iain Taylor. 1993. *Teach Yourself Gaelic.* London: Hodder & Stoughton.

Butler, Christopher. 2003. *Structure and Function: A Guide to Three Major Structural-Functional Theories.* Parts 1 and 2. Amsterdam: Benjamins.

Cartier, Alice. 1972. *Les verbes résultatifs en chinois moderne* [Resultative verbs in modern Chinese]. Paris: Klincksieck.

Chao, Yuen Ren. 1948. *Mandarin Primer.* Cambridge MA: Harvard University Press.

Chao, Yuen Ren. 1968. *A Grammar of Spoken Chinese.* Berkeley & Los Angeles: University of California Press.

Chomsky, Noam. 1957. *Syntactic Structures.* 's-Gravenhage: Mouton.

Chomsky, Noam. 1965. *Aspects of the Theory of Syntax.* Cambridge MA: MIT Press.

Chomsky, Noam. 1970. Remarks on nominalization. In Jacob, R.A. & P.S. Rosenbaum (eds). *Readings in English Transformational Grammar.* London: Ginn. 184–221.

Chomsky, Noam. 1995. *The Minimalist Program.* Cambridge MA: MIT Press.

Daneš, F. (ed.). 1974. *Papers on Functional Sentence Perspective.* The Hague: Mouton.

Dik, Simon C. 1978. *Functional Grammar.* Amsterdam: North Holland.

Dik, Simon C. 1989. *The Theory of Functional Grammar. Part 1: The Structure of the Clause.* Dordrecht: Foris.

Fawcett, R.P. 2000. *A Theory of Syntax for Systemic Functional Linguistics.* Current Issues in Linguistic Theory 206. Amsterdam: Benjamins.

Fillmore, Charles. 1968. The case for case. In Bach, E. & R. Harms (eds). *Universals in Linguistic Theory.* New York: Holt, Rinehart & Winston. 1–88.

Fillmore, Charles. 1977. The case for case reopened. In Cole, P. & J.M. Sadock (eds). *Grammatical Relations.* New York: Academic Press. 59–82.

Firth, J.R. 1950 / 1957. Personality and language in society. *The Sociological Review,* xlii.2. Reprinted in J.R. Firth. 1957. *Papers in Linguistics.* London: Oxford University Press. 177–189.

Firth, J.R. 1956 / 1968. Linguistics and Translation. In Palmer, F.R. (ed.). 1968. 84–95.

Firth, J.R. 1957 / 1968. A synopsis of linguistic theory, 1930–55. *Studies in Linguistic Analysis*. Special volume of the Philological Society, 1957, 1–31. Reprinted in Palmer, F.R. (ed.). 1968. 168–205.

Foley, William A. (ed.). 1993. *The Role of Theory in Language Description*. Berlin: Mouton de Gruyter.

Foley, William A. & Robert Van Valin Jr. 1984. *Functional Syntax and Universal Grammar*. Cambridge: Cambridge University Press.

Graffi, Giorgio. 2001. *200 Years of Syntax: A Critical Survey*. Studies in the History of the Language Sciences 98. Amsterdam: Benjamins.

Gruber, J.S. 1965. *Studies in Lexical Relations*. Ph.D. Dissertation, Massachusetts Institute of Technology.

Halliday, M.A.K. 1956. Grammatical categories in Modern Chinese. *Transactions of the Philological Society*. 177–224.

Halliday, M.A.K. 1961. Categories of the Theory of Grammar. *Word*. 17.3. 241–292.

Halliday, M.A.K. 1966. Syntax and the consumer. *Monograph Series on Languages and Linguistics*, 17. Washington: Georgetown University Press. 11–24.

Halliday, M.A.K. 1967–68. Transitivity and theme in English, Parts 1–3. *Journal of Linguistics*. 3: 37–81, 199–244. 4: 179–215.

Halliday, M.A.K. 1970. Language structure and language function. In Lyons, J. (ed.). *New Directions in Linguistics*. Harmondsworth: Penguin. 140–164.

Halliday, M.A.K. 1985. *An Introduction to Functional Grammar*. 2nd edition 1994. Oxford: Arnold.

Halliday, M.A.K. 1986. On grammar and grammatics. In Hasan, R. et al. (eds). 1996. 1–38.

Halliday, M.A.K. 1993. Systemic grammar and the concept of a 'science of language'. In Zhu, Yongsheng (ed.). *Language, Text, Context*. Beijing: Tsinghua University Press. 1–22.

Halliday, M.A.K. 2005. On matter and meaning: the two realms of human experience. *Linguistics and the Human Sciences*. 1.1:59–82.

Halliday, M.A.K. & Edward McDonald. 2004. A metafunctional profile of the grammar of Chinese. In Caffarel, A., J.R. Martin & C.M.I.M. Matthiessen (eds). *Language Typology: A Functional Perspective*. Amsterdam: Benjamins. 305–396.

Harris, Zellig S. 1951. *Methods in Structural Linguistics*. Chicago: University of Chicago Press.

Hasan, Ruqaiya. 1987. The grammarian's dream: Lexis as most delicate grammar. In Halliday, M.A.K. & R. Fawcett (eds). *New Developments in Systemic Linguistics*. Volume 1. London: Pinter. 184–211.

Hasan, Ruqaiya & Peter Fries (eds). 1995. *On Subject and Theme: A Discourse Functional Perspective*. Amsterdam: Benjamins.

Hasan, Ruqaiya & Peter Fries. 1995. Reflections on subject and theme: an introduction. In Hasan, R. & P. Fries (eds). 1995. xiii-xlv.

Hasan, Ruqaiya, Carmel Cloran & David Butt (eds). 1996. *Functional Descriptions: Theory in Practice*. Amsterdam: Benjamins.

Hjelmslev, Louis. 1935,1937. La catégorie des cas [The category of cases]. *Acta Jutlandica*. 7. i-xii, 1–184; 9. ii-vii, 1–78.

Hjelmslev, Louis. 1943 / 1953 / 1961. *Prolegomena to a Theory of Language*. English translation by Francis J. Whitfield. 1951. Baltimore: Indiana University Publications in Anthropology and Linguistics (IJAL Memoir 7). 2nd ed. (slightly revised). 1961. Madison: University of Wisconsin Press.

Hockett, Charles. 1968. *The State of the Art*. The Hague: Mouton.

Hockett, Charles. 1987. *Refurbishing our Foundations: Elementary Linguistics from an Advanced Point of View*. Current Issues in Linguistic Theory 56. Amsterdam: Benjamins.

Hopper, Paul & Sandra A. Thompson. 1980. Transitivity in Grammar and Discourse. *Language,* 56.2. 251–299.

Hou, Baolin & Guo Qiru. 1980. *Xiangshengji* [Crosstalk Collection]. Beijing: China National Radio.

James, William. 1890. *The Principles of Psychology*. New York: Henry Holt. Reprinted New York: Dover. 1950.

Kuhn, Thomas. 1962 / 1970. *The Structure of Scientific Revolutions*. International Encyclopedia of Unified Science, Vol.2, No.2. Chicago: University of Chicago Press. 2nd ed. 1970.

Lamb, Sydney M. 1966. *Outline of Stratificational Grammar*. Washington: Georgetown University Press.

Lamb, Sydney M. 1999. *Pathways of the Brain: The Neurocognitive Basis of Language*. Amsterdam: Benjamins.

Lamb, William. 2001. *Scottish Gaelic*. Munich: Lincom Europa

Lehmann, Winfred P. 1993. *Theoretical Bases of Indo-European Linguistics*. London & New York: Routledge.

Li, Charles N. & Sandra Thompson. 1981. *Mandarin Chinese: a Functional Reference Grammar*. Berkeley & Los Angeles: University of California Press.

Li, Jinxi. 1924. *Xinzhu Guoyu Wenfa* [A New Grammar of Mandarin]. Shanghai: Commercial Press.

Li, Rong. 1952. *Beijing Kouyu Yufa* [Grammar of Spoken Pekingese]. Translation of Chao 1948, Part One: Introduction. Beijing: Kaiming Shudian.

Li, Yen Hui Audrey. 1990. *Order and Constituency in Mandarin Chinese*. Dordrecht: Kluwer.

Liu, Yuehua, Pan Wenyu & Gu Wei. 1983. *Shiyong Xiandai Hanyu Yufa* [Practical Chinese Grammar]. Beijing: Foreign Languages Teaching and Research Press.

Lockwood, David G. 2002. *Syntactic Analysis and Description: A Constructional Approach*. London: Continuum.

Lu, Zhiwei. 1964. *Hanyu de goucifa* [Word formation in Modern Chinese]. Beijing: Kexue chubanshe.

Lü, Jiping.1958. (ed.). *Hanyu de zhuyu binyu wenti* [The problem of subject and object in Chinese]. Beijing.

Matthews, P.H. 1981. *Syntax*. Cambridge Textbooks in Linguistics. Cambridge: Cambridge University Press.

Matthews, P.H. 2001. *A Short History of Structural Linguistics*. Cambridge: Cambridge University Press.

Martin, J.R. 1996. Metalinguistic diversity: The case from case. In Hasan, R. et al. (eds). 323–374.

Martinet, Andre. 1960. *Elements of General Linguistics*. Translated by Elisabeth Palmer. London: Faber & Faber.

Mathesius, Vilém. 1929. Zur Satzperspektive im modernen Englisch. [On sentence perspectives in Modern English.] *Archiv für das Studium der Neueren Sprachen und Literaturen* 155. 202–210.

McDonald, Edward. 1994. Completive verb compounds in modern Chinese: A new look at an old problem. *Journal of Chinese Linguistics*. 22.2. 317–362.

McDonald, Edward. 1996. The 'complement' in Chinese grammar: A functional reinterpretation. In Hasan, R. et al. (eds). 265–286.

McDonald, Edward. 2002. Humanistic spirit or scientism?: Conflicting ideologies in modern Chinese language reform. *Histoire, épistémologie, langage*. 24.2. 51–74.

McDonald, Edward. 2004. Verb and clause in Chinese: issues of constituency and functionality. *Journal of Chinese Linguistics*.

Newmeyer, Frederick. 1980. *Linguistic Theory in America: The First Quarter-Century of Transformational Generative Grammar*. New York: Academic Press.

Newmeyer, Frederick. 1998. *Language Form and Language Function*. Cambridge MA: MIT Press.

Ò Maolalaigh, Roibeard & Iain MacAonghuis. 1996. *Scottish Gaelic in Three Months*. Hugo's Language Books.

Palmer F.R. (ed.). 1968. *Selected Papers of J.R. Firth 1952–59*. London: Longmans.

Palmer, F.R. (ed.). 1970. *Prosodic Analysis*. London: Oxford University Press.

Pawley, Andrew. 1993. A language which defies description by ordinary means. In Foley, W. (ed.). 87–129.

Pike, Kenneth L. 1982. *Linguistic Concepts: An Introduction to Tagmemics*. Lincoln: University of Nebraska Press.

Quirk, Randolph & Sidney Greenbaum. 1973. *A Concise Grammar of Contemporary English*. New York: Harcourt Brace Jovanovich.

Radford, Andrew. 1997. *Syntax: A Minimalist Introduction*. Cambridge: Cambridge University Press.

Radford, Andrew. 2004. *Minimalist Syntax: Exploring the Structure of English*. Cambridge: Cambridge University Press.

Robins, R.H. 1961. Syntactic Analysis. *Archivum Linguisticum* 13, 78–89. Reprinted in Hamp, Eric P., Fred W. Householder & Robert Austerlitz (eds). 1966. *Readings in Linguistics II*. Chicago: University of Chicago Press. 386–395.

Robins, R.H. 1993. *The Byzantine Grammarians: Their Place in History*. Berlin & New York: Mouton de Gruyter.

Robins, R.H. 1997. *A Short History of Linguistics*. 4th edition. Cambridge: Cambridge University Press.

Sag, Ivan A. & Thomas Wasow. 1999. *Syntactic Theory: A Formal Introduction*. Stanford: CSLI Publications.

Saussure, Ferdinand de. 1916 / 1959. *Course in General Linguistics*. Trans. by Wade Baskin. New York: Philosophical Library.

Shannon, Claude & Warren Weaver. 1949. *The Mathematical Theory of Communication*. Urbana: University of Illinois Press.

Siewierska, Anna. 1991. *Functional Grammar*. London: Routledge.

Simon, H.F. 1958. Some remarks on the structure of the verb complex in Standard Chinese. *Bulletin of the School of Oriental and African Studies*. 553–577.

Starosta, Stanley. 1988. *The Case for Lexicase: An Outline of Lexicase Grammatical Theory*. London: Pinter.

Tesnière, Lucien.1934. Comment construire une syntaxe [How to construct a syntax]. *Bulletin de la Faculté des Lettres de Strasbourg*. 12.7. 219–229.

Tesnière, Lucien. 1953. *Esquisse d'une syntaxe structurale* [Sketch of a structural syntax]. Paris: C. Klincksieck.

Tesnière, Lucien. 1959. *Éléments de syntaxe structurale* [Elements of structural syntax]. Paris: C. Klincksieck. Second edition revised and corrected 1965.

Thompson, Sandra A. 1973. Resultative verbs in Chinese: A case for lexical rules. *Language*. 49.2 361–379.

Van Valin, Robert D. Jr. 2001. *An Introduction to Syntax*. Cambridge: Cambridge University Press.

Wang, Li. 1944. *Zhongguo Xiandai Yufa* [Modern Chinese Grammar]. Shanghai: Commercial Press.

Zhou, Chiming. 1957. Hanyu de liandongxing fushi dongci [Conjoined complex verbs in Chinese]. *Language Research*. 2. 23–58.

Zhu, Dexi. 1982. *Yufa jiangyi* [A Grammar Course]. Beijing: Commercial Press.

Index of names

Index of terms

CPSIA information can be obtained at www.ICGtesting.com
Printed in the USA
BVOW011745140413

318109BV00004B/59/P